Loose Canon

A portrait of Brian Brindley

Loose Canon

A portrait of Brian Brindley

_____

Edited by
DAMIAN THOMPSON

continuum
LONDON • NEW YORK

Continuum

The Tower Building   15 East 26th Street
11 York Road   New York
London SE1 7NX   NY 10010

www.continuumbooks.com

First published 2004

British Library Cataloguing-in-Publication Data
A catologue record for this book is available from the British Library.

ISBN 0 8264 7418 7

All photographs reproduced by permission of the estate of Brian Brindley, with the
exception of 'Historians at Stowe', 'Brian on Holiday' and 'Brian in a Victorian Set',
which have been supplied by Colin Anson and reproduced by his kind permission.

Typeset by RefineCatch Limited, Bungay, Suffolk
Printed and bound by MPG Books Ltd, Bodmin, Cornwall

Contents

Introduction

DAMIAN THOMPSON

BRIAN BRINDLEY (1931–2001) possessed the essential qualifica-
tion of a great English eccentric: he did not know how eccentric he was. When I was a reporter on the *Reading Chronicle* in
the 1980s, I would sometimes run into the then Canon
Brindley striding through Sainsbury's, panting from his heavy
shopping bags, dressed as an eighteenth-century Roman
monsignor. His buckled shoes with red heels – painted by
himself – clopped like horses' hooves against the linoleum as
he scoured the aisles for ever creamier puddings; his fatness
was disguised by a soutane with 39 red buttons, 'one for each of
the Articles I don't believe in'. (As the highest of high church-
men, he had a robust disrespect for the Church of England's
Protestant heritage; his organists had it written into their con-
tracts that they must never play Luther's 'Ein feste Burg'.)
There was a touch of the pantomime dame about Brian, which
could cause sniggering behind him in the checkout queue.

If this makes Brindley sound like a caricature, the truth is that he turned himself into one. The process was deliberate, in so far as every sartorial flourish and flirtatious advance was carefully planned (far more so than his sermons, which were improvised and wandered all over the place). It was also unwitting, in that he had no idea how silly he looked, even to admirers. 'What does he *see* when he looks in the mirror?' I remember one of his friends, a Labour MP, asking. One might have applied the same question to his spirituality. On a number of occasions I asked him, as tactfully as possible, how he squared his Christian faith, which never wavered, with the sexual self-indulgence that was cruelly exposed and exaggerated by the *News of the World*. His answers were complicated and unsatisfactory; I don't think he really knew. There was undoubtedly a tension between his religious beliefs and his inordinate love of beautiful things. This tension could be destructive or it could be creative, and often it was difficult to tell the difference.

As Vicar of Holy Trinity, Reading, from 1967 to 1989, Brian choreographed liturgically extreme High Masses in what Gavin Stamp called 'an undistinguished Gothic box' near the railway-line. On feastdays, the rubric of Fortescue's *Ceremonies of the Roman Rite Described* was infused with the spirit of Busby Berkeley; the results could have been awful but were in fact superb – and, for his congregation, a path to God. 'I have a perfect sense of colour,' declared Brian, and it was true. The Brindleian liturgy reached its apotheosis at his Silver Jubilee Mass in 1988, over which the Bishop of Oxford presided from a throne worthy of a Borgia pope: one visitor joked that he would not have been surprised if, through the clouds of incense, one of the participants had clutched his throat and slumped, poisoned, to the floor. Brian was delighted by this thought.

So the caricature was real, but it was often misunderstood. People sometimes assumed that the grandest Anglo-Catholic priest in the country must be deeply embedded in a culture of 'gin, lace and backbiting'. Lace, yes; but Brian had no interest in alcohol and, almost uniquely among clergymen of his persuasion, did not enjoy gossip. He had a high doctrine of the priesthood: I never heard him refer to his colleagues by women's names, and woe betide anyone who reminded him that many people (including his rural dean) knew him as 'Brenda'. Moreover, the caricature was not the whole story. Having created it, Brian undermined it in unexpected ways.

The Holy Trinity ceremonial, however brilliantly executed, was not an unprecedented achievement: there is a tradition dating back to the Oxford Movement of dazzling services performed in the back streets of industrial towns. What was unusual about Brian was his refusal to engage in Anglo-Catholic solipsism; to behave as if the rest of the Church of England did not matter. As an office-holder in the General Synod, he saw it as his duty to protect Anglicans of other traditions from experimental services disfigured by ugly language and sloppy theology. He was not, however, opposed to change in principle. He saw the Alternative Service Book as an opportunity, already exercised by the Roman Catholic Church, to rediscover the authentic worship of the early Christians. It is a paradox that a clergyman who appeared to be so much in love with spiky rubric was also concerned with liturgical purity: underneath the gilded carapace of the

Solemn Mass at Holy Trinity lay the skeleton of the *Novus ordo* of the Second Vatican Council, the product of recent scholarship, rather than that of the Tridentine Rite ('a Mass for peasants', he sniffed). As a member of a Synod committee charged with revising the liturgy, Brian was partly the author of a eucharistic prayer, based on the Hippolytan canon of the early third century, that was moulded to fit Catholic requirements; he thus made it easier for Anglo-Catholics to remain in the Church of England after he himself had become a Roman Catholic.

Brian's decision to resign his orders was an immediate consequence of the vote for women priests in 1992; but there can be no doubt that it was made easier by what he called 'my troubles'. He had always lusted after fame, and there is something rather sad about the fact that he achieved it, fleetingly, twice: when his career was destroyed by the *News of the World* in the summer of 1989, and when he dropped dead in the middle of his 70th birthday dinner party at the Athenaeum twelve years later. Only in retrospect did his friends come to see that neither of these events was quite the disaster that it appeared at the time.

Brian deliberately never read the tabloid article about him that cost him his job, his house and his seat on the General Synod, but he was told of its contents a few hours before it was published. I visited him on that bleak Saturday, as he sat in his drawing room, methodically telephoning friends, family and legal advisers to warn them what was about to happen. 'There will be no bishopric now,' he said (though there never would have been: he was far too exotic a beast for the Crown Appointments Commission). He blinked in disbelief, but there was no panic or wringing of hands. I was surprised by how bravely he accepted a punishment that, as he admitted, he had brought on himself. Just as famous holy men are often secret prima donnas, so this most worldly of clerics – capable of Bunteresque boastfulness when things were going well for him – revealed a streak of humility. 'Self-pity is the least attractive of emotions,' he used to say, and he rarely exhibited it, either in the aftermath of his fall or during the years of miserable ill-health caused by heart failure. His courage was deeply impressive.

Alan Bennett remembers that, as a young man, Brian was kinder than he liked people to think. That became obvious during the 1990s. Released from the burden of unrealistic ambitions, Brian relaxed; more and more time was spent in long telephone calls to his friends in which he dispensed good advice and held forth amusingly about things that few other people knew (or cared) about. If I needed information on, say, the Jacobite peerage, I knew I could ring Brian; listening to him was as comforting as settling into a favourite armchair. More than anything else, I miss those phone calls. But my sadness at his death is mitigated by its circumstances, and here I know I speak for most of the guests at his farewell dinner party. It was an almost perfectly judged exit – I say 'almost' because Brian was looking forward to the *boeuf en daube* – in the best Holy Trinity tradition. He was ready to go; we felt honoured to be with him.

This volume begins at the end, so to speak, with an account of Brian's death that I wrote in the *Spectator*. Brian's schooldays are described by his friend Colin Anson, and his time at Oxford by his contemporaries Alan Bennett, P. J. Kavanagh and

Ned Sherrin. Nicholas Krasno and Peter Sheppard describe life and worship at Holy Trinity; Fr Seán Finnegan of the London Oratory writes about Brian's curious love affair with the computer. The longest contribution is a biographical essay by Fr Anthony Symondson SJ, who untangles the personal, cultural and theological roots of Brian's ministry. Finally, there is a selection of the marvellously opinionated articles Brian wrote for the Charterhouse Chronicle slot in the *Catholic Herald.*

It was Brian's idea that his friends should collaborate on a volume of articles about him after he died. He would not, I think, have been pleased by some of the more candid observations in this book, but what choice did we have? This was a man who chose to exercise prodigious but essentially secular talents in an arena that was not obviously appropriate to them: the postwar Church of England. In doing so, he did not always respect the traditional boundaries of good taste and morality. It would be wrong, not to say impossible, to take him at his own estimation; yet he was a magnificent self-creation and a lovable man whose achievements are worth celebrating. Just as great English eccentrics contribute to the gaiety of the nation, so great clerical eccentrics add sparkle to the liturgical year. As an Anglican priest and, later, a Catholic journalist, Brian enriched the fabric of two great churches – whether they liked it or not.

CHAPTER ONE

*Death at the Athenaeum**

DAMIAN THOMPSON

MY FRIEND BRIAN BRINDLEY had spent months planning a dinner party to mark his 70th birthday. He was very clear about its purpose: he was not trying to assemble a collection of the prettiest or most amusing people he knew, but, rather, 'those who have played a significant part in my life'. His boyhood was to be represented by a senior civil servant; Stowe by a clergyman and an art historian; Oxford by Ned Sherrin. Several of us knew Brian from his days as Vicar of Holy Trinity, Reading, a drab Victorian box that he had transformed into a gilded Anglo-Catholic confection of Gothic and baroque. The youngest guest, a jeweller, had met him only in his final incarnation as a Roman Catholic journalist, a career move forced on him by a skirmish with the *News of the World* and the Church of England's decision to ordain women priests. Women were no more capable of being priested than donkeys, he once said; it was to be an all-male dinner party.

* From the *Spectator*, 3 August 2001.

Brian was worried that a guest might drop out, leaving us a sinister thirteen, so another friend agreed to spend the afternoon by the telephone, ready to don a dinner jacket at a moment's notice.

There was only one possible venue: his beloved Athenaeum. Every week, Brian would come up from Brighton to air his High Tory views at the club table, and, after lunch, would ascend in the mahogany-panelled lift (shaped to accommodate a coffin) to tea and a snooze in the drawing room. His membership of the club was doubly precious because he had nearly lost it: when the tabloid article appeared, Lord Coggan led a nasty campaign to expel him. Brindley always brought out the worst in evangelicals.

A legendary epicurean, he had managed to boil down the menu to just eight courses: prosciutto and figs; *avgolemono*; 'drest crab'; lime sorbet; *boeuf en daube*; summer pudding; angels on horseback; and fruit for dessert. The beef was to be accompanied by samphire – an endangered species, he told me proudly. (This was a man who refused to wear fur unless it was 'cruel fur'.) The invitations, in the style of William Morris, announced drinks in the south library at 7.30 p.m., dinner in the north library at 8 p.m., and instructed guests to wear 'Black Tie and Short Coat (Smoking or Tuxedo)'.

When I first knew Brian he was enormously fat and modelled himself on an eighteenth-century monsignor. I once watched him sail into a civic dinner in Reading in a cream tropical cassock with scarlet buttons. 'My auntie's got a frock like that', sang out one of the Labour councillors. The figure holding court in the south library last Wednesday was dressed in a white dinner jacket, a waistcoat reproducing the wallpaper of Brighton Pavilion and a psychedelic bowtie; I told him he looked like the next Doctor Who. He sat there with a stockinged foot resting on a gout-stool, barking instructions at a club servant. But ten years of heart disease had shrunk him, and guests who had not seen him recently were shocked by his frailty. Ned Sherrin bounded in and pressed a pot of caviar into his hand with the words, 'I thought I'd get you something perishable, Brian, as neither of us has got long to go.' Everyone laughed.

We trooped down the corridor into a cube-shaped room lined to the ceiling with books and filled by an oval table laid with Athenaeum silverware. Brian sat at the far end next to Ned. The Jesuit architectural historian Fr Anthony Symondson said a Latin grace. During the first two courses I listened with half an ear to our host's conversation. He recommended his favourite fish restaurant to Ned, then moved on to the subject of the state of Israel, which he was convinced (and hoped) would go the way of white South Africa. I also heard him mention his hero Michael Portillo, whose elimination from the Tory leadership race he regarded as a far greater disaster than the general election defeat.

As the shadows lengthened in Pall Mall, the butler lit the candles. The drest crab was magnificent, which pleased me for Brian's sake, but I was worried that he seemed to be pausing between sentences, bowing over the table as if before the sacrament. Then he turned to me and said, 'I need to go outside for a moment. If I'm not back in five minutes, come and get me', and he tottered out.

The next thing I remember is looking up to see Brian, back from the loo, being helped into a chair by Martin Taylor, the young jeweller. He closed his eyes, then his white head lolled forward. Martin was saying, 'Can you hear me, sweetheart?' There was no response. Fr Symondson made the sign of the cross over Brian's head, whispering absolution. Someone else went out to call an ambulance. We carefully lowered Brian to the floor and put him on his front in the recovery position. Half the diners were still in their places, standing with one hand on the table and the other clutching a napkin, like figures in a Victorian tableau, their faces frozen in a very English mixture of embarrassment and concern.

A doctor who had been dining in the club appeared at the doorway. He knelt down, searched for a pulse, shone a light into Brian's eyes, and told us, apologetically, what we already knew: 'I'm afraid he has passed away.' There was a long silence as we gazed down at our host. The flickering candles, the rows of leather-bound books, the body on the carpet: all the scene lacked was Hercule Poirot. Fr Symondson recited a beautiful formal prayer in the measured tones in which he had said grace: Brian detested the mateyness of improvised worship.

There was no question of continuing, of course: the only person I knew who might conceivably have carried on eating in these circumstances had himself just died. (The Athenaeum later refused to accept any payment for the dinner.) We wandered sadly into the drawing room, where we reflected on the tragic appropriateness of what we had just witnessed. Brian had expired surrounded by people from every strand of his life, in front of a feast of his own devising, in the arms of a good-looking young man. A tail-coated waiter approached us and asked Martin, who had removed his dinner jacket while trying to revive our friend, if he would put it on again. Brian would have approved: like Bill Shankly, he felt that some things were more important than life and death.

Only later did I discover that, during the afternoon, he had seen a chiropodist who took one look at his ulcerated foot and told him that if he did not go to hospital immediately he would lose his toes. 'You could even die at your own dinner,' he said. 'Then so be it,' replied Brian. 'I shall go down in flames.'

CHAPTER TWO

With Brian at Stowe

COLIN ANSON

IN MY SECOND TERM at Stowe a clever new boy called Brindley arrived. It was the summer of 1945. We were in the same house, the same dormitory and the same form, and became friends almost at once. We soon discovered another sympathetic new boy in our house called Peter Jameson. The three of us remained close friends throughout our schooldays and beyond.

Brian's father owned a small electrical engineering factory in London, off the Holloway Road. By his own efforts in the 1920s and 1930s, he had built up this successful business, which continued to flourish during and after the war. The Brindleys had two children. Brian, born in 1931, was some years younger than his sister Nancy. The family lived in a comfortable house, with a gravel driveway and a large garden, in Bushey Heath. I was impressed on my first visit to notice in Mr Brindley's study a prewar television set calmly awaiting the resumption of normal services. Brian's parents must have been bemused by their unusually intelligent son, so unlike anyone they had met before; they treated the cuckoo in their nest with kindness, even indulgence. Unlike them, Brian always spoke with an educated, middle-class voice. Its slightly imperious tone developed much later.

Stowe itself could hardly fail to make an impression on us. We were living in an abandoned neoclassical palace of considerable grandeur, stripped of its princely furnishings. From its south portico a great flight of steps led down to an extensive landscaped garden containing artificial lakes and many ornamental buildings. Just after the war, everything was in a forlorn state of disrepair. Brian, Peter and I were enchanted as well as dismayed by the romantic decay of the temples and follies and drew up impracticable plans to rescue some from their derelict condition.

Brian and I were physically much the same, both wearing spectacles and with mouse-coloured hair, his with the wavy remains of angelic curls. Our thin, almost muscleless bodies were especially ill-suited to sport. We abhorred all physical exercise. Peter was equally averse to it, though less painfully thin and with normal vision. Obliged to play house games about three afternoons a week, we did so in a perfunctory manner until shouted at, when we might make a brief show of enthusiasm before relapsing into our usual lethargy. For rugger we evolved a technique of continual motion, following the ball at the furthest possible distance from it, swirling round the pitch as if at the end of a comet's tail. Such an obvious contempt for games would have been hard to sustain alone, but as allies – at a tolerant school – we survived.

Promoted shortly to the Middle School, Brian and I were already on our way to School Certificate exams the following summer. He was put in a higher form than mine; academically he was already pulling ahead. He would finish his prep with time to spare for doodling or reading unsuitable books. He passed all his exams with ease, while I scraped through with my credit in art. At just under 15, we had to choose one main subject in which to specialize for the rest of our time at school. The dashing prewar history tutor Bill McElwee had just returned from his Highland regiment with a heroic war record to take up his old position. Beside the rest of the staff he stood out as a distinctly glamorous figure, darkly handsome and stylishly dressed. He was determined to re-establish the History Side as both an intellectual elite and an exclusive club, though his criteria for choosing those he would teach could seem capricious. I passed muster because he had heard of my eccentric Irish grandmother, while Brian was accepted on merit. His decision to study history instead of science was a blow to his father's hope that he would one day take over the family firm.

The main advantage of promotion to the Upper School was being able to leave the noisy House Room for a study, which we were allowed to decorate as we liked. Brian and I decided that we must cheer up our bleak little cell by painting the walls a cyclamen pink. The effect was pleasingly outrageous. When Brian's parents visited and his father expressed amazed disapproval, his mother countered, 'But Fred, it's a lovely *warm* colour.' As another Upper-School privilege allowed us each to order an improving magazine of our choice, we soon became keen followers of London's social scene and women's fashions in our copies of the *Tatler* and *Vogue*. Even the broadminded McElwee was driven to suggest that *Esquire* would perhaps have been a more appropriate choice. He was equally stuffy about Brian's saucy parody of a schoolgirl story, 'No Mail for Monica'. Peter joined us when we were eventually given a study for three, and remained with us for the rest of his time at Stowe. Over the years, our study gathered an increasing amount of ornate bric-à-brac, including some wax fruit under a glass dome. Sadly, Peter had decided to read modern languages and physics, so missed the many entertaining activities that Brian and I were to enjoy as historians.

McElwee was a kind and painstaking tutor, treating us all like undergraduates rather than schoolboys. In his classroom lectures he enthralled us with his perceptive interpretation of the past. He set us weekly essays, either on history or general subjects, in confident preparation for our scholarships to Oxford or Cambridge. At just 15, we had little idea how to write on a subject such as 'Men are not hanged for stealing horses, but that horses be not stolen', which was among the first we were given. However, we had over three years to find out. Perhaps his most helpful teaching occurred in the tutorials, when he paid almost more attention to thinking clearly and writing decent English than to history itself.

McElwee lived with his wife Patience and their young daughter in an early nineteenth-century house called Vancouver Lodge, just a short walk across fields from the school. Anyone accepted as a historian was adopted as part of the McElwees' extended family. In term time we enjoyed their hospitality every Saturday evening and the company of any distinguished visitor who came to stay. Life at Vancouver Lodge thrillingly subverted all the cherished norms of our middle-class upbringing. The McElwees shared their house with a number of animals: a bulldog, a corgi, sometimes a pair of foxhound puppies, various cats, rabbits bred to eat and a hunter in the stable. Away from the school, Bill saw himself more as an impoverished hunting squire – he regularly hunted with the Grafton – and Patience, though industrious in the kitchen, considered it very suburban to waste time on house-work. These alternative values were not always understood by parents. Mr and Mrs Brindley could just excuse the dust and shabbiness on the grounds of poverty, but thought it most discourteous of Patience to entertain them in the sitting room while peeling potatoes, perhaps being prepared for more important guests.

Bill and Patience McElwee jointly undertook a far wider kind of education that can be taught in the classroom. We imbibed their views on how a gentleman should behave and what was really important in life. They became our surrogate parents, our own seeming so dull by comparison. The general conversation at Vancouver Lodge, often ribald and extremely disrespectful to other masters and their wives, meant that historians suffered the disapproval of many members of staff, but we were too haughty to care. Brian and I became especially frequent visitors after our housemaster was persuaded that a number of ends would be served if we looked after the McElwees' garden instead of playing games. Thereafter we spent almost every afternoon at Vancouver Lodge, doing little in the garden, but enjoying tea and gossip with Patience. She would occasionally take us by taxi to Buckingham, where we bought more bric-à-brac for our study at the local junk shop. We showed our gratitude with birthday and Valentine cards consisting of an amusing poem by Brian and an illustration by me. Our most ambitious collaboration was a mildly scurrilous *Vancouver Book of Nursery Rhymes* in our last summer term.

Boys at Stowe had many opportunities to become involved with theatricals, in school plays, house plays and the historians' Shakespeare play during the summer. In Agatha Christie's *Ten Little Niggers*, Brian played an elderly spinster, whom I murdered in my role as a judge turned serial killer. Perhaps Brian was too convincing, as he was cast as another an old lady in Emlyn Williams's *Night Must Fall*. Brian's most successful performance, an impressive comic creation, was as Sir Andrew Aguecheek in *Twelfth Night*. The following summer I was given the part of Richard III, and once again I callously killed off Brian, who was playing the Duke of Clarence. By the time I left school, my craving to dress up and perform before an audience had been fully satisfied, while Brian's seemed to intensify and to have lasted the rest of his life.

In 1948 McElwee revived a prewar historian tradition by taking a group of boys to Italy for two weeks in the summer holidays. This was the most exciting adventure of our lives for an age group that had been prevented by the war and its aftermath from travelling abroad. On our first day in Milan we visited the cathedral. While exploring the vast, cool and almost empty interior, Brian and I suddenly found ourselves in a crowded, low-ceilinged crypt, its atmosphere thick with incense. The spectacle before us was of a richness and splendour we had not witnessed before. A portly prelate in glittering vestments was conducting a service with attendant priests and acolytes, everything a profusion of white, silver and gold lit solely by candlelight. Enraptured by what he saw and determined to capture the moment, Brian brought out his father's prewar camera and aimed its long, concertina-like proboscis at the altar, but sadly nothing appeared on the negative. Witnessing that scene, I often thought, was for him a revelation of how strongly he was attracted to the glamour of church ceremonial. However, though knowledgeable about liturgy, as he seemed to be about many arcane subjects, Brian was not noticeably religious at school. It never occurred to me, nor I think to him, that one of his career options might be to become a priest.

At the end of the summer term of 1949, Peter left Stowe with a place at Trinity College, Cambridge, while Brian and I stayed on for two more terms. It had been McElwee's boast that given time he could get any boy a scholarship to Oxford or Cambridge, and he was successful with almost all the historians of our generation. While Brian fulfilled everyone's expectations by gaining a scholarship to Exeter College, Oxford, my own failure even to be offered a place may have slightly dented McElwee's self-confidence; it certainly dented mine. However, for the spring term of 1950, I was made a prefect and head of our house; it gave me pleasure to be taking Brian with me to the prefectory, an altogether more pres-tigious study than we'd had before. We both enjoyed the status this brought us in our last term. Unable to change our ways, we covered its walls with some of my great-grandmother's collection of fans.

After being scattered by National Service, during which none of us was made an officer, we took up our separate student lives. While undergraduates, both Brian and Peter were independently drawn to Anglo-Catholic worship. As an art student in London, I found myself living almost next door to St Mary's, Bourne Street, well known for its extravagantly high church services. I never entered the church and remained unaware of its reputation until, in 1954, I discovered that both Brian and Peter were worshipping there. Our student days over, Peter and I embarked on our first jobs, his in an architect's office and mine at the Arts Council. Brian, meanwhile, had joined an Inn of Court with a view to being called to the Bar. As a law student he was obliged to eat three dinners a term for three years and during that time to pass two Bar exams. Unknown to his parents, Brian was not even attending his dinners, let alone studying law; he was instead writing a novel at the Junior Carlton Club. But the novel was not going well, leaving him in a bit of a fix. In 1959, when I was working in St James's Square, he invited me to join him one afternoon at his club. While we sipped our China tea in the Smoking Room, he announced that Peter had given up architecture and planned to be ordained. 'Well,' continued Brian with note of resolve, 'if Peter has a vocation, so have I!'

CHAPTER THREE

A Bubble Bubbling

P. J. KAVANAGH

THE EARLY YEARS OF the 1950s have gone down in history as particularly grey – postwar depression, rationing, Victor Sylvester – but to those of us who were young at the time they did not seem so. Perhaps it was only because we were young that they seemed coloured, but sufficiently colourful they were and they needed defending. Oxford was full of exotics, and among them was Brian Brindley, but he was importantly different from the others. They too often seemed merely ambitious, or malicious, or so eager *pour épater* that you suspected they would abandon their pose as soon as there was advantage in that.

Brian was surrounded by his own bubble, himself bubbling away inside it, indifferent, or so it seemed, to any impression he might make. Always expensively, exquisitely (and conventionally) dressed, his hair neatly parted in the middle, he seemed to represent some past age that had never existed anywhere outside Brindleyland. He was so theatrical a personage that you wondered at first why he didn't take part in plays, and then you saw that he could never be an ensemble player: the world was his stage, himself never off it, and daily life his play. This might have been ridiculous were it not for an obvious and joyous kindliness, an open invitation for everyone to join in his fun. Some may have found him tiresome, but I never knew anyone who did.

He could also be wise. It was he who suggested that if I was ever disgusted by contemporary ugliness in a town, I had only to lift my eyes above the shop-fronts and enjoy the architecture that remained, the fenestrations, the weird and pointless towers and glassed-in turrets that the past delighted in. I am grateful to him for that; every bus-ride since has been a revelation; he made me a connoisseur of ingenious drainpiping.

There were also his jokes, doubtless worked over, but they seemed impromptu. He founded the Bowdler Society to find out what bits of Shakespeare brought a blush to a maiden's cheek. For the first and last meeting of the society, the *Daily Express* was alerted and sent a photographer. Did Brian arrange that? Perhaps he did. The maiden chosen was Sally Philipps, later my wife, and in one of the photographs she has obediently swooned. Brian bends forward anxiously, with a soda-syphon, ready to revive her. The period interest of the picture is the excessive neatness, by contemporary standards, of the male participants' hair: very 1950s.

He wrote a masque to be presented in front of visiting Princess Margaret called, inevitably, *Porci ante margaritam* ('Swine before a Pearl'). I was in it in black doublet and hose,

Sally in a frightful wig, but remember nothing else about it, except the Brindleyesque nature of the script and the high wind that swept across the lawn of St Hilda's and blew most of the swines' voices (and Brian's lines) away, to the probable bewilderment of the pearl.

We lost touch for half a century, but, saddened, I went to his funeral, with its rococo extravagance, its surplices and choirings and flutings, and I understood, happily, that Brian had never changed. Its excesses were entirely appropriate: a recognition that life is serious, of course, and often tragic, but, when possible, is best taken as a generously shared joke.

CHAPTER FOUR

The Sound of Breaking Glass

NED SHERRIN

BRIAN BRINDLEY, AS I first saw him, lit up my gauche provincial eyes to the prospect of an Oxford that was a good deal more fun and sophisticated than my grammar-school years in Somerset. I cannot now remember when Brian came into the rooms opposite mine on our staircase, or when he moved out. I recall only his colourful occupancy. Tapestries and Victorian pictures filled the walls. Great glass domes housed stuffed birds and preserved fruit and flowers. Bric-à-brac and bibelots covered every surface. A fire blazed from autumn to spring, and in front of it we ate thin cumber sandwiches and white toast with Gentleman's Relish. I had never come across Gentleman's Relish before.

For two years, I shared the rooms across the landing with D. B. (Dai) Williams, a mercurial Welshman who went on to a distinguished career at the Bar and on the Bench. Below us were Firth and Mucklow, medical students whose names we spoonerized. Dai had pyromaniacal tendencies. One morning I complained to Brian that on the previous night he had entered my bedroom bearing a blazing wastepaper-basket that he tossed playfully at me. I was sufficiently awake to catch it and lob it back over his shoulder and out through the open window into the Turl. Firth and Mucklow, standing at their window, thought it must be some sort of meteor. Brian thought it was hilarious.

I saw in his obituaries that Brian read modern history, but I do not think that we ever discussed it. We did speculate on what he might do when he came down. For quite some time he considered a career as an interior decorator of churches, inspired perhaps by his architect friend Roddy Gradidge. In fact, he lingered on at Exeter, trying law before he eventually decided to go on to Ely Theological College.

Exeter was a small, friendly college. In his welcoming address to our year, Rector Barber described it as the second oldest in the university, or the fourth if you count lodging-houses. Mrs Barber, a bubbling Swiss, did much to break the ice between new arrivals when she mixed up the decanters at an early cocktail party and Brian and I found ourselves plied with neat whisky instead of the sherry she thought she was pouring.

Brian was rightly flushed with his first university triumph, the masque *Porci ante margaritam*. Much later, I produced an OUDS pantomime, *The Sleeping Beauty*. The first half, which I asked Brian to write, was his brilliant parody of a Victorian pantomime after Planché. The Beauty pricked her finger in 1853, just before the interval, and awoke in the modern pantomime world of 1953. The result was an anticlimactic second half that could not compete with Brian's virtuoso rhyming couplets. The line which stayed in my mind, and which I included in the *Oxford Dictionary of Humorous Quotations*, was given to a character who finds a letter pinned to a tree in the forest and exclaims: 'It would have been less heterodox if he had put the letter in the letter-o-box.'

We stayed a close group of half a dozen friends throughout my years at Exeter. Membership of the Adelphi, the college dining club, which started its meals in the Hall and then moved for various courses to different rooms, was another unifying factor. Sadly it is no more, but Brian did ask me as a guest soon after I had gone down and pandarously seated me next to an undergraduate with theatrical ambitions.

To visit Brian in Reading, and later in Brighton, was to witness the re-creation of his rooms at Exeter. To attend a service or parish function at Holy Trinity was to realize immediately what a lively and devoted congregation he had gathered and inspired. I read in one of his obituaries that when Bishop Henry Carpenter appointed him to Holy Trinity he said that he had put his most impossible priest into his most impossible parish. Brian summed up his predecessors vividly. He told me: 'One committed suicide, one was removed for immorality, and one went to London to visit the Boys' Own Exhibition and never came back.'

At some point in the 1970s, I bought at auction a file of correspondence between King Edward VII and his sometime mistress Daisy, Countess of Warwick. Part of a settlement she made with lawyers for King George V was an undertaking that her lover's personal letters, 'To my own, lovely, darling, little

Daisy', should be destroyed. They were; but before that she had them photographed, and the glass-plates survived in the bundle I purchased. I hoped to make a film about the romance, but the opportunity passed, and some years later I heard that the story was to be told in a play starring Coral Browne. I asked her to dinner to look over Daisy's effects. Brian was another guest. After dinner we spread the bills, *billets-doux* and solicitor's notes on the floor and got down on our knees to examine them.

Brian stood up suddenly to leave the room, and trod heavily on two pieces of transparent glass he had failed to see, smashing them into hundreds of pieces. For someone who had tripped so elegantly and in such a considered fashion through life it was mortifying – but it reminded me of another incident at Oxford.

Brian had a glass walking stick that he sometimes took out for an airing. One afternoon he was happily swinging it as he picked his way down the High. Somewhere around the Turl, he attracted the attention of a group of Teddy boys, who followed him, jeering. Brian pointedly ignored them, but with an unconcerned whirl of the glass stick he accidentally shattered it against a lamp-post. The jeering increased, but Brian affected not to notice and continued on his way, holding only the surviving crook in his raised hand.

Odd how two of my most vivid memories of Brian concern shattered glass.

I had no idea he was so ill when I attended his 70th birthday feast at the Athenaeum. I lunched with him there a couple of times, and he chaired a talk dinner at which I spoke some months earlier, so it was an innocent gesture when I handed him a pot of caviar as his present, saying: 'Something perishable, Brian, as neither of us has got long to go.'

The manner of his death, surrounded by friends, in the middle of a meal that he had so meticulously planned, was a typical refinement of the popular desire to die peacefully in one's sleep. Brian always knew how to go one better.

CHAPTER FIVE

'Like Some Fat Blackbird'

ALAN BENNETT

WHEN I MET B. D. F. T. Brindley in October 1954, he was the first person I had ever come across with four first-names and the only person I had ever met one of whose names was Titus. Both the number of his initials and the 'Titus' marked him out in my callow provincial eyes as indubitably a member of the upper classes, an impression which his dress and demeanour and above all his voice tended to confirm. If in the course of time I came to see that this wasn't quite the case, and though I came to like him, more to understand him and always to be amused by him, he never ceased to intimidate me.

I had gone up to Oxford as a history scholar at Exeter College after two years national service. Brian had done national service too, three or four years earlier, when he had served a stint as a disc-jockey on the British Forces Network in Germany. He was teamed with Karl Miller, an abrasive Scot of the Leavisite persuasion, who was subsequently editor of *The Listener*, founding editor of the *London Review of Books* and Northcliffe Professor of English Literature at University College, London. Sergeants both, they must have been an unlikely pairing, and I long to have heard some wordplay of Miller and Brindley as they vied to introduce the latest pressings of Anne Shelton and Dorothy Squires to the bemused barrack-rooms of the British Army of the Rhine.

I was 20 at the time of our first encounter, which would probably have been in the Lodge at Exeter, though Brian would also often preside at the head of the scholar's table in Hall. He seemed years older than we did and more like a don than someone who had only graduated the previous term. He was attempting a second Honours School, in law, but his attitude to academic matters was tangential.

He wore a three-piece suit, generally in charcoal grey, though occasionally favouring tweed with a discreet check. The waistcoat would be double-breasted, invariably with lapels, and across what was even then a discernible paunch stretched a gold watch-chain. Shirts might be coloured but the (detachable) collar was always starched and white, the tie probably from Hall's in the High. Exeter was at this time a prosaic, even dowdy, foundation, so Brindley stood out, though since eccentrics were in short supply I think the college, dons and undergraduates alike, were rather proud of their exotic cuckoo.

It might be thought that Brian's self-conscious elegance precluded hurry, but in my mind's eye he is always on the move, rushing round the front quad in agitated spurts, like some fat blackbird. His hands flapped in agitation, too, though wherever possible, as it was an elegant accoutrement, he was enveloped in the billowing folds of his bachelor's gown. And in the cartouche of memory that is how I see him, framed by its furls and folds.

At a time in the early 1950s when prudence might have dictated otherwise, Brian made no secret of his homosexual predilections, though they were generally expressed with such verve that even the objects of his affections found him easy to forgive. He was keen, or professed to be keen (with Brian you were never quite sure), on one Ogilvy, a blond fellow-lawyer and stalwart of the rugger team. In those days the lavatories at Exeter were off the back quad in an institutional block of a score or so cubicles where the lavatory paper was of the Izal interleaved variety. Brian procured two dozen or so packets of this brand and with a John Bull printing outfit painstakingly stamped 'Oggers is Lovely' on each individual sheet before carefully interleaving them again and replacing them in their various receptacles. The patience and application required in the accomplishment of this prank seemed to me in itself an education, the lesson being that if a thing is not worth doing, it's worth doing well. The same could be said of the exuberantly silly confections with which Brian decorated the JCR Suggestions Book – a drawing, for instance, of himself in cope and mitre presiding over the elevation to sainthood of some beefy South African Rhodes Scholar who had lately taken his fancy.

In my second year Brian was elected President of the JCR, which gave him rooms in college. His taste was for Soane and the Gothick, and his rooms were crowded with religious images and (though I did not know the word then) *bondieuserie*.

It was a decor to which on one occasion I unwillingly contributed. Outrageous, witty, but kinder than he would have liked you to think, he was also a bit of a bully. When he called on me in my attic room at the top of staircase 5 – the call a mark of significant social favour as much as was a visit from Lady Bracknell – he spotted among my sparse possessions two blue Bristol glass dishes, liners from some long-vanished salt-cellars. He begged one from me in order to use it as an incense burner, and so overawed was I by this arbiter of taste that (though it had not been cheap and they were after all a pair) I reluctantly gave it to him. I still have its fellow, and somewhere among the exquisite clutter of his Brighton house (for his taste had not altered one jot since he was an undergraduate) languishes, I imagine, its twin.

If I have portrayed him as being frivolous, which he seemed to me then, he was far from being a fool, and when he was interested in a subject he could be pre-eminent, as is testified by his later authority on ritual and ceremony and his position as a proctor in convocation. Still, when I read in Nancy Mitford's *Love in a Cold Climate* how at an Oxford dinner party Cedric Hampton had charmed the Waynflete Professor of Pastoral Theology, it rang a bell.

Cedric, the Professor and Alfred followed in a bunch, still pursuing a conversation that seemed to be interesting them deeply.

'Just a narrow edging of white,' Fanny heard Cedric say, as they came down the passage.

Later, Fanny is told by her theologian husband that they had been having a most fascinating talk on burial customs in the High Yemen, and that just because Cedric is a glutton for gossip does not mean that he is not nevertheless a most intelligent young man. Fanny is sceptical. 'The fact was Cedric could bring out edges of white to suit all tastes.'

And so, I think, could Brian.

But little edgings of white can only take you so far, and the carefree days when a whole morning could be whiled away in an armchair in front of the JCR fire, chatting and elaborating some architectural fantasy in the Suggestions Book, inevitably came to an end. Examinations loomed, and Brian's nerve failed: he had a sudden but short-lived nervous breakdown, which precluded attendance at the Schools, and for a few days thereafter remained sequestered in his rooms. Then he bounced back as if nothing had happened and ended his time at Oxford with all his usual style.

And I never saw him again, so the face that stared out at me from the obituary pages from behind a voluminous beard looked more like some Green Man peering through the foliage of a medieval boss than the plump young dandy I remembered.

This, though, was of my own choosing, as we had arranged to meet several times over the intervening years, with me always the defaulter. Latterly, he was always trying to get me to lunch at the Athenaeum, but with no more success: my feeling always being that, confronted with this personality I had as a young man found so intimidating, I would revert to what I had been then and become once more the awkward stammering youth I was happy to have left behind.

Besides, I could imagine that lunch, with Brian still calling me 'dear boy' and every detail of the conversation audible in the farthest corner of the dining-room.

Thus it was when Peter Sheppard asked me to read at Brian's funeral I told him of our history of non-meeting, saying that to play any part in a celebration of Brian dead when I had so often let him down living would seem like hypocrisy.

'Yes,' Peter Sheppard agreed, 'it would. But then, Brian would have loved that.' Which, of course, was true.

So, together with his other Exeter contemporary, Ned Sherrin, I read a lesson.

CHAPTER SIX

A Priest Remembered

NICHOLAS KRASNO

READING THE OBITUARIES AND reminiscences of Fr Brian Brindley at the time of his death was a moving experience for those of us who knew him well. There were precisely remembered anecdotes, memories of photographic exactitude conjured up after 50 years or more, even spurious tales related by those who hadn't met him. What I did not see – except for the occasional offhand remark – was any reference to the core of his existence and his true calling: that of a parish priest.

The first time I saw Brian Brindley he was walking up the aisle of Holy Trinity Church with a red rose in his black soutane. It was St George's day, 23 April 1969. I was 16, very impressionable, and I had been brought to Holy Trinity by my great-uncle and (appropriately enough) godfather, who was a stalwart of Reading's rival Anglo-Catholic parish, St Giles. I was not disappointed.

The Mass that day was like nothing that I had seen before: the Burgess propers, sung by a slightly quavering voice up in the gallery; the *outré* hymns to St George; sacred ministers in lace and gold vestments, wearing strange hats (I had not then ever seen a biretta). At that time, the altar was still in its position against the east wall, in a mean chancel. There was little to remember there, save for vases of gilt lilies on the gradine (I had never seen metal flowers before). There was an eclectic and good-looking crowd of servers and congregation.

My great-uncle and my grandfather had together attended Holy Trinity at various times in their youth, and I was sufficiently aware of the church's past to note the arrival of Brian Brindley announced in the *Reading Chronicle*, complete with photograph. His parish magazine carried the unusual title *Battle*. A friend and I giggled at the salutation, 'Dear little flock', with which the Father's letters were addressed each month. We also giggled a few years later at the suggestion that the Pugin screen that Brian proposed to buy from Birmingham would make Holy Trinity a 'place of pilgrimage' for lovers of Victorian Gothic. All these impressions, and my godfather's amused conspiratorial invitation, were in my mind as the door to the rest of my life opened that 23 April.

Though with a much older Anglo-Catholic tradition, St Giles was not as 'advanced' as Holy Trinity. One of Reading's three ancient parishes, it retained a ponderous air of respectability. Into this staid establishment occasionally flashed Brian Brindley, to assist in the distribution of Holy Communion at High Mass. He showed – I noted with approval from my place in the choir-stalls – understandable irritation with the disorganized, ill-mannered and overbearing servers. Brian and the vicar of St Giles had already formed a partnership in the town; there were joint pilgrimages to Walsingham.

Brian realized that special events gave people who wanted to stay loyal to other churches a chance to worship at Holy Trinity. The highlight of the year was the Feast of Title; to enable visitors to attend, a grand Evensong and Benediction of the Blessed Sacrament was held on the preceding Saturday afternoon. This was the occasion of my first significant encounter with Brian, when he thrust into my hands a copy of Briggs & Frere's pointed psalter with the command: 'You can read music, can't you? We'll need you to sing.' To be not only noticed but given a part in this liturgy was an empowering experience.

Even before I was a regular at Holy Trinity there were other experiences. There was a concert by 'Nadine, Countess of Shrewsbury' (it was indeed the opera singer and former wife of the Earl). My first Corpus Christi processions were memorable for the flowers scattered ankle-deep on the floor, and of course the experience of an outdoor procession. The herb-filled scent of the church and the unique smell of incense out of doors have never left me and, as fragrances often do, take me instantly back when I smell them again. Brian's extreme Anglo-Catholicism was in no way inconsistent with a love of ancient hymnody; back at home, I searched for the hymn-tunes we had sung. I felt I was on the edge of a great discovery.

Inevitably, I made Holy Trinity my regular place of worship. At Brian's command I began for the first time to serve regularly at Mass: it was a powerful and rather terrifying experience. It was also in those early 1970s that Brian encouraged me to contribute to the decoration of the church. A first project was the transformation of a large nineteenth-century, high-backed Gothic chair, with dingy and sagging upholstery, into a worthy bishop's throne. A paint process that Brian had discovered produced a distressed look of 'instant age'; the creation of a grand piece of furniture from a dingy relic was entirely new to me. Next came the marbling of the organ-case. I had no experience of marbling, or indeed painting on such a large scale, but my objections were dismissed and scaffolding was hired. The work took some weeks, and was an encouraging success. Brian suggested the colour scheme, and together we improvised the details and techniques, some of which involved chemically alarming mixtures of different paints. The Latin inscription was devised by Brian and applied using Letraset, one of his favourite design materials. I thereby also learned about lettering – another of his skills. Later, the new pedal towers were painted to match. It was all extraordinarily rewarding work.

And this, I think, was the secret of his success in building a community around him. His enthusiasm communicated itself through his personality when you first met him – and, before that, in his flair for publicity in the newspapers or the parish magazine. The breadth and depth of knowledge provided answers to one's questions and made him a sound teacher. He emphasized the emotional appeal of holy things, and the blend of the sacred with the familiar that is the hallmark of a now rather old-fashioned Anglo-Catholicism. His knowledge and enthusiasm were not to be admired only at a distance; one was dragged forcibly into the experience, given tasks to do, made part of the enterprise he was leading. For the young and provincial – this was Reading 30 years ago – it was heady stuff. This was not what 'church' was supposed to be like, and for many of us the experience caught and held us at that crucial (and dangerous) period in our lives. For some of us it holds us still.

The spiritual life of Holy Trinity was centred on the public liturgy: the high and solemn occasions as well as the daily celebration of the Mass. The extent and nature of Brian's personal piety was unclear, though this was a matter I did not consider my business. Though he did not appear to say the daily office, or pay much attention to parish calls, he rose early and worked hard, either at his desk or at meetings of the Church Union and the General Synod in London – and, above all, by keeping an open house for his flock. His love of, and obvious enjoyment of celebrating, the liturgy was matched with an insistence that only the best things were for God. I recall commenting on the purchase (in Italy, of course) of a holy-water stoop and suggesting that it would look good in the church. 'Not really good enough for the church – it's for the house,' he said. At the same time, there was a lingering element of reserve, of dignity. Brian had a high concept of priesthood, of its rights and responsibilities.

In 1983 he came to stay for a week with me in New York. He preached at St Mary the Virgin, a large and gloomy Episcopal church off Times Square, which I attended only occasionally. I preferred, as would Brian, some of the better Roman Catholic churches in the city, with their more familiar liturgy and more interesting buildings. Brian and I walked down Broadway from my apartment, he in soutane and *curé* hat attracting curiosity (and great respect from my Hispanic doormen). His sermon, illustrated with a description of the Pantheon in Rome, was far above the heads of the congregation, and the ensuing stiff and humourless lunch in the rectory provided little amusement. But we had other more jolly engagements, including dinner at a friend's 1830 town house in the city, and a bloated performance of *Porgy and Bess* at Radio City Music Hall, where the dressed-to-the-nines audience provided as much entertainment as the show. When in 1987 I went to live in New York again, Brian asked me where I would attend church. I was undecided, but he directed me quite plainly: 'I think you really have to attend and support St Mary's, even though it is not our style.' I did so obediently for ten years exactly, though it was increasingly uncomfortable and I gritted my teeth (and prayed for him) every Sunday.

After Brian retired to Brighton, I saw him often when I returned briefly to live in London again in 1994. By then, his illnesses were becoming more pronounced, and he complained about his increasing feebleness, without apparently doing much to remedy it. Our meetings followed a predictable pattern: he would tell me of his doings, first at Diocesan Church House, where he was doing great work, and then, after his retirement and reception into the Roman Church, at the Sacred Heart, Hove. He would show me his latest writings – at that time a vital source of income. It was apparent from the sales of his possessions, including his collection of vestments, that his financial situation was dire. He would also give me samples of typography that he had devised, many of them for friends he had in Brighton. Lunch on these visits was often at a small bistro round the corner – in later years, journeys to the centre of Brighton were impossible. He was not much interested in my doings, but this was more than made up for by flashes of the old wit and his inexhaustible source of knowledge on the most surprising subjects.

He enjoyed his new parish of the Sacred Heart, Hove, though it was perhaps less congenial than he made out. They allowed him to do certain things: a reading course for aspiring lectors (no doubt at his prompting, and why not – he was superb); elaborate typographical notices for the church; a setting of a Mozart aria to a sacred text; but he was still viewed with suspicion. A pretty church, and popular, it was nevertheless a far cry from the heady days at Reading, yet he never complained. He could be caustic about people he regarded as foolish, but he spoke with enthusiasm about the kindness of old friends, lay and clerical.

Though Brian was undoubtedly a gentler person in those post-Reading days, this seemed quite distinct from his membership of the Roman Catholic Church. Certainly, after his financial problems were solved by the generosity of others, he expressed great contentment in certain areas of his life, his health being the main exception. But his sometimes gloating satisfaction at being in the arms of the 'True Church' did not ring quite true. In part, it gave him a new role to play; and it also provided a way for him to break with the recent and painful past. He had destroyed his career through a silly indiscretion, but the Church of England and his diocesan bishop had treated him badly, if not quite as badly as he considered. This was a way of getting back at them.

During his parish career, Brian had relatively little contact with Roman Catholics. He had little time or inclination to mix with the local Roman parish clergy, who would have found his productions of 'their' *Missa normativa* bizarre and unsympathetic. On his trips to London he showed no interest in visiting their more glittering shrines – the Oratory, say, or Spanish Place. He experienced the Roman Catholic Church fleetingly when on holiday in Europe, of course, but he despaired of it liturgically, and probably pastorally as well. No: the Church of England was his natural habitat, and he was too intelligent to nurture any expectation that he would find a comfortable niche as a convert priest, or mould it to his way (the vain hope of many recent converts from the Church of England). But, though his conversion may indeed have been a reaction to recent events in his life, and not some deeper mystical Damascene revelation, the ministry of the clergy at the Sacred Heart, and the faint glimmers of good liturgy that it represented, were enough to prevent a loss of faith.

Of his past calling and work in Reading he spoke often. He remembered how he had led members of his flock towards paths they had scarcely known existed. He specifically asked that they tell their tales, in the form you see here. But, although he did not stress his spiritual influence on their lives, we should not assume that he did not consider his to have been the true ministry of a Catholic priest. Brian was as reluctant as any Englishman to talk about personal faith; but this does not mean that he had none, or that he thought his priestly calling had been a sham. His much-repeated 'vacuum-cleaner' joke – he said he felt like a salesman who had spent decades selling vacuum-cleaners, only to discover that they did not work – needs to be understood in the context of his desire to shock and to amuse. If he truly felt that his 25 years of work in the Church of England had been a fraud, such an intelligent and driven individual would have shown more convincing evidence of despair. Just as the appointment of his immediate successor at Holy Trinity had been in his view a mistake, and was a source of pain, so the next incumbent, and his sympathetic restoration of much of what he had built up, caused him great pleasure and satisfaction. This was not the view of a vendor of non-functioning vacuum-cleaners. Brian was delighted to see Holy Trinity restored as the living centre of a worshipping community, building on the work that he had accomplished 30 years previously. Those of us whose faith was nurtured at a crucial stage in our lives by this extraordinary pastor, teacher and friend will pray for his successors as they take up the challenge.

CHAPTER SEVEN

A Life Less Ordinary

PETER SHEPPARD

'ARE YOU THE CELEBRATED Fr Brian Brindley?' I asked. The year was 1968. I was a precocious 17-year-old schoolboy at a local performance of the Chester Mystery Plays. He was the parish priest of Holy Trinity, well known in the Reading deanery for being extravagantly high church and for his flamboyant appearance. He had a cherubic face, eighteenth-century curls and long sideboards, and wore a stiff Roman collar with a black clerical suit enhanced by a considerable embonpoint. I was immediately invited back to the presbytery – 'vicarage' was too C of E – for supper along with Tim Clarke, my English teacher. I remember that first meal: delicious vegetable soup made with coarsely cut cabbage, bacon and herbs, followed by a whole punnet each of English strawberries and clotted cream. Brian produced the supper in his kitchen: a narrow galley piled high with utensils and washing-up. Holofernes, a poodle with matted grey hair similar to Brian's own, scavenged, while Judith, a black cat, meandered along the dresser meowing. Very soon I was a regular at Holy Trinity.

The presbytery at 32 Baker Street, Reading, was Brian's home for twenty years. He had decorated it only a year or two before, but it was like entering another century. Even before one entered it there were signs that this was no ordinary house: next to the front door were chalked the names of the three wise men, Caspar, Balthazar and Melchior. Brian introduced the custom of the blessing of chalk after the Epiphany Mass, and encouraged his parishioners to write those legendary names by their own doors.

The black-glazed front door opened on to a hall of bright crimson. To the right was a study decorated in midnight-blue and dark green William Morris wallpaper, studded with religious pictures and lined with books; the desk was covered with layers of papers, books and inks. Nestling in the middle of the chaos was a portable Olivetti typewriter on which Brian would thump out his letters and articles with two fingers. Over the mantelpiece was a Victorian picture in a gilded frame which showed the face of Christ; but as you moved to the left and right St Joseph and St Francis mysteriously appeared. Luminous green Morris curtains added to the dark magic. Returning to the scarlet hall, one turned right through two full-length Morris willow curtains into the inner hall, also papered in willow, and then into the dining room. Painted in the darkest green, this was filled with a large oval mahogany table and William IV chairs with the stuffing beginning to show. White porcelain cherubs, vases and candlesticks were set off by a side table groaning with silver-plated tureens and crystal decanters.

Going through the swing-door into the kitchen, one never knew what to expect. If Mrs Payne had been in, the breakfast room – decorated in baroque blue and yellow Portuguese tile wallpaper and covered in instructions to mythical servants – would be a pleasing arrangement of china and unfamiliar foods such as tinned palm hearts and Bath Olivers. If Mrs Payne had not been in, and Brian had prepared supper, plates and dishes would be piled on top of each other. He was an imaginative but untidy cook: another meal, and he would reach out for any clean available pot, pan and plate until every single one had been used. My task was often to make fresh coffee in a complicated 1960s glass contraption. The smell of gently decaying food and coffee was not unpleasant for a day or two, but if a week had passed and the cleaning lady was away, Brian would have to be rescued by his kind parishioners Sue Stevens and Elizabeth Utting.

The most comfortable room in the presbytery was the upstairs drawing room. It was also wallpapered in Morris – a diagonal swirling pattern of ochre and chrome yellows. Brian had inherited his parents' furniture from their house in Bushey, and huge comfy red chairs and a boudoir grand piano invaded a room already over-furnished by 1960s standards. There was a lovely Regency sofa in striped terracotta and yellow velvet, and the centrepiece of the room was a copy of a Raphael painting of Our Lady. Every surface of the piano was covered in domes of waxed fruit, boxes of chocolates and sugared figs. Brian had a knack of putting things together. Collections of pop-up books, kaleidoscopes and alabaster eggs were mixed with pieces from his past: a glazed pot by Walter Crane, a bronze figure of a youth holding a three-pronged candlestick. By the hearth sat a silver-plated Gothic kettle purchased from one of his jumble sales. On the television sat a glazed Buddha, softening the technological intrusion.

I would often spend the afternoon with Brian discussing the Act of Settlement, the pointlessness of fish-knives or the art of typography. On other afternoons, Brian would settle down to read Jane Austen, a paper opposing the Anglican–Methodist Union or the *Daily Telegraph*. Brian was not much interested in music until 1975, when he decided that he ought to be, and then he bought every classical record available. Similarly, his backyard was a jungle until he decided to make a garden, which he did skilfully by planting the most correct flowers and herbs. The garden was an extension of the house, populated by concrete statues of Apollo, Pan and the Three Graces, with a gazebo and terrace. Few objects in the house or garden were of great value; it was the effect that he loved. He said that he wanted his home to look like one which had been developed by a family of taste, almost as though the house had always existed. It didn't, of course: it was unmistakably his personality and past. The exotic, the historical, the theatrical, the learnedness, the trivial, the camp, the grandeur and the chaos were all features of the house, and of Brian himself.

I once heard Douglas Bean, the Rural Dean of Reading, exclaim: 'How can anyone take him seriously, looking like that?' Brian was wearing a cassock, cloak, broad-rimmed black beaver hat and buckled shoes. His lay dress was hardly quieter: a three-piece suit in Prince of Wales check, with gingham shirt, clashing tie and two-toned shoes. Facially, he looked like a cross between George IV, in the cartoon by Rex Whistler, and Oscar Wilde, with the grand manner to match.

Brian like to mix his loyal elderly parishioners – Miss Harris, who made the most delicious cucumber sandwiches, and Mrs Goodall, her posh arch-rival – with his eccentric London friends and young parishioners. Ivy Harris was a very singleminded old lady whom I once discovered putting a parcel of clothes under a rug and standing on it 'to make it lighter and cheaper to post'. The circle was further enhanced by the strange Trevor Brown, who provided partridges and smoked salmon but whose cheques invariably bounced. A part of all our lives, he mysteriously disappeared for ever. A solitary postcard from South Africa told us he was well and begged us to write. There was no address.

Characters from London would visit. Roderick Gradidge shared Brian's passion for architecture and high church. Brian thought Roddy's appearance outrageous. He disapproved of his earrings, long hair and tattoos. The curate's wife once complimented Roddy on 'that beautiful shirt with the dragon on the back'; it was actually a plain white see-through shirt. Roddy longed to be a Teddy boy and often wore a 'drape' with a velvet collar and suede brothel-creepers. The tall, elegant Simon Blow arrived in a vast pink American car with his smaller, grander friend, Tatton Sykes (now Sir Tatton Sykes of Sledmere Castle), both of them attired in fur. Simon, whose flat in South Audley Street was in the latest modern style with silver walls, donated all his clothes to Brian's jumble sale. I bought Turnbull and Asser shirts, Mr Fish suits and kipper ties for a fiver. Ned Sherrin made rude jokes when opening Holy Trinity's Christmas market. The *Carry On* actress Liz Frazer was photographed on Brian's sofa for the local paper

Loose Canon: A Portrait of Brian Brindley

under the headline 'More Tea, Vicar?' Peter Levi SJ, the distinguished poet, preached.

For a teenager from suburbia, meeting these colourful personalities was like entering the world of Ronald Firbank. At this time I lived with my mother and father and my two younger brothers in a very ordinary semi-detached house, four miles south of Reading's centre. My mother, on discovering that a Regency house was for sale opposite the presbytery, was encouraged by Brian to buy it, and my whole family became part of the parish. From the moment I met Brian I hardly ever went back to school. We travelled up to town together. On alternate Wednesdays Brian would have his haircut at Stephen August's in Chester Row. Stephen was a good-looking and sophisticated hairdresser who specialized in cutting the hair of the rich and famous. It was a centre of gossip, and next door to Brian's beloved St Mary's, Bourne Street. After haircuts we would go to the copper-lined Chelsea Drug Store in the King's Road. This might be followed by tea at the Ritz, drinks with Felix Hope-Nicholson and dinner at the Chanterelle in Brompton Road, then the last train back to Reading.

Once a year Brian organized 'Food Week', which involved eating in the best restaurants listed in *The Good Food Guide* and visiting country houses in between. Brian had a prodigious appetite and rarely did lunch or dinner consist of fewer than four courses. I still remember with nausea a dinner (after a gargantuan lunch) at Thornbury Castle, where the wrong first course of avocado and prawns had been given to me, to be replaced by artichoke mousse with crab. By the time the navarin of lamb arrived, I was sick. Brian had little interest in wine or alcohol in general: he was intoxicated by cream, butter and rich food, as well as by young men and good conversation.

Brian once told me that his mother, when she fell out with one of her relations – which she did often – would carefully cut out that person from every photograph using a pair of nail-scissors. It was a family trait. Brian fell out with people he didn't agree with or approve of. I once grew a beard and he refused to speak to me: 'No *nice* person has a beard,' he said. (As an old man he grew one himself.) He generously took me to Venice, Florence and Rome. But when I told him, sitting in a coffee bar by La Fenice, that I had once worn a false earring, he declined to talk to me for two days. He had a way of insisting that we meet. Postcards would arrive when I was at art college trying to pin me down, and eventually he got so cross that he stopped speaking to me. This was around 1976, when he demanded that we go to the country for lunch and I told him I couldn't spare the time, as I was trying to run my own design business.

For the next thirteen years we hardly spoke, despite the fact that I became the churchwarden and master of ceremonies at Holy Trinity and lived across the road from his church. On one occasion I went to confession thinking that it was the curate behind the curtain, but to my horror it was Brian who peered out through the grill. I once received a bottle of claret from him with the message: 'With Good Wishes for Christmas. This is a gift for you as my churchwarden. It is not a personal present.'

In 1988 I bought a house in Cheyne Walk. Returning home one morning, I was approached by a little man in a raincoat who wanted 'to have a few words'. Suspecting that he was from the Inland Revenue, I asked him in. He then revealed that he was from the *News of the World* and that there was about to be an exposé of Canon Brian Brindley in his paper. He tried to blackmail me into corroborating his story, which was based on a tape-recording of Brian at dinner after too much wine and in the company of a charming and apparently interested young reporter. I refused and threatened to sue the paper if they printed anything about me.

After he left I immediately rang Brian, who was already aware of the calamity that had befallen him. Our long silence was broken and we became firm friends again. For a while he disappeared into his small basement flat in Brighton. After three weeks of battering in the tabloid press and plenty of local coverage, his face was infamous in Reading. He still hoped to return to his post, but the tapes were five hours long and despite his excellent memory he couldn't remember how much material was left. The *News of the World* was knocking on local people's doors, and they got one publicity-seeking woman to make up a story.

After six weeks he did return and, accompanied heroically by my mother Joan, made shopping expeditions into Reading. He came to a garden party in my Reading house, St Giles's Old Rectory, wearing a white cassock piped in crimson. One day he called me over to his garden and asked what he should do. The Bishop of Oxford, Richard Harries, was under great pressure from Brian's evangelical opponents, and was finding it difficult to support him, especially as no one knew what was left on that tape. By the next day, Reading's most colourful character had gone and the parish life, which he had nurtured, began to ebb away.

Visiting Brian in Brighton in his damp flat, I found him remarkably cheerful. He grew a pigtail and wore a red polka-dotted bandanna and denim shorts. Freed from the onerous chairmanship of the business sub-committee of the General Synod, a position he had once prized, he became a sweeter person. His friend and former tutor Eric Kemp, the Bishop of Chichester, found him a job as assistant secretary of the Chichester Diocese. After the Synod's vote to ordain women priests in 1992, he announced that his orders had always been invalid and that his life as a priest amounted to nothing. He was received into the Catholic Church at Sacred Heart Church, Hove. Damian Thompson and I were his sponsors and, much to our embarrassment, he insisted on kissing us both on the mouth during the Kiss of Peace.

By this time something very nice had happened. A forgotten life-assurance policy matured, and Brian received a cheque for £60,000. He made an offer on a house in Brighton by the Regency architect, Amon Wilds, and managed at the age of 63 to get a 30-year mortgage. This was the project he needed. Number 4, Western Terrace, is the last house of five in a cul-de-sac, opposite an onion-domed house known as the Western Pavilion. Designed in 1827, the terrace looks like a single grand house, with pediment, pilasters, ammonite capitals and asymmetrical bow windows, painted white with iron balconies. The houses were totally rebuilt with new interiors, and aspire to the highest principles of design and decoration.

Instead of the chalked names of the three kings, two concrete lions guard the front door. A stone fountain trickles water, and some of the clear window-panes have been replaced with coloured glass. The matt green and grey front door opens on Brian's masterly re-creation of Sir John Soane's hallway in Lincoln's Inn Fields. Classical statues line the hall, which has a Venetian *trompe l'œil* floor. A marble bust and two pots sit on an arch dividing the space. Over the top of the meticulously painted walls are pasted engravings, including an enormous one of ancient Rome. A grandfather clock stands on the quarter-turn of the stairs. A politically incorrect and badly executed Moor holds a letter-tray. A notice behind the bust of a Roman emperor proclaims in elaborate letters: 'I have just gone to visit old Mr Waitrose – back soon.'

The panelled doors into the drawing-room have been grained rich red with black outlines with black bosses, and on the other side tiny circular mirrors. Our Lady of the Drawing-Room presides over walls painted in pink with hand-painted azure birds, lanterns and flowers and other Chinese motifs copied from the Pavilion. Icons, gilded lilies, candlesticks and Chinese porcelains cover every inch of surface. A television with a cornucopia of videos spills into the room. The parental furniture is now well worn. A vast gilt chandelier, ingeniously fitted with tiny bulbs and wax candles, is joined by table-lamps, standard-lamps and wall-lights. Brian adored playing with the effect of lighting; while he hated modernity, he loved technology.

The dining room (though Brian never actually ate here) is dominated by a mural of Brighton Pavilion, with Brian in period clerical dress walking through the garden. On the opposite wall are views of the seaside, including sailors and dandies. Having commissioned the mural from Gary Sollars, Brian insisted on having a green trellis design painted over it, much to his friends' consternation. Teapots on plinths are mounted on the mural, as well as the wax fruit that sat in his rooms at Exeter College

The boudoir grand piano is stacked with benediction candle-sticks; there is a photograph of Brian smiling patronizingly at Pope John Paul II during a visit to Rome. The silver serving dishes, decanters and furniture have found a new home here. Over the architraves are plinths that carry glazed mythical creatures, not in pairs but in sixes. Little piles of letters and papers lie everywhere. Copies of the *Catholic Herald*, for which he wrote regularly, are still in their poly-thene envelopes. When we went through the room after his death, we found unopened bills – Brian was perpetually about to be cut off from this or that – and twenty uncashed cheques amounting to nearly £2,000.

To many people, Brian's houses and church were over-decorated and over-furnished. His liturgy was old-fashioned and over-the-top. But that was how he liked it. He did not conform to the conventions of good behaviour; he always believed he was right and it was very hard to make him change his mind. The pigtail he grew at the age of 60 when he was trying unsuccessfully to find a new living in the Church of England was a typical example. His friends pleaded with him to cut it off to make himself more acceptable to parochial church councils. Eventually he did remove it, and pinned it up on the wall with the motto: 'A Sacrifice to Ambition'.

Brian showed his friends what life could be like. Homes did not have to be dull. Food could be exotic, and 'things' put together an interesting way. He was the master of making the most of all that he had – his middle-class upbringing, his appearance, his church, his ordinary houses, his few distinguished friends, even his sometimes limited knowledge of a particular subject. In a bland and conventional world, he was determined to prove that life could be less ordinary.

CHAPTER EIGHT

Brindley at the Keyboard

SEÁN FINNEGAN

IN ALL THE OBITUARIES and comments that followed Brian Brindley's death, one word appeared again and again: flamboyant. And there was another that could equally well have been used: cluttered. There was scarcely an aspect of his life that was not both of these things. Most people's experience of Brian will have been during his public ministry, when the flamboyant and cluttered Holy Trinity Church inspired and certainly entertained the locals, as well as those borne on the 'fast trains from London' advertised in the parish magazine. I did not know Brian at this time, but I can imagine what it was like, for in many ways he was a consistent man. The notorious *News of the World* article and his conversion to Rome turned his world upside-down, and he retired to hold court in a little house in Brighton which was to become the epitome of flamboyant clutterdom for the next eight years or so. And it was here that he was to achieve a strange late flowering of his remarkable artistic skills. No longer able to put on vast liturgical spectacles, he gave vent to his talents in a new and surprising way. He took to the Apple Macintosh computer.

This may come as a surprise to those who did not know him in this retired phase of his life; Brian was not naturally one to embrace modern technology unless it could do something seriously useful, like his ice cream-maker or his bread-maker. But the Apple Mac enabled him to produce beautiful things on paper. He had long had an interest in typography: he had read and possessed most of the classical works on the subject. At Holy Trinity he used an old Amstrad computer with a dot-matrix printer to produce fantastical frontispieces for parish magazines, with columns and pediments and inscriptions. But now he had a much more powerful machine. The discovery that there was an infinite range of fonts at his disposal led him to spend almost every free moment peering myopically at the huge screen provided for him by Peter Sheppard, trying not to entrap his long nails between the keys. He eagerly seized on the facility of Macs to be customized by their user, colouring his screen so dazzlingly ('Isn't it lovely, Father?') that one almost required sunglasses to look at it. The programme's name, appropriately, was Byzantium.

When Brian first got the computer, I had just moved to join a religious community in Oxford. For weeks, the wires were hot with new discoveries. One day my superior came in with several pages of fax paper; 'I think this must be for you,' he said, disapprovingly. They turned out to be page after page full of huge ampersands from about a hundred different fonts, without a word of explanation. I rang Brian. 'Aren't they particularly handsome, Father?' he said. Always impecunious, he would think nothing of using up a whole expensive inkjet cartridge to print something in reverse: there was, I remember, a verse from some operatic ensemble printed so that the background was entirely green and the very few words in white.

Our tastes did not coincide: I love a classical appearance on the page, with little decoration and plenty of white space. This was anathema to Brian. His pages were a sort of typographical Barnum's Circus, and he was dissatisfied if there were fewer than seven or eight fonts on a single page, often of the most disparate nature: Gothic, Old English, Fraktur, Plantin, outlandish poster fonts and one that had every letter in the shape of a distorted Christmas pudding. It wasn't to everybody's taste – to my eyes, the result resembled nothing so much as a ransom note – but he was, as always, supremely confident that he had produced a masterpiece. 'Isn't that good?' The staff of the *Catholic Herald* enjoyed the arrival of his weekly contributions by fax, not least for their improbably glorious frontispieces, always surmounted with the greeting *Fax vobiscum* and occasionally ending *Dona nobis facem*.

'I never joke' was another of Brian's lines, and this was true so far as it went: he never 'told' jokes. But his satirical wit was magnificent, and his skills with the computer were put to good use in this regard. He produced a hilarious notice, supposedly from Archbishop Geoffrey Fisher, on the precise use of the gentlemen's lavatory in Lambeth Palace, and claimed that it was a very accurate typographical representation of a contemporary notice. I am not convinced that Eyre & Spottiswoode (the alleged printers) would have quite such an eclectic taste in typefaces, but naturally Brian could not resist putting in as many as possible.

LAMBETH PALACE, S.E.1.

USE OF THE GROUND-FLOOR RETIRING-ROOMS
A Memorandum by His Grace the Archbishop.

T HE ground-floor retiring-rooms (known locally as "Δ τόπος") are clearly divided into three chambers by the transverse gothic arches.

The "**Inner Sanctum**" (sometimes jestingly called the "*Holy of Holies*")
is customarily reserved for the use of *Bishops* (diocesan, suffragan,
colonial, and retired,) & other members of the House of Lords,
& of deans (*but not provosts*) of *English* cathedrals.

The same facility is extended by courtesy to the
Moderator of the General Assembly of the Church of Scotland,
to the
Moderator of the Free Church Federal Council,
& to
Roman Catholic bishops for England & Wales.

The "**Middle Court**" is reserved for the use of other deans & provosts,
canons, members of the House of Commons,
Lords Lieutenant, Lord Mayors, members of the Church Assembly,
foreign bishops, & the inferior clergy generally.

The "**Outer Court**" ("Γαββαθᾶ") is available to laymen generally.
Please note, however, that, to avoid congestion, on occasions of larger concourse,
(including the Lambeth Conference, & garden parties,)
The "Inner Sanctum" may also be used by provosts & canons, Lords Lieutenant, & Lord Mayors.

✠ ✠ ✠

[N.B.: Distinct arrangements for ladies & women, in another part of the
Palace, have been made under the direction of Mrs. Geoffrey Fisher.]

* SMOKING IS NOT PERMITTED *
in any part of the ground-floor retiring-rooms.
Facilities for smokers are provided in a room on the lowest floor of the Lollards' Tower.

W HILST it is appreciated that these arrangements of use and wont cannot have the force of Law, it is hoped that they will be cheerfully observed by all those concerned, in the interests of seemliness, due order, the equality (rightly understood) of man and man, and ease of social intercourse, bearing in mind the injunction of St Paul:

"Let all things be done decently and in order." I Cor., 14. 40.

≠ Geoffrey Cantuar:

EYRE & SPOTTISWOODE, LTD,
PRINTERS TO HIS MAJESTY.

About the same time, he produced a series of what he called tablemats (he was rather vague about the process by which these pieces of A4 paper might be transformed into something you could put a hot plate on), showing satires on many of the bench of Anglican bishops, all in the style of nineteenth-century tradesmen's advertisements. George Carey was a 'pork Butcher', Graham Leonard a 'funambulist, who studied under the best Italian masters', Eric Kemp, the prodigiously long-serving bishop of Chichester, was 'shy, but not retiring'. There was also one in a very faint typeface telling of a forth-coming series of mats depicting the 'lovable eccentricities' of the Roman Catholic hierarchy; in the interests of accuracy, they were to be left entirely blank.

Unsurprisingly, although Brian rapidly learned to drive the computer, he kept his distance from what went on under the bonnet. I knew a little bit more than he did, and so from time to time I would get a phone call. 'I was wondering if you would like to come to lunch, Father.' I knew what that meant. And so I would drive down from Oxford or, later, from Guildford, to see a Brian a little iller and a little more unwieldy than last time. 'You go upstairs first, Father, and I'll take my time after you,' he would say. I passed one day on the stairs a picture of a curly-headed infant: 'Your sister, Brian?' 'No, that's me. Wasn't I a beautiful child!' By the time he had made it upstairs, I was already trying to make sense of the computer. It was a frustrating experience. Once one's eyes had adjusted to the visual riot of Byzantium, one had to negotiate one's way down through layers of abandoned documents, homeless programmes and aliases, all in no particular order – the electronic counterpart to his desk, his house, his life –

so that it took ages just to find the software files. And the prodigious quantities of fonts he had loaded slowed up the machine excruciatingly; it trundled along at a grinding two miles a fortnight that he somehow never seemed to mind. I was rarely of much use to him; what he really needed was a new, powerful machine, but that simply could not be afforded.

Then there came the Internet: once online, I expected Brian to take off with delight, but he used to complain that he couldn't find anything at all of interest or use on the web. 'Then you are not Brian Brindley, but an imposter,' I thought. But it was Brian all right, just a very ill Brian. On my last visit to him he spoke with me frankly and calmly about his funeral: we had never talked much about religion, just about its periphery. I was very moved by his deep faith, which we discussed on this occasion; famously, not every aspect of his life had been holy, but he told me that, once an adult, he never for a moment doubted the goodness of God nor the truths of the Christian Gospel, and I believed him.

It was fitting that our last communication, a few days before his death, should have been electronic. I had sent him an email telling him that I was joining the London Oratory. His response was entirely characteristic, just five words: 'So handy for Harvey Nicks.'

CHAPTER NINE

'Renovating Heaven and Adjusting the Stars'

ANTHONY SYMONDSON SJ

IN THE SUMMER OF 1995 I was invited to give a talk to the Friends of St Michael and All Angels, Brighton. At the tea-party afterwards, I noticed an eccentric figure with a head swathed in a white beard and long hair, wearing a Hawaiian shirt, shorts, sandals and gold-rimmed spectacles. He looked like the Old Man of the Sea on a SAGA holiday. With a slight sense of dismay I noticed him coming in my direction and I flexed myself for a conversation with a queer fish. As soon as he spoke in a grand Oxford drawl I knew who he was: Brian Brindley. I had not seen him for many years and he had become unrecognizable.

The last time significantly, I think, must have been at my ordination to the Anglican priesthood in St Peter's, De Beauvoir Town, Hackney, in 1977, when he turned up with an elaborate haircut that looked like an eighteenth-century clerical wig, and wore an extravagant cotta with lace falling from his pectoris to below his knees. Some asked afterwards if he was a visiting woman priest from America, and when I told him he was not at all pleased.

Brian was then approaching the zenith of his fame as vicar of Holy Trinity, Reading, and had become a notable member of the General Synod. He was on the way to becoming the most renowned Anglo-Catholic priest in the Church of England. He had already achieved notoriety for his wit and debating brilliance in the chamber, and for the idiosyncratic magnificence of the services and furniture of his church. Yet, although he was a powerful advocate for the cause, he was not trusted by the Anglo-Catholic establishment.

Brian cannot be dissociated from extreme Anglo-Catholicism or from his career in the Church of England. They composed the greater part of his life and energy. When I renewed my friendship with him, both of us had independently become Roman Catholics and moved on to an entirely different state of life. I had joined a religious order; Brian remained a layman. I had not known that he had become a Catholic and I was pleased that he had entered the Roman Church and to see him again. But I was cautious and a little shy, because much water had passed under the bridge in the intervening period and some of it was opaque. Later that evening we went for a drink with Prebendary Gerard Irvine and his sister Rosemary, at their delightful stuccoed, Morris-papered house in Montpellier Road. In a curious way this brought my acquaintance with Brian round full circle to the time when I first met him and Gerard, when I was about to leave school in 1958.

I had been taken by a relation to see St Mary's, Bourne Street (Pimlico), and, together with Wren's St Magnus-the-Martyr (London Bridge), thought that it was the most exotic and beautiful church I had ever seen. Both churches embodied Anglo-Catholic Congress Baroque: the services had remained unchanged in their polished, Roman perfection from the period when they had been fixed as a model of the Netherlandish liturgical ideals of the Society of SS Peter and Paul and Adrian Fortescue's *Ceremonies of the Roman Rite Described* at the end of the First World War. They embodied the liturgical precepts of St Pius X. High Mass was faultlessly celebrated as a sensuous work of art. The music was contrapuntal polyphony, specializing in the Tudor masters. Achieved by the virtuosity of Martin Travers, these churches made self-consciousness appear natural, they possessed a magnetic quality that was difficult to resist, and seemed altogether persuasive as an expression of classic Anglo-Catholicism.

I first met Brian at a party one Sunday after High Mass at St Mary's. The curate, David Davies, formerly of Little St Mary's, Cambridge, brought together his flock after they had come to London and, as many had been to school together, they brought their friends. Women never featured at these gatherings. Brian was one of a group of three Stoics, including Peter Jameson and Roderick Gradidge, both of whom were studying architecture. Fuelled by rage, Gradidge started a wearisome row with me about most things that ran, with occasional remissions, for the next 40 years. Brian introduced a formidable, impossibly ostentatious, element of Oxford sophistication. He alarmed as much as he fascinated.

Imagine a somewhat raffish ecclesiastical party, with gin flowing, cigarette smoke, laughter and loud conversation. Brian, aged 26, was standing against a bookcase holding a glass, wearing spectacles, dressed in tweeds and a moleskin waistcoat with a thin gold watch-chain, his hair standing up and parted in the middle, a grey complexion and slightly yellow teeth. He talked about the miracles of St John of Capistrano, *contra lumini del gradini*, osculations, holidays in Spain and Italy with his mother, and Bernini's polychromatic statue of the death of St Stanislaus Kostka, recumbent on a couch of marble that resembled watered silk, in San Andrea al Quirinale, in Rome. It was his favourite piece of sculpture. 'Larvely,' he said, with a long emphasis on the first syllable. In a tuneless voice he unexpectedly broke into a humorous hymn he had written which started 'Mary is a mystery, she is the Mother of God'. I only vaguely remember how it continued but it had an ending that shocked me keenly. The room found it deliciously funny. I thought he was a grandee, a young man of fashion, and when I mentioned this to the others after he had gone they snorted. 'Old Brindlebelly,' said David, and everybody laughed.

At this point I should say that this was not my world. After the wholesome, serious, suburban Anglo-Catholicism of my boyhood, St Mary's, its Oxbridge religion and aesthetic perfectionism, was caviar to the multitude. I was highly strung, shy, socially awkward, and Bourne Street opened up an enticing new world that had the excitement of danger and an escape from a restrictive sphere of discouraging respectability in South London. It represented madder music and stronger wine. One of the curates at our church at home warned me against St Mary's and West End religion. That made it all the more attractive. David's group was a rockpool and Brian was its most highly coloured anemone.

The Vicar was F. E. P. S. Langton, who had suffered appalling injuries in the Royal Flying Corps during the First World War when a propeller pierced his stomach. He was a cynic and a snob who spoke in a cracked, strangulated voice and was reputed to be the ablest casuist in the Church of England. Fr Langton had sailed the extremes. Influenced by N. P. Williams's *Northern Catholicism*, and the liberalism of the Cambridge school, he had, like many of his generation, embraced non-papal Catholicism. This seemed an odd position at a church that was a simulacrum of Rome and effectively turned it, I came to think, into a gilded sepulchre. He took a keen delight in the opposition of some of the French clergy to the definition of the dogma of the Assumption in 1950, yet observed the feast with panache. St Mary's used the Holy Communion service of The Book of Common Prayer disguised as the Roman Mass. The parish's line was that Bourne Street represented what the Church of England could be. Fr Langton once embarrassed me by saying, with a salacious smile, that somebody had said to him that Solemn Benediction at St Mary's was like the chorus at the Chelsea Palace dancing the cancan in crumpled nylon panties. I thought he was vile.

St Magnus-the-Martyr was a more serious venture. London was full of old smells in those days. After the delicious camphor-scented air of the fur warehouses lining Upper Thames Street, Lower Thames Street provided a rank contrast. Buried in the stink of Billingsgate fish-market, against which incense was a welcome antidote, St Magnus was the most extreme Anglo-Catholic church in the Church of

England. It is a graceful composition of Wren, Gibbons and Travers and looks like a seventeenth-century Catholic church in the Low Countries. Eliot had described the 'inexplicable splendour of Ionian white and gold' in *The Waste Land*.

H. J. Fynes-Clinton, the aged and learned rector, was kindly satirized as Fr Chantry-Pigg in Rose Macaulay's *The Towers of Trebizond*. Like Fr Langton, Fr Fynes-Clinton was of old clerical stock; but he was grave, grand, well-connected and holy, with a laconic sense of humour. He said the Roman Mass in English and offered delights such as Low Mass with music, said at side-altars, accompanied by an elderly organist who had studied in Paris in 1911. While accepting everything Rome taught, he was opposed to conversions because he had known some that had led to atheism. Anglo-Catholics had a duty to stay and convert the Church of England from within until corporate reunion was achieved. The more advanced the position, he believed, the sooner this would be realized.

Fr Fynes-Clinton spoke with an almost inaudible, late-nineteenth-century aristocratic intonation that lent itself to the silent Canon. His church was so beautifully appointed and ordered that, before the war, distinguished Roman Catholic priests would sometimes come to see how things should be done properly. I had become a solicitor's articled clerk at a Dickensian practice in Lincoln's Inn Fields and used to go there to Mass in my lunch hour; so too, I discovered, did Brian and we became servers. Fr Fynes-Clinton insisted that we should wear leather slippers with rubber soles to protect the black and white marble of the sanctuary. 'I always thought rubber was middle-class,' objected Brian, but not to the Rector's face.

Off-stage, Brian was less intimidating, as there was not so much need to swagger. His mind was captivating. If you went into a church he would imagine how it could be transformed into something very High if it was very Low, and even Higher if it was already High. He liked the terms 'High' and 'Low', and would tease Anglo-Catholics who insisted on using 'Catholic'. Expeditions with him to look at churches, buildings and pictures were illuminating and enjoyable; but I wearied sometimes of his desire to improve everything. However great the architect, Brian could always do better. He wanted, for instance, to hang Gibbs's St Mary-le-Strand in rose-red damask and turn it into a small Roman church with a baroque reredos, a sarcophagus altar with a tabernacle in the form of a *tempietto*, diagonally flanked by altars made from Kent tables, one of them crowned by a portrait of King Charles the Martyr. After Brian was ordained, Roddy said he hoped Brian would never get a decent church as he would ruin it.

Brian invited me to stay at his parents' house in Bushey Heath. Fred and Violet Brindley had bought it in 1948, when Brian was 17. Previously they had lived at Northwood Park, in Middlesex, and before that in Harrow, where Brian was born on 4 August 1931. His London, school and Oxford friends had talked of his croquet and fireworks parties and their treasure-hunts. I was intrigued to see where he lived. I remember travelling down in a Green Line bus for dinner. It was a large, brown-brick, gabled, stockbroker's Tudor house in a large garden full of lawns, shrubs and rose-beds. It was opulent and comfortably furnished in the style of Harrods and Maples, and I saw for the first time pieces of furniture, pictures and ornaments that would accompany Brian through life in his own houses as symbols of continuity in an ever more heavily layered palimpsest. At dinner we were waited on by his mother's maid, Louise, in a starched cap, black dress and apron; I had already heard of her at Bourne Street, where she was mockingly described by David as a 'maid in streamers'.

Brian's study was extraordinary. Papered dark green, lined with books, it was hung with Victorian steel engravings in gilded frames, dominated by a large copy in oils of the Madonna and Child by Franciabigio. There were winged arm-chairs upholstered in rose-red damask; the surfaces were covered in wax fruit beneath glass domes and *objets de piété*. It was there that I realized how interesting he was. It was, I suspect, an overflow from his Oxford days – but it also showed the influence of Stowe.

The greatest formative influence in Brian's life was Bill McElwee, Stowe's charismatic Head of History, who lived with his wife Patience in elegant disorder in Vancouver Lodge. The gatherings there of the historians were influential not only on the way Brian thought but also on his taste, as were McElwee's 'culture tours' in France and Italy. In 1948 they visited Arles, Nîmes, Carcassonne, Vezelay and Rheims; and in the following year Milan, Venice, Florence, Ravenna and Siena. McElwee took the boys to decent hotels and let them drink. The exposure to foreign food, wine and light was intoxicating. The germ of Brian's eclectic informality of style was sown by the McElwees. So were his social attitudes, code of manners, High Tory politics, broad culture, love of travel and food. McElwee taught Brian that pleasure was the basis of civilization.

Betjemanism pervaded the life of Vancouver Lodge, inspired by the snobbish unmasking of social pretensions in the poem 'How to Get on in Society', first published in 1951. Betjeman liked to use the language of the upper class; so did others at that time who were, like him, middle class. His mockery started as a private joke, and was given general currency in 1956 when Nancy Mitford published *Noblesse Oblige*, which contained essays by her and Alan Ross on 'U' and 'Non-U' vocabulary. It was an infection easily caught, and throughout his life Brian never recovered from it.

Brian had presented Patience McElwee with an epergne made of red glass, which he felt would be a perfect table centre-piece. He celebrated this event by writing a Betjemanesque parody, 'The Pellucid Moment', and in doing so also, perhaps, recalled life in Bushey Heath:

Amid the humdrum cares of life just think what joy you're
    giving
By spreading, as a Clever Wife, the cult of gracious living;
It's not alone the polished floors, the windows gleaming brightly,
But other less familiar chores that must be done politely;
These small refinements should be shown in cottage or in
    chateau:
The doyley crisp beneath the scone, the frill around the gateau,
The sweet that's topped with whipped cremette, the salad plates
    all hot,
The folding of a serviette to represent a yacht,
The dainty tea, the frozen pea, the glass of empire wine,
The gleam of spotless napery, the fragrant hint of pine;
The tin of beans, the fingered fish, achieve a real panache

If in a silver entrée dish. Here's how to make a splash:
Place on your board some grand epergne with ivy twining
    through it;
Rub up the ornamental urn and fill again the cruet.
Make sure your bathroom has appeal – neglect is sure to spoil it,
For who can feel at all genteel who cannot flush the toilet?
China and silver must be clean: this task at least is easy
For anybody who has been presented with – a Squeezy.

Brian found Vancouver Lodge a refuge from school life, and it also paved the way for an escape from his father's ambitions. Fred Brindley was an orphan who was born in Birmingham, came south and became a self-made man. He was an innovative electrical engineer whose work had helped the evolution of television, and he had successfully established a small specialist firm, F. Brindley & Son, in Holloway. He added 'Son' on the day of Brian's birth. As well as electrical goods it also manufactured stylishly designed household products: plated cake stands, entrée dishes, tea services (Brian retained many examples). Fred was one of the earliest people to have a television set, and his licence number was in single figures. He was affluent but suburban, exceedingly generous, took family holidays in good hotels at Bournemouth and an occasional cruise, and gave Brian and his sister Nancy a happy childhood. Violet was short, pretty and sweet, and Fred did not like her to wear lipstick. When the family moved to Bushey Heath he bought a Daimler. When a young friend asked how many miles it did to the gallon he replied that if you were rich enough to buy one there was no need to worry about that. On his 21st birthday Brian was offered a car, but he declined the present because he had no interest in driving. It was from Fred that Brian inherited his cleverness.

Fred wanted Brian to study something technical in order to join the firm. Colin Anson asked if he would take him to see his father's factory, but he refused. Brian enlisted McElwee's support in pursuing a quite different career.

What Brian did not like about Stowe was the school religion. Stowe had been founded in 1923 by an evangelical group who wanted to correct the growing threat of Anglo-Catholicism. Brian disliked the coercive methods and the low church religion of the chapel; it left him wholly uninfluenced.

The Brindleys were not a religious family, yet from his prep-school days at Gadebridge Park Brian had been captivated by religion. The school worshipped in the north transept of Hemel Hempstead church, and he enjoyed the hymns. He hankered after high church worship without knowing what it was and had an instinctive liking for clergymen. Colin James, a later chaplain of Stowe who became Bishop of Winchester, described Bill McElwee as a 'God-fearing low churchman, with a penchant for high church company, which could perhaps ease his conscience in his enjoyment of non-puritanical tastes'. There was little spiritual help there, and Brian would slip away to look at churches; at home he was excited to discover St Mary's, Kenton, a local Anglo-Catholic centre. It made him even keener on high church ways.

It was when he had left school and was doing eighteen months National Service in Germany that Brian met Captain Hayes, a Church Army captain, and became part of what he described as a cave of Adullam for crypto-Anglo-Catholics, many of whom were ordinands. He learned about the sacraments and became a server. The Church of England was strong immediately after the Second World War, and the Anglo-Catholic movement was approaching the height of its postwar recovery. But it was when Brian went up to Oxford in October 1951 to read modern history at Exeter College that his latent interest in a full-blooded expression of Anglo-Catholicism was fulfilled in a form as final as the cultural influences he had received at Vancouver Lodge.

Brian had a good fill of Oxford religion: he dutifully went to Pusey House for Mass, to the Cathedral for the music, and to Exeter Chapel for evensong. His college chaplain and tutor was Eric Kemp. The austere restraint of the Cowley Fathers did not appeal to him. He made friends with Peter Levi, the Jesuit poet, at Campion Hall, but occasional attendance at Mass at the Old Palace, where Mgr Valentine Elwes was chaplain, did not convert him to Rome. Nor did a conference preached by Mgr Ronald Knox, in which he made the point that members of the Church of England who had made any study of history always stopped calling themselves Protestants and called themselves Catholics. After Brian had become a Roman Catholic, he remembered: 'From this I drew at the time the wrong inference – that they *were* Catholics. I have now come to see, as Knox had come to see, that this was what we *called* ourselves, not what we were.'

He met Colin Stephenson, the Vicar of St Mary Magdalene's, and was irresistibly attracted by a combination of faith, wit, charm and sophistication. He had never met a clergyman who was so magnetic, so amusing, so fashionable, so ultra-High. They became friends. Fr Stephenson sailed through life in a gale of laughter, and managed through his personal appeal to empty every other Anglo-Catholic church in Oxford. On most Sundays there was Pontifical High Mass celebrated from the faldstool by Bishop Roscow Shedden – bluff, hearty, irascible – who had made his home at St Mary Mag's after his retirement from Nassau. Brian was one of Fr Stephenson's most notable neophytes. At home, his new-found interest in religion was received with bewilderment rather than hostility, and he was interested to discover that at Bushey Heath the parish church had graduated from Matins to a sung Eucharist. The level of churchmanship was rising throughout the country to Moderately High with a Western liturgical tinge. Not even the Parish and People Movement could stop six candlesticks rising on altars around the country. Fr Stephenson turned Brian into a man of the Church.

Despite his good brain, Brian was not bothered by a notion of Catholicism that was seen as a solution of intellectual difficulties. The higher levels of philosophical and theological speculation were not for him, and he was not interested in ideas. His understanding of dogmatic theology, doctrine and the Bible was systematic, governed by reason. He responded to a constant tendency in Catholic theology which attempted to put everything on the basis of sheer logic. Many theologians of that time spoke as if articles of faith, including the system in which the Roman Church became the speaker of faith, could be proved beyond all reasonable doubt. Brian was much concerned with the 'evidence' of faith. He was not attracted to Catholic spirituality, mysticism or asceticism; his idea of faith left little room for emotional reaction, and he dismissed apologetics that spoke to the heart.

Brian was not a pious person and rarely mentioned God. He never for a moment doubted that Catholicism was the historic faith of Christendom. He also believed that the strength of Catholicism is that it is a great religion, the only one to which he could own and feel an allegiance. He had a secure belief in the ordered certainty of the Church's teaching, guaranteed eventually by an allegiance to Rome. Unusually for an extreme Anglo-Catholic, he was an enthusiast for the Bible and regretted the work of liberal scholars to obscure its unvarnished truth. Brian was, despite his inconsistencies of character, a believer.

While Brian was in the army in Germany he worked in the British Forces Network, broadcasting with the bleaker personality of Karl Miller, later editor of the *London Review of Books*. From boyhood, Brian showed a talent for humorous verse and satire. At Stowe, the historians put on a puppet pantomime of a rhyming version of *The Barber of Seville* that Brian had written. At Oxford he was involved in the Oxford University Dramatic Society with Ned Sherrin. They directed a mid-Victorian production of *Sleeping Beauty*, set in 1852, which Neville Coghill said was exactly what an OUDS pantomime should be. He made suggestions for Alan Bennett's sermon, which was eventually incorporated in *Beyond the Fringe*, and would tease him by saying he had modelled it on Eric Kemp (which Bennett denied). Brian's humorous sympathies were wide: he was a great fan of Max Miller. He set Betjeman's poems to hymn tunes, and Victorian ballads, notably 'Death in Leamington', to the tune of 'The Lost Chord'. They were sung at his parties, and he hoped the poet would hear of them. His talents pointed to a future in revue, broadcasting and the theatre, and Roddy would later indignantly declare that Brian had thrown away his chances. He admitted that there was something in that, but said that behind a confident façade he was too shy and diffident to follow that path.

Brian's principal theatrical triumph was a masque he wrote in the manner of Dryden, *Porci ante margaritam* (or 'Swine before a Pearl'), performed before Princess Margaret, who sat on a dais on a sunny lawn at St Hilda's in 1954. It gave royal pleasure, but Brian was unable to attend as he was sitting his finals. The text of the masque was designed in the elegant eighteenth-century typography of Baskerville, printed by the Clarendon Press, bound in buff card, and was the finest example of printing that Brian had so far achieved. He was obsessed with the eighteenth- and nineteenth-century typefaces of Caslon and Bodoni, but he came to see that the best book ever printed was the Kelmscott edition of the *Works* of Geoffrey Chaucer, printed by William Morris with woodcuts by Edward Burne-Jones. Both had been undergraduates of Exeter, and on the open shelves of the college library, in an attached cloister, were copies one and two. There, on quiet afternoons when it was not warm enough for the river, Brian would sit, usually alone, and take down one of these precious volumes. He knew that he was highly privileged to read Chaucer from them. Thereafter Morris, the Pre-Raphaelites and the Arts and Crafts found a place in Brian's aesthetic hierarchy and were represented in his houses.

Brian's Oxford years were among the happiest of his life. When he went up there was still a sense of postwar euphoria. Socially, the public schools dominated the university, and the degree of snobbery that prevailed would be intolerable to the present generation. Yet Oxford and Cambridge in the 1950s were largely grammar-school universities and less 'elitist' than they are today. It is hard to associate Brian with austerity. Rationing was still in force, bread was scarce, and in his first term as an undergraduate he had to take scraps of butter to hall for breakfast. Perhaps that partly explains his passion for rich food. The 1950s were a golden age of hope and good feeling. Brian greatly enjoyed the Festival of Britain in 1951 with its light and flimsy Modern architecture and it gave him an interest in modern design. Unlike the majority of his contemporaries, however, he was pleased about the defeat of Attlee's second Labour administration and welcomed the return of Churchill. McElwee had turned Brian into a High Tory. He remained a Conservative and, with the exception of a period in the 1980s when he read *The Times*, a reader of the *Daily Telegraph* for the rest of his life. He was elected to the Junior Carlton Club and supported the status quo.

Brian was appointed President of the Junior Common Room for 1955–56, and he carried out his duties with humour. The JCR book records many of his witticisms. There was a suggestion for the floodlighting of Sir Gilbert Scott's delicate French Gothic spire of the College chapel, and Brian's reply: 'Suggestion noted, but though the spirit is willing, the flèche is weak.' He founded the Bowdler Society, which made a pilgrimage to Dr Bowdler's grave. Its members wore straw hats bearing fig-leaves. It had only one meeting, to which Brian invited the *Daily Express*, and a photograph of him was published poised with a soda siphon to revive a female member from her swoon brought about by a Shakespearean allusion.

Brian made a considerable impression; but academically his Oxford life ended disappointingly. He only secured a Third – a mischance he subsequently rarely mentioned. Brian rationalized the class by saying that it was better to get a Third than a poor Second. He stayed on for a further two years, ostensibly to read law, but he had a mental breakdown before the examination and went down in 1956 without taking a degree.

Brian dashed his father's hopes by not wanting to go into the family firm. He reminds us of other figures whose backgrounds were very similar: Ronald Firbank and John Betjeman. All came of well-to-do parents: the money one generation made in business the next squandered on art. Brian tried to redeem his failed degree and spent two years in London desultorily reading law at Gibson Weldon, a crammer. Fred believed that Brian was working hard. Instead, he went every day to the Junior Carlton Club to write a novel, but he did not have the stamina to complete it. For much of the time he spent the day reading newspapers. He was at Gibson Weldon when I first met him, and few of his friends took his legal aspirations seriously. Brian had the mind to be a good lawyer and he might have succeeded at the Bar, but he lacked application.

Religion became of increasing interest. He never drove,

and the Green Line bus took him to Anglo-Catholic churches locally and in central London: St John's, Watford; St Augustine's, Kilburn; and Our Holy Redeemer, Clerkenwell. Most of his friends went to St Mary's, Bourne Street, and that soon became his church. In 1959 he began to contemplate reading for holy orders. This was received with mixed feelings by his friends and family, but they eventually came round. When Fred and Violet retired to a nursing home in Bushey they became communicants, and that was entirely due to Brian's influence. He was accepted by the Central Advisory Council for Training for the Ministry, but despite initial encouragement from Arthur Couratin, the Principal, he was not accepted by his preferred choice of theological college: St Stephen's House, Oxford. It was the first of a string of disappointments that bedevilled his ecclesiastical career. Instead, Brian went to Ely Theological College in the Fens, one of the last-but-one intake before the college closed.

Ely had had a strong Anglo-Catholic tradition, and many of the leaders of early twentieth-century Anglo-Catholicism had been there, including Fr Fynes-Clinton. Brian did not get on with Canon Douglas Hill, the trenchant Principal, whom he described as a spoilt Catholic (meaning that he had moderated his early convictions). It would have been difficult for Brian to fit easily into any theological college, whatever its complexion. He was too forceful in character and intelligence, too arrogant, and his sophistication was strong meat for most of his contemporaries. But he brought gaiety and laughter to the college and influenced some of the more impressionable young theological students against the regime.

Brian was desperately unhappy there, disliking Ely's

Cambridge liberal Catholic position and Prayer Book funda-
mentalism. He delighted in teasing Hill and would sometimes
kick his door as he passed in the corridor. Canon Hill simply
could not cope with him, and put Brian's ordination to the
diaconate under question. He said, at a difficult interview,
that he would not recommend Brian, and was on the point
of dismissing him. This gave Brian two of the worst days of
his life, when he was racked by uncertainty, bordering on
despair. He thought the game was up. Canon Longford, who
taught singing in the college and prepared the final-year
students to celebrate Mass, intervened, persuading Hill that
there was more to Brian than unconventionality, and he
went forward. Many years later, after Hill had mellowed,
Brian made it up with him. As a result of Brian's work in the
General Synod, Hill had come to a different conclusion
and generously told him that he was his best pupil with the
greatest promise.

Brian wanted a title in London and he was promised one by
Gerard Irvine who in 1961 had become vicar of St Cuthbert's,
Philbeach Gardens, Earls Court. Gerard drove a 1929 Rolls
Royce that had formerly belonged to Buckingham Palace; he
had also been a contributor to *Time and Tide*. He was a priest
of outstanding pastoral gifts with a sparkling intellect, and he
was an ideal choice for St Cuthbert's. It is the most sumptuous
late-Victorian Anglo-Catholic church in London. Gerard's
old friend Betjeman called it St Philbert's. Brian was eagerly
looking forward to going there. Then his expectations were
dashed. David Davies persuaded Gerard to offer the title to
Brian's schoolfriend Peter Jameson rather than to Brian, and
justified his intervention by saying that St Cuthbert's did not

need a member of the chorus. Brian described his distress to Roddy in an undated letter from Ely:

I suppose you will have heard by now that Gerard is to offer the Title to Peter. David will doubtless have some plausible explanation for his conduct in the matter, but at the moment I feel that this marks the End between myself and him, myself and Peter, myself and S. Mary's and – once Peter is there – S. Cuthbert's. I am not being selfish – I should have been selfish weeks ago . . . I am in the depths of despair at yet another setback – especially as there has been a conscious plot to deprive me of the benefit of a long-standing promise. Gerard should never have allowed himself to be persuaded into the position of either Brian/or Peter, in which he was bound to hurt *one* of us. However, he *did* promise me. I don't know where I can go now. Sorry to be so gloomy, but I am.

The letter showed Brian's acute hypersensitivity, which was easily activated, but seldom as profoundly as this. Invariably reverses resulted in a breach and a cessation of good terms. Explanations were rarely given; few understood Brian's archaic code of manners; and many were unaware that they had crossed invisible boundaries. The decision divided Brian's friends. I remember how distraught he was, behind an outward display of composure. He was never reconciled to David, and for a long time he was estranged from Peter, but he never blamed Gerard. Yet I remember Gerard telling me that he could not possibly have had him. So who really was to blame?

It was difficult for Brian to find a title, as he was hard to place. A solution came from Cyprian Dymock Marr, Rector of Clewer, near Windsor, in the Diocese of Oxford.

St Andrew's, Clewer, was a bulwark of the Tractarian tradition: a parish where the Victorian Rector, Canon T. T. Carter, had founded the Community of St John the Baptist in magnificent conventual buildings. Fr Dymock Marr offered Brian a title, and at Petertide, 1962, at the age of 30, he was made deacon by bishop Harry Carpenter in Oxford Cathedral. Brian circulated a baroque ordination card printed in red and black on cream handmade paper by the Curwen Press in the style of the Society of SS Peter and Paul. At Oxford he had taken the names Dominick and Titus, and thereafter became the Revd B. D. F. T. Brindley. ('B. F. Brindley!' exclaimed a master at Stowe. 'What *were* your parents thinking of?')

Brian moved into a small modern house at 25 Parsonage Lane. It was his first private residence, and he said how good it was to have his own front door. One of his greatest pleasures were the Windsor antique shops, where he made many purchases, including a lustre pot by Walter Crane, marked 'not old'. It was a good period for making such discoveries. He would decorate plain modern plates of pleasant shape with inscriptions such as JESUS, MARY & JOSEPH in bold nineteenth-century faces applied from sheets of Letraset. I remember a delightful mix of generations at sherry parties in his house after the High Mass. Brian was imbued with Oxford; he added glamour and a cultural dimension to the parish. The monthly magazine was enlivened by his pen. The novels of Barbara Pym were making an impression at the time. At a literary evening he organized, which was addressed by a local lady novelist who wrote romantic fiction, a small group of us, including an amusing bluestocking curate's wife, talked enthusiastically of *A Glass of Blessings* because it described a world we knew. Conspiratorially we applied the characters to the room. It was fun to be High.

Brian's first Mass was as elaborate as he could get away with. St Andrew's was not an extreme church, but it had a good Catholic standard and the Mass was the centre of its life. It was a medieval church that had been restored by Woodyer and thereafter largely left alone. It had a wooden screen and, in the chancel, carvings of lilies, vines, wheat and saints. Brian soon used his influence to improve it and Roddy and Anthony Ballantine were brought in to decorate the screen, make better steps for the font, restore and electrify the Victorian coronas in the nave and aisles, and, with Brian's help, improve the sanctuary furniture. In the churchyard, Brian's graphic skill was used for gravestones in an eighteenth-century style decorated with flourishes.

From early in his ministry, Brian went to Walsingham, where he was welcomed by Colin Stephenson, who had become administrator of the Shrine, and made part of an inner circle. He could not fail to be noticed, not least for his exaggerated style of celebrating Mass, which was jerky and involved awkward gesticulations. The general view was that he had taught himself and it was no use telling him as he would take no notice. Brian held that it was more Continental to celebrate Mass fast rather than slow, and this affected his entire view of ceremonies: he had no time for slow, dignified, Anglican solemnity. Brian had to be larger than life, and his fame spread.

In 1967 he was appointed vicar of Holy Trinity, Oxford Road, Reading. Bishop Carpenter said that he had put the most impossible priest into the most impossible parish. Holy Trinity was not an architecturally distinguished building. It was designed in 1826 by E. W. Garbett as a proprietary chapel in the lancet style and was given a new, correct, stone façade and a higher pitch roof by William Webb in 1845. Henry Fox Talbot (the English inventor of photography), who worked nearby, made a study of it, and it is possible that Holy Trinity is the first church ever to be photographed. 'Sir Nikolaus Pevsner,' Gavin Stamp observed, 'in writing up Berkshire for the *Buildings of England*, did not see any need to mention Holy Trinity, and it is essentially the sort of brick box with a tiny chancel that Pugin would have ridiculed.'

Holy Trinity did not offer inviting prospects. It had had a long Anglo-Catholic tradition, dating back to the late nineteenth century, and was at one time extreme. In the 1920s Martin Travers had designed an elaborate baroque scheme for the sanctuary, but it was never executed. Apart from a hanging rood there was little good furniture. It was in serious decline, with a small congregation of not more than 30, and its liturgy had been moderated: it now used what was known as the Sandwich Rite, the 1662 Prayer of Consecration sandwiched between the first and third parts of the Roman Canon, which was said silently.

Brian's main task was to revive the parish, and this was achieved in conjunction with the refurnishing of the church. Within fifteen years, Holy Trinity was transformed, and Brian remained there for 22 years. It was here that he embraced the highest extremes of Anglo-Catholicism and indulged his love of self-projection and dressing up. But it had a solid base, and he gave a course on the liturgy during his first Lent in order to carry his people with him.

Brian came to Reading two years after the conclusion of the Second Vatican Council. The effects of the Council upon the Anglo-Catholic movement were every bit as decisive and bewildering as they were in the Catholic Church, perhaps more so. There were once two schools of thought among those initiating the liturgical revival in the Church of England: those who founded themselves on modern Western Catholicism, and those who looked back to the Sarum Rite of medieval England. Brian belonged to the former school. He ridiculed Sarum ceremonial, saw it as representing an aesthetic dilution that further diluted Catholic doctrine, and was more than happy to embrace the 'degraded' taste of the eighteenth and early-nineteenth centuries. Indeed, Brian revelled in it; nothing could equal baroque Catholicism. In time, his sense of the ridiculous was applied to all aspects of conventional Anglican taste, old and new. He enjoyed injecting a healthy dose of vulgarity into the slightly effete veins of the Established Church. He nurtured a particular aversion to white Gothic chasubles with blue orphreys, edged with black and white diced braid, and mocked moderate clergymen who thought they were suitable for feasts of Our Lady.

All of this dramatically and unexpectedly changed in 1963 when the Second Vatican Council's Constitution on the Liturgy was published and applied in the following year. Between 1964 and 1970 Latin was virtually abandoned; Mass was said facing the people in hastily adapted sanctuaries; ceremonies and vestments were simplified; worship became congregational and populist music replaced Gregorian chant, polyphony and the classical repertoire. A consequence of these changes was a wave of iconoclasm throughout Europe and the world, and the wholesale discarding of vestments, plate and church furniture that had not been paralleled since the aftermath of the Napoleonic wars. Antique-dealers were sated with church furniture, textiles and ornaments, and Paris in particular was a place where magnificent vestments could be found, gathered from all over France. Another development in Britain was the start of redundancy measures in the Church of England which led to the closure of many churches, some of architectural worth, which had been finely furnished. At no time had good church furniture and ornaments been so freely available on such an extensive scale.

As Brian approached his ordination, he bought modern Latin vestments in Spain and his mother gave him an attractive set of green vestments made of flowered brocade. He also acquired ornate continental *bondieuserie*, statues of St Dominic and St Sebastian, a head of Christ in agony, among much else. Shortly before he came to Reading he had discovered a long-established Armenian dealer, Souhami, who had premises in the Prince's Arcade, Jermyn Street. Souhami had great discrimination and wide continental connections, and he enabled Brian to start a valuable collection of antique vestments. Some were of princely splendour, which appealed to his courtly taste.

This gave an idea to John Milburn, the vicar of St Paul's, Brighton. He began to deal privately in continental vestments, linen, lace, altar-plate and established useful connections in Paris. Consignments regularly came to Brighton and met a ready market among extreme clergymen. Anglo-Catholics were not happy about giving up their hard-won externals. The opportunity of making worship more glamorous, while Rome was abandoning its baroque past, was eagerly seized. As a result of Fr Milburn's and Brian's enterprise there was a general transformation of Anglo-Catholic worship which made it more dazzling than it had been before. Never before had so much lace been seen in Anglican chancels. The liturgical reforms became twice as splendid as what they had replaced.

Brian quickly began to take advantage of the liturgical revolution. As soon as he arrived at Holy Trinity he began to make changes. The parish had £14,000 in the bank and he regarded the church as a blank canvas. In 1968 a radical reordering of St Chad's Roman Catholic Cathedral, Birmingham, had led to the removal of Pugin's screen. Roddy suggested that it should be installed in Holy Trinity. An appeal for £500 was launched, supported by Betjeman and by Pevsner, who described its removal from St Chad's as 'vandalism unmitigated'. The screen was placed across the entire width of the church. A new section of gallery cornice was provided beneath the existing rood, and new decorative panels in gilded gesso were made by Anthony Ballantine. Six wooden candlesticks flanked the rood. The installation of the screen proved decisive for the reordering of the church. It enabled a new sanctuary to be made in front of it and turned the chancel into a Jesus chapel.

Brian also acquired the high altar of St Paul's, Walton Street, Oxford, with its seventeenth-century tabernacle, bright with red and gold, rescued from a Belgian church during the First World War. It replaced Holy Trinity's own high altar and

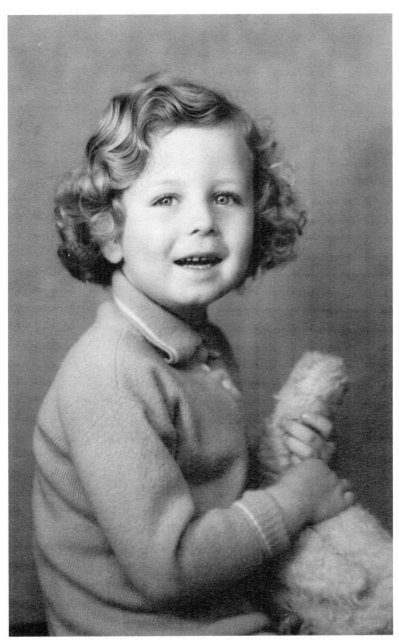

Brian with his teddy bear

Brian, aged three, with his sister Nancy (right) and Keith and Margaret Jeffery (left)

Historians at Stowe – Brian, front row, centre stage

Brian on holiday

Brian in a 'Victorian set', in the Art School at Stowe

Meeting of the Bowlder Society, Oxford 1955. P. J. Kavanagh and Brian in the back row. In the centre, Kavanagh's first wife Sally, daughter of the novelist Rosamond Lehmann

The young Anglo-Catholic priest

Established in Reading

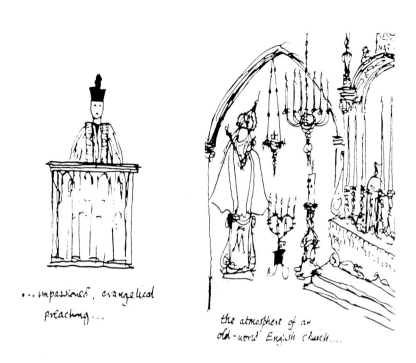

... impassioned, evangelical
preaching...

the atmosphere of an
old-world English church....

.. for nothing

Brian's drawings for St Mary's Church, Bourne Street, London

With Liz Fraser of the 'Carry On' films

The High Altar prepared for Mass at Holy Trinity, Reading. The occasion was Brian's Silver Jubilee Mass in 1988

On the way to Mass with acolytes in Reading

Brian and his sister visit The Holy Father in Rome

Brian, the Roman Catholic

The sitting room in Brighton

was enriched by a crucifix and six magnificent neo-classical candlesticks, smaller versions of those used for Napoleon's coronation. Above the altar was hung a contemporary old master copy of a painting of the Virgin and Child by Guido Reni. Another windfall came Brian's way from Oxford when All Saints, in the High, was converted into the library of Lincoln College. Brian secured the splendid high pulpit of dark oak with a large sounding-board enlivened with urns, stairs with twisted balusters, marquetry panels decorated with ogee shapes. He took the organ of 1780, had its case marblized and enlarged, and installed in the west gallery of Holy Trinity; he also took Sir Thomas Graham Jackson's gilded lectern. Last came Jackson's pews with their baroque profiles. Some experts were cross that the pulpit was installed in 'so wonderfully wrong an architectural setting'. Gavin Stamp thought it made Pugin's screen look a little tawdry.

These additions provided a setting for the new sanctuary. The work was started in 1970. Brian's principle was that nothing should be temporary and that as far as possible the best materials should be used. The spacious sanctuary was paved with a pattern of black and white linoleum tiles. He designed altar-frontals, which were made by Watts & Co. Brian let few opportunities pass to help forward the decoration of Holy Trinity. It could not be beautiful enough. He attended the sale at Beaumont College, the Jesuit school at Windsor, when the chapel furniture was auctioned. He scoured antique shops and church furnishers, redundant churches and closing convents for gaudy objects – reliquaries, gilded lilies, spangled lace, elaborate Benediction candlesticks, embossed sanctuary lamps – that would make the church ever more resplendent.

The most significant of his later acquisitions was the high altar designed by Martin Travers in the form of a gilded sarcophagus for Nashdom Abbey, which Brian installed in the Lady chapel. A blue dossal from the Lady chapel designed by Comper's pupil W. H. Randoll Blacking was rehung behind the statue of Our Lady. It was the only example of the taste of the English use in the church. Sprung stocks were made for all the candlesticks, Irish altar-linen was ordered woven with patterns of the Agnus Dei in a sunburst, and every piece of altar-plate was gilded and paid for with money given at the Epiphany. The entire effect was enhanced by an ingenious and sophisticated lighting scheme designed by Peter Freeman: the lights could be dimmed and raised at strategic moments. 'Through clouds of incense,' noted Brian's obituarist in *The Times*, 'a liturgical *son et lumière* was performed, high-lighting the elevated Host, the reliquaries and the pulpit at dramatic points during the service.' Brian had created a unified work of art that was *sui generis*; the result was extraordinary.

Brian wanted Holy Trinity to embody the ceremonial precision of St Mary's, Bourne Street, the geniality of St Mary Magdalene's, Oxford, and the pure Roman tradition of St Magnus-the-Martyr, London Bridge. From the start of his time in Reading, he advertised Holy Trinity's services in the *Church Times* with the phrase 'Fast trains from Paddington'. (The vicar of St Mary's, Paddington Green, responded with an advertisement for his own church mentioning the 'Fast trains from Reading'.) He was determined to put the church on the map, and he had no scruples about attracting an eclectic congregation.

In the summer of 1983, when Brian had got Holy Trinity as he wanted, Gavin Stamp attended High Mass one Sunday morning in preparation for a chapter in *The Church in Crisis*, written in conjunction with Charles Moore and A. N. Wilson. It gave a well-observed account of what he found:

It is ... possible to hear an intelligent, witty and profound sermon from an Anglican pulpit. The pulpit at Holy Trinity, Reading, is a high one in every sense. The vicar, Fr Brian Brindley, is one of the most conspicuous and flamboyant clergymen in the Church of England, and he has enlivened a dull Gothic box of the 1820s with splendid furniture thrown out of other churches ... This beautification, combined with impeccably performed ceremonial and excellent music, has attracted a loyal congregation and the church is full of life. Naturally the tradition of the church is extreme Anglo-Catholic; the 'Missa Normativa' is used and this is one of the few Romanising churches left – both in the Anglican and Roman Catholic Churches – where birettas are still worn ...

There was a congregation of about fifty present for the Parish Mass at 11 o'clock on July 17th, 1983. Many, but by no means all of these were elegant, youngish men. There was also a (male) choir of seven and four servers. Priest, curate and deacon were all fully vested. The sermon, delivered by Fr Brindley from his magnificent pulpit, was concerned with the 150th anniversary of the Oxford Movement which had been celebrated the day before in Oxford by the Archbishop of Canterbury ... Considering that 'the Church of England is as beyond hope of improvement now as in 1833', Fr Brindley discussed the positive attributes of the heroes of the Oxford Movement: Froude, 'extravagance and joy'; Newman, 'integrity'; Keble, 'sweetness'; and Pusey, 'firmness'.

In his eccentricity, of course, Fr Brindley is supremely Anglican.

He shows how unorthodoxy can be positive and not negative, creative rather then destructive. Holy Trinity is a centre of ritual and tradition, which is clearly appreciated and therefore needed. Although he believes that both the Oxford Movement and his ceremonial are 'a gesture of defiance to the stodginess of the Church of England', he does not become a Roman Catholic. He could exist only within the Church of England. But he has been in Reading for eighteen years: a man of talent, intelligence and style could surely achieve much elsewhere. But he is offered no preferment: he is too extreme.

The mid 1980s were the crowning point of Brian's years in Reading. In 1985 he was appointed an honorary canon of Christ Church and this opened up the potential for an entire new clerical wardrobe. He dressed in lavish Roman monseigneural attire, including buckled shoes with high heels that he painted red. Some of his clerical neighbours thought that nobody would take him seriously if he dressed like that.

Only once did I take part in one of Brian's elaborate ceremonies. It was in 1976, and he invited me to be the deacon at the Forty Hour's Devotion, an observance that involved High Mass before the Blessed Sacrament exposed. It was an uneasy and unsettling experience. I stayed in his presbytery in Baker Street and, on one level, enjoyed the luxuriant extravagance of the house. But life behind the scenes was hardly relaxing. Brian talked continuously of the pounds of beeswax in the great number of candles on the altar, its cost to the last ounce, what vestments he would use, the minutiae of the ceremonial, where he could find a bannerette for the monstrance. He engaged in edged banter with a group of young men (few of whom could match his wit) drooped around the upstairs drawing-room: the spider in the midst of the web.

In the sacristy the preparations resembled a dressing room for a pantomime. There was little sense of preparation beyond getting the vestments right, and I remember fighting with mounting impatience to get into an impossibly complicated lace alb, spread over black satin, with hidden hooks and eyes. Others undoubtedly enjoyed this coterie, but, perhaps because of the idealism of being newly ordained, I priggishly could not bear it, and resolved never to officiate at Holy Trinity again. Brian got his own back by remarking later to a common friend that I was like Mrs Whitehouse. She obviously enjoyed sex, but did not think that others should; I obviously enjoyed ceremonial but wanted the same prohibition. Maybe. But liturgically I remained happy with reserve in a splendid setting; it was closer to the Fynes-Clinton model and the austerity of one of my heroes, Mgr Ronald Knox.

The summit of Brian's liturgical extravagance took place in 1988, when he celebrated the sacerdotal silver jubilee of his ordination to the priesthood. There were 40 concelebrating priests wearing matching Latin vestments. The Bishop of Oxford's chair was covered by a sumptuous canopy decorated with plumes of pink ostrich feathers. It lasted for a very long time and when Bishop Harries ascended the pulpit he said that he came uncertain what to expect, but had resigned himself to enjoying the experience. The function had more than an element of the *opera buffa* and he was treated like a Counter-Reformation prelate.

None of this, however, was in any sense Lefebvrist. Brian was not inclined to reject the Second Vatican Council. He found the revised Roman Missal an inexhaustible mine of riches and followed the rubrics meticulously. He had no desire to abandon the cultural legacy of the West, but wanted to prove that the new should be no less splendid than the old. When Brian became a Catholic he had no patience with the Tridentinist movement and believed that the Old Rite had gone with the wind. His liturgical ideal was the *Novus ordo*, celebrated in Latin, with elegant ceremonial.

Brian was not a conventional parish priest. He took an interest in his people, knew them and was kind, but he left the pastoral work to the curates (especially Andrew King and Graeme Rowlands) as his work in the General Synod grew more demanding. He would often spend three days a week at Church House or at Faith House, the headquarters of the Church Union. He was not negligent, but from time to time he fell out with those close to him and was quite often not on speaking terms. It was a strange ministry; but one of the strangest aspects was that he seldom forfeited the affection and loyalty of those surrounding him. They never quite knew what to make of his eccentricity but cherished him for it; he had injected new colour into their lives.

In 1970 the General Synod of the Church of England came into being. Brian secured the nomination by the Rural Dean of Reading for the Diocesan Synod and Fr Dymock Marr nominated him for election to the General Synod because he thought he was a good debater. But he failed to get official Anglo-Catholic backing. 'I don't think we want to be represented by Holy Trinity, Reading,' commented Canon Charles Smith of St Mary Magdalene's, Oxford, the rival candidate. In 1975 Brian was elected as an independent representative of the Oxford diocese. In 1980, when he had become an established member of the Synod, he recorded in the *Church of England Year-Book* his appointments and interests. He served on the Council of the Society of Mary and the executive committee of the Church Union; he was chairman of the Church Literature Association and the Society of SS Peter and Paul, the publishing sections of the Union. His interests were listed as 'Catholic renewal and liturgical restoration; the preservation of the English language; printing and publishing; church architecture and liturgical reordering', His appointments in the Church Union and membership of the Catholic Group in the Synod showed a degree of acceptance, but they were hard-won. It had taken a long time for him to be recognized by the Anglo-Catholic political wing. The leadership never trusted him, but the Catholic Group, composed of the rank and file who formed the voting fodder, was glad he was there.

Brian's maiden speech in 1975 was on the proposals for a revised marriage service. He mocked the drafts, but his arguments were accepted as a useful contribution, and he was elected on to the revision committee. In those years there was a general sense of evangelical triumphalism, encouraged by Colin Buchanan, architect of the eucharistic rite of Series III. Brian described this as 'the most Protestant liturgy the Church of England had known since 1552'. Anglo-Catholics were forced onto the defensive. Brian had a wide knowledge of liturgy, and he felt he had to rescue the

Catholic liturgical position. It was a hard task. Ronald Jasper, Dean of York and Chairman of the Liturgical Commission, treated him as an amateur. Jasper was largely responsible for the experimental services and wanted one eucharistic prayer for all in the Anglican way. Brian was far more outspoken than his predecessors. In debate he could be as rough as Buchanan; he made bold speeches and did not pussyfoot about his uncompromising promotion of an Anglo-Catholic demand.

Brian exerted an important influence on the proposed Alternative Service Book. His ambition was to loosen up Anglican liturgical requirements to allow them to be as close as possible to the revisions made by Rome in the *Novus ordo*. Against conservative opposition, he argued for a common-sense adoption of Roman revisions, and got much of his own way. He successfully moved the adoption of the Roman two-year weekly lectionary and unsuccessfully attempted to get the three-year Sunday cycle in place of the proposed Anglican Sunday cycle. He worked on the services for Lent, Holy Week and Easter. He joined the Calendar Revision Committee and helped to include many new names, move some saints' days, and made many minor changes in the arrangement of the seasons.

Of the four alternative eucharistic prayers, that based upon the canon of Hippolytus (which also provided the basis for the second eucharistic prayer in the 1970 Roman Missal) eventually secured a rite which made it possible for Anglo-Catholics to use the Alternative Service Book in good conscience. The genius of Brian's influence lay in the drafting of ambiguous rubrics that enabled the rite to be celebrated in the Roman order. Indeed, it was largely due to Brian that the recent liturgical reforms of the West were incorporated into Church of England services, not simply on a purely party basis but because they had sound credentials and scholarship, universal authority and application.

None of these gains could have been achieved single-handedly. Brian was an astute politician. He secured the support of Bishop Cyril Bowles of Derby, an old-fashioned but eirenical evangelical who, on the basis of Anglican comprehensiveness, wanted to achieve a rite that would be acceptable to Anglo-Catholics. Brian, too, argued for Anglican liberality and formed an unexpected alliance with Roger Beckwith, the Principal of Latimer Hall, Oxford, a centre of conservative evangelical intrigue. Beckwith wanted a version of the Book of Common Prayer of 1662 in modern English. Brian proposed a policy of political tolerance. Why should not they have it, if Anglo-Catholics were also allowed a rite they could use? When the Alternative Service Book, with its two rites and multiple eucharistic prayers, was authorized by the General Synod in 1979, Colin Buchanan paid Brian a pointed compliment. He thanked him for helping to produce a service-book which he (Brian) never intended to use. And there he put his finger on an issue.

The reality of many Anglo-Catholic parishes through-out the country, including Holy Trinity, Reading, was that increasingly they were using the 1970 Roman Missal without amendment. The Church Union was quick to publish a Catholic version of Rite A for use in parishes, taking full advantage of its rubrical subtlety, and it was widely distri-buted and used. Protests were made but silenced because it was demonstrated that the options used were, as a result of the ambiguous rubrics, legal.

The General Synod is not a noticeably light-hearted body. It is earnest and serious, and perhaps invests itself with a little too much gravity. 'Stodgy' was Brian's description of it. Within this subfusc setting he stood out as being too clever for his own good. He was hard to handle, his appearance and style were against him, and nobody was quite sure how often he was trying to pull a fast one. What he enjoyed was playing games, and the opportunities to do so were many and irresistible. But others recognized the formidable abilities, seriousness and efficiency which lay behind an at times preposterous façade. The Synod was also the place where Brian was most vulnerable. 'Though many found him amusing,' observed *The Times*, 'many also disliked him intensely for his flamboyance, his sharp wit, his confident buffoonery and his church-manship.' But the reward for his work in liturgical revision was that for the first time he was seen by Anglo-Catholics as not merely an eccentric court-jester but somebody who knew what he was talking about, was orthodox and had an unshakeable commitment to the cause. He had at last found a constituency.

In this light it is both a little extraordinary, and also not altogether surprising, that after his re-election to the Synod in 1985 he was elected, with George Austin and Gareth Bennett, on to the influential Standing Committee. This was due, he believed, not only to his ability but to his popularity. Derek Pattinson, the Secretary-General, worked behind the scenes to make a way for his appointment. Many had come to value his interventions and humour. His speeches were welcomed by some as light in darkness, if resented by his enemies. Committees like mediocrities, men who will not make waves. In the context of the Church of England's liberal ascendancy, Austin, Bennett and Brian were not prepared to play the role of safe Anglo-Catholics who had slipped through and were expected to make no trouble. They decided to be as awkward as they liked. Brian regarded their policy as a unilateral declaration of independence for the Catholic Group.

Soon after Brian was installed as an honorary canon of Christ Church in 1985, largely in recognition of his Synod work, he was chosen to be chairman of the Business Subcommittee. The committee is in charge of the Synod's agenda, and it enabled him to exercise considerable influence. His administrative proficiency was greatly admired. In ten years he had learned how to work the Synod; he knew the standing orders and he knew how to get things through. 'I am the tribune of the plebs,' he declared. To see him chair any meeting was to view a master of the art at work.

Privately, Brian knew that his claws had been drawn. But he loved the power and prestige the chairmanship gave him. Walking with a friend in London, he passed a diocesan bishop. 'I have more power in my little finger than he has in his whole body,' Brian observed. He acknowledged in later years that recognition went to his head a little and ministered to his vanity. It gave rise to an expectation among some of his friends, which Brian did little to discourage, that he might become a bishop. 'He usually gets what he wants,' said Nicholas Krasno. Indeed, Brian avowed that he would accept a bishopric anywhere in the country, no matter how obscure.

But others remained silent; they knew that the possibility was remote.

About five years after Brian had been inducted to Holy Trinity he told me, perhaps in a moment of dejection, that he wanted to move on. Reading was not really his milieu, and he longed for the prestige of a London parish. There were several possibilities. In 1975 St Augustine's, Kilburn, fell vacant. Two strong candidates emerged: Brian and Derek Allen, formerly Principal of St Stephen's House, Oxford. Neither was chosen by the Society of the Maintenance of the Faith, the patrons. In the following year came the Annunciation, Bryanston Street, Marble Arch, but Bishop Gerald Ellison had no desire to see the church become a strong Anglo-Catholic centre. If Brian had been presented, his work on the Synod and in the Church Union would have been considerably strengthened and he would have attracted a large congregation.

In 1983 St Magnus-the-Martyr, London Bridge, was vacated on the death of Fr Gill. He had an immensely grand Solemn Pontifical Mass of Requiem, celebrated by Bishop Graham Leonard, and the ranks of the Anglo-Catholic clergy rallied from all over the country. Brian amused me afterwards by declaring in a loud voice, not once but many times, to whom-ever was within earshot, that he had no desire to go there. But of course he had and, once more, despite representations made on his behalf to the Diocesan Board of Patronage, he was not chosen. Finally, in 1986 he sought Our Holy Redeemer, Clerkenwell, but although he had friends among the trustees he was disappointed again. There is little argument that Brian would have succeeded in making an impression in London.

He would have elaborated already elaborate churches – perhaps too much – and injected them with even greater glamour. But, in the end, perhaps it was best that he remained in Reading, as the difficulties which broke upon him in 1989 might have come sooner. Brian was seen, in the broadest context, as a risk. Bishops and patronage committees like safe men.

I became a Roman Catholic in 1985, and quickly lost touch with most of my Anglo-Catholic friends, including Brian. It was the usual pattern in those days. In the summer of 1989 I read an article by Andrew Brown in the *Independent* that referred to some articles about Brian that had been published in the *News of the World*. Brian's disaster began when he invited a young reporter from the *Reading Chronicle* to dinner. The conversation became recklessly indiscreet. In fact, it was a case of entrapment. The reporter posed as a man who did not know where his orientation, heterosexual or homosexual, lay. Unknown to his host, he had come with a concealed tape recorder and eventually filled five cassettes. Brian had slit his own throat.

'The indiscretions captured on tape,' wrote George Austin, Archdeacon of York, in the *Church Times* after Brian's death, 'were mostly fantasies, and for the most part less serious than those actually committed by some other clergy, whose views and connections were such that they survived and sometimes prospered.' A sensational story was offered to the *Reading Chronicle*, but the editor refused to publish it. It was then submitted to the *News of the World*, which ran it over three weeks. Brian was remorselessly hunted off the General Synod by two evangelical members, Jill Dann and the Revd David Holloway. Shortly before the summer session they had circulated photocopies of the articles to the entire member-ship. The circumstances in which this happened left nothing, morally, to choose between any of the parties. The evangelical vendetta continued, and the former Archbishop of Canter-bury, Donald Coggan, tried unsuccessfully to have Brian expelled from the Athenaeum.

As soon as the articles were published, Brian rang up the Bishop of Oxford and was sent to stay quietly at St Mary's Convent, Wantage. While he was away, his presbytery was broken into, ransacked, and much of his collection of china was smashed. He later resignedly commented to a friend that it was not the loss of the china that upset him, it was the pleasure of collecting it that he had enjoyed. Two friends of Brian went to see the editor of the *News of the World*, Patsy Chapman, to discuss the future. She was adamant that the paper was determined to hound Brian out. So far she had used only two tapes and there was more damaging material in the rest. Nobody knew what they contained. Brian realized that this was the end, and resigned his canonry, his parish and his membership of the Synod. Not even his friendship with Robert Runcie could save him. So ended 22 years in Reading, a period during which he had become the most famous Anglo-Catholic priest in the country and had made a career that had admitted him into the most powerful echelons of the Church. It was a great fall.

Brian took refuge in a flat he had bought some years previously in Devonshire Place, Brighton. His friends supported him. Many considered that he had been convicted without committing a crime. Keith Jeffery, who had known him since they were small boys and was his oldest friend, invited him to stay in the Dordogne, but Brian said, 'I must face this out.' Bishop Kemp, his old friend and tutor, showed characteristic loyalty and gave him the job of Diocesan Pastoral Secretary in the diocesan office in Hove. This post had three strands: running the Diocesan Advisory Committee for the Care of Churches; the pastoral reorganization of the diocese; and serving the Redundant Churches Uses Committee. Brian devised the machinery for the last's implementation and exercised a good influence on those who would listen. Chichester has some of the best churches in the country, notably the great Anglo-Catholic shrines that line the South Coast. It was a successful appointment that used Brian's enthusiasm and knowledge of church architecture and liturgical reordering.

What people admired was the way Brian could synthesize his erudition and make it applicable to a given situation. He had a good grasp of the Pastoral Measure and is remembered for writing eloquent letters and for calming the waters in difficult situations. Brian gave five years to the job, but he hated office routine. He longed for a parish and vainly began to dream of St Bartholomew's, Brighton. Nevertheless, it was an ideal appointment and after Brian became a Catholic he stayed on until the collapse of his health made retirement unavoidable.

Soon after Brian was appointed to the Chichester post, he received an invitation from the Prince of Wales to a luncheon at Kensington Palace given for people who had an interest in the protection and preservation of English churches. To the guests' surprise the Princess of Wales was present, looking astonishingly elegant, dressed in a stylish pale pink suit, and sat next to Brian. She knew exactly who he was, they got on like a house on fire, and had an animated conversation not on churches but on press harassment and intrusion. Brian was a loyal monarchist, but his meeting with the Princess converted him to her side. He noticed that whenever the Prince said something she disagreed with, she rolled her eyes. Brian regarded this as the summit of his social ambition and would later recall it with enormous pleasure. He little expected such recognition.

Brian was received into the Roman Catholic Church in 1994 at the Easter Vigil at the Sacred Heart, Hove. His reception was decided by the Church of England's fateful vote on 11 November, 1992, for the ordination of women to the priesthood. He waited to see what would develop, and did not make a move until the measure had been passed by parliament. Brian's motives were not entirely misogynistic: they were more subtle. No church could call itself Catholic, he believed, and follow such a course when the matter of ordination was defective. It was a breach from the Apostolic Tradition, church order, and Catholic sacramental doctrine. 'For me,' Brian recalled, 'it was as if scales fell from my eyes on that Black Wednesday. I saw, all at once, that Leo XIII had been right after all. The ministry of the Church of England was not, as I fully believed it to be, a continuation of the Apostolic Church, but a new creation of the sixteenth century, with which the Church of England was free to do whatever it chose.' 'Women are no more capable of being priested than donkeys,' he bitterly observed. And he told a friend: 'I felt as if I had been a commercial traveller who had been selling vacuum-cleaners for 50 years, only to discover suddenly that they didn't work.'

Emotionally, Brian's decision was very hard. He loved cultural Anglicanism, the union of Church and state, the historic place of the Church of England in the life of the nation and the ancient universities. He cherished its buildings, music and traditions, the powerful influence it had had on the evolution of the English character and identity. He saw himself as part of the line represented by the Caroline divines, the high church tradition, the Non-Jurors and the Oxford Movement. He liked the atmosphere of English churches: grey, soft and bleak, patched with Victorian stained glass, memorial brasses overlooked by Puritan ravages, Jacobean and eighteenth-century monuments, cartouches, hatchments and a few regimental flags. He appreciated the old Anglican clerical tradition where literary men, scholars, indigent younger sons, unfulfilled geniuses, could be slid into livings by private patrons. I discovered a reference to a post-Reformation decorator's bill surviving from Telscombe in Sussex which amused him: 'To renovating heaven and adjusting the stars, washing servant of the High Priest and putting carmine on his cheeks, and brightening up the flames of hell, putting a new tail on the Devil, and doing odd jobs for the damned, and correcting the Ten Commandments.' 'Exactly what I did at Holy Trinity,' said Brian.

It is a hard transition to move from a beautiful dream to a messier reality. Doctrinal crises in the Church of England have, from the reception of Manning as a result of the Gorham Judgment onwards, led to many conversions, and Brian's reasons should not be seen in purely negative terms. He was not a one-issue convert. As he put it:

My principal feelings on being received into communion with the See of Rome have been those of liberation and relief: liberation from the (supposed) necessity of maintaining a number of propositions about the Church of England the truth of which was not immediately obvious, and relief at no longer having to reassure myself and those in my spiritual care that our sacraments were valid and certain, when the majority of Christians believed that they were not.

Brian worshipped at the Sacred Heart, Hove, a Catholic church which then maintained a good standard of liturgy and had architectural interest. He contrived the decoration of the organ-case in the west gallery, took a critical interest in the liturgy, and designed and typeset a fine *Guide to the Order of Sung Mass as it is Celebrated on Sunday and Holy-days in the Church of the Sacred Heart, Hove*. Brian made discreet enquiries about priestly reordination but was, equally discreetly, discouraged. He found contentment in a new career as a Catholic writer, and the past more positively rearranged itself.

Brian had always written well, and he became a regular contributor to the 'Charterhouse Chronicle' and to the literary page of the *Catholic Herald*, while his Anglican memory was kept green by supplying sumptuous, old-fashioned recipes to the cookery column of the *Church Times*. He was incapable of enjoying even a simple quiche, a friend remembered, without smothering it in double cream 'to make it less rich'. 'The range of subjects on which Brindley could hold forth was breathtaking,' wrote Damian Thompson in his obituary in the

Daily Telegraph. 'They included heraldry, typography, English detective fiction, the architecture and food of Florence and Rome, the gardens of Jekyll, the operas of Rossini and the prose of Thomas Cranmer (which he thought overrated).'

Brian's best articles were autobiographical, recalling his parents, boyhood and university days. He caused annoyance to some of the Catholic clergy by writing critically about liturgy and ceremonial, to the extent that threats were made to cancel parish orders. He extolled the place of order, beauty and theatre in the worship of God; while traditionalists were incensed by his dismissive views of the Tridentine Rite. Dr William Oddie, the editor of the *Catholic Herald*, had to restrain him. For the most part, however, Brian's work was widely enjoyed by the readers and, as memories of the scandal faded, many came to a revised view of him.

The welcome surprise of a forgotten life insurance policy opened the final chapter of Brian's life. It enabled him to move in the early 1990s to the centre of Brighton and buy 4 Western Terrace, the end house of a stucco terrace of five forming a single composition in the style of Sir John Soane, with Ammonite pilasters and a central pediment, built in the 1820s by Amon Henry Wilds. It is part of an enchanting enclave surrounded by Wilds' confections: the remains of the Gothick Priory Lodge in Western Road and the Western Pavilion in the style of the Royal Pavilion.

There is genius in what he created at Western Terrace. Nash at the Royal Pavilion and Soane provided the inspiration. He brought together young decorators: Gavin Houghton, who painted the walls of the hall and staircase in imitation of Siena marble, decorated with plaster *tondi* and prints of Rome in simulated frames; and Gary Sollars, who painted the floor in a pattern of tumbling blocks and a *trompe-l'œil* frieze and cornice. On the half-stair the decoration switched from neo-classicism to the late nineteenth century. The landing walls were hung with paper by Morris, but Soane returned in Brian's bedroom and library on the first floor. The walls of the Chinese parlour on the ground floor had a pattern of flowered branches painted by Sollars on a pink ground. The shutter-cases in all the rooms were fitted with reflective glass, 'to increase the light, and give unexpected vistas'.

Brian's taste was sometimes the subject of mockery. 'To be invited to a party at the Reading presbytery,' recalled his obituarist in *The Times*, 'was like passing through a junk shop of exaggerated bad taste, perhaps to move into the garden where stone cherubs had been equipped with trays to hold drinks or olives.' But that is to misunderstand it. Brian hated the lifelessness of the dead hand of taste. He understood its principles and beneath what superficially appeared to be a garish, tinselly *mélange* lay discrimination, knowledge, good judgment and a cultivated discernment.

I am always pleased when people become Catholics, and I was particularly happy about Brian's reception. Soon after I had seen him I was told that he was not well: he had congestive heart failure, and I rang him up to ask how he was. It was the beginning of a resumption of our friendship and, although I was not able to see him often because I was working in the North of England, I noticed that there was a difference in him that was not simply the result of age, poor health and waning energy. He had become a much kinder person, and I knew that this was due to grace because the strands of his life had been brought together on the right soil.

In the Roman Catholic Church, Brian had no need to make a statement or defend a party position. There was no need to be competitive, nor to show off, nor to be on parade, and his touching vanity was as fulfilled on a journalistic stage as it had been as a prominent member of the General Synod. He enjoyed the *réclame*. Brian showed unexpected kindness to people whom at one time he would have dismissed. A maddening friend from years past, who had also become a Catholic, had retired to Brighton and wanted to see his house. Brian was far from well and very short of breath. He must have been irked by his guest's crass comments, but the latter left him feeling welcomed and valued. There were fewer barbs.

The general reaction to Brian's reception among his friends was not antagonistic. They expected it. An exception was Roderick Gradidge, who remained loyal to St Mary's, Bourne Street, and could never understand why friends deserted the numinous ritual of Anglo-Catholicism for Rome. They could expect to experience the rough side of his tongue. Brian tired of his anti-Catholic tirades. Roddy did not appreciate how unwell Brian was, nor what his conversion had cost him. 'Be amusing! Be amusing!' he shouted in his penetrating upper-class voice in a restaurant before launching into another verbal onslaught on Rome.

Brian and I spoke on the telephone, sometimes twice a week. His intellectual powers were undiminished and he gave good advice. I came to know and like him better than before. A year or two previously I had published an obituary in the

Independent of Brian Masters, Bishop of Edmonton. I consulted Brian about some details and found that his own mind was turning towards death. He had been impressed by a sung Latin Mass on the Epiphany at St Etheldreda's, Ely Place, and decided that he would like his funeral to be there. He surprised me by asking if I would write his obituary and give a panegyric at his funeral. I agreed, and later spent two days with him in which he gave an account of his life.

It was one of the most truthful, lucid and honest interviews I have had, and was like receiving a manifestation of conscience. Periodically we moved to different rooms in the house, surrounded by the outward symbols of Brian's life, and gradually they came to resemble its grain. It had become, in a personal sense, a house with a genuinely continuous history rather then an inventive contrivance. And again he had succeeded in making it look as if he had lived there forever. For lunch we went to his favourite Brighton restaurant, La Fourchette, in Western Road. There was no sense of self-pity, no whinging or self-justification, nor did he ever complain about the deteriorating health that slowly circumscribed his activities. He did not repine. His account was not simply a chronology of achievements and vicissitudes: he talked of his inner thoughts and his disappointments.

Few realized that behind Brian's confidence lay shyness and diffidence. This did not only affect his arrested satirical and theatrical prospects. Much of his arrogance, self-assertion and pleasure in scoring is explained by a desire to prove himself. He was very amusing, but that shows, as a rule, a lack of confidence. It was a way of hiding timidity and unease under a constant lightning of sparklers. As a young man in the 1950s and 1960s, he believed he could be emotionally and personally independent, but he realized as the years went by that it became less true. One of his fundamental principles, he said, was that it was vitally important in life to get your own way and this drove him after his early disappointments. It had involved an enormous effort of the will. He had enjoyed being a prima donna. He admitted to loneliness and regretted that he had been unable to form a stable relationship with a close friend. His poor health made him feel depressed and disorientated and evidence of this was found after his death in a diary which briefly and desolately recorded his fluctuating moods and state of mind as well as his engagements and telephone calls. Brian used his wit as well as his mind, which is why he could be devastating. But wit and melancholy are frequent companions and I suspect had been with him for much of his life.

Brian's lasting achievement, he believed, lay in his *protégés*. He said that he wanted to give to others what McElwee had given to him. To those who were susceptible to his influence, Brian exercised a Svengalian sway. He was able to turn a spark into a flame, a goose into a swan. Those transformed described it as the sowing of a golden seed. It was a dangerous power and may have led to casualties. When acolytes adopted Brian's ruthless logic they saw life in absurdly programmatic terms that ruled out development and surprise, and did not always arrive at the right conclusion. Brian could always present a clear, logical analysis of a problem and situation and point to a solution; but it was sometimes off-beam because he did not always know how systems and circumstances beyond his experience worked.

He encouraged a taste for the good things of this life that could easily develop into prodigal materialism. Mortification was unknown to him. And, where religion was concerned, his influence invariably led to its reduction to style and appearance reinforced by rational arguments. But those who were changed will bear lasting gratitude to him that their talents were fulfilled. His friendships might well form, after his achievement at Holy Trinity, Reading, his monument.

Brian's deteriorating health brought many privations. He fluctuated from egregious size to rake-thinness. He took strong drugs to control his weight and heart, and life slowly became circumscribed. A period of time was spent in hospital. He was still able to go to the Athenaeum to meet friends, but at parties he had to sit down. None of this affected his writing, and his mind became, if anything, clearer and more logical. I have not known anybody as unwell as Brian who bore the ills of life so well. He had an extraordinary knowledge of physiology, and an aversion to doctors and dentists, that made him think he could be his own physician. He was neglectful of himself and allowed minor complaints to get worse.

Brian had never had looks, and this affected the way people reacted to him and also became a source of frustration. I once asked him if he had known Oxford dons such as Maurice Bowra and John Sparrow. 'No,' he replied, 'they only liked the pretty ones.' But, if anything, he grew more handsome, in a rather Caligulan way, as he grew older. His long white beard was cut to a reasonable size, and then he went back to being clean-shaven, because he thought it made him look younger. He kept his hair, but abandoned its wig-like style. He was incapable of being an old man. I complained, when I was tired, of feeling old. 'You've had a lifetime's practice,' he replied.

In the spring of 2001 Brian asked me if I would pencil the first of August in my diary for dinner at the Athenaeum. He said, a little mysteriously, that he was giving a party, but would not say why. Gradually, it emerged that he was to celebrate his 70th birthday. Details began to come to light. He said he wanted it to be in the north library; he wondered if he could run to lighting the *flambeaux* outside, but decided against it; he mentioned the menu; he hoped the club would provide a certain waiter he liked (it could not); he did not mention the other guests. He planned to celebrate his actual birthday three days later at Stowe with friends.

I had found an early-nineteenth-century silk picture of Our Lady of the Rosary which I thought he might like. It was a pleasant evening in high summer, and the sun brought out the light and shade of the stucco architecture of Pall Mall and was reflected in the gilded figure of Pallas Athene above the club's portico. All promised well for an entertaining evening. Brian did not look well, sitting in a chair before the fireplace of the card room, with his foot, in a blue canvas shoe, on a green gout stool. But he kept up a brave front, and as each of the guests greeted him and offered their presents he waved them to a table. The only one he opened was from Martin Taylor, a young jeweller, who had made some malachite cufflinks. 'Larvely!' he joyfully exclaimed. Most of the guests knew, or knew of, each other, and it quickly emerged that each one represented a significant strand in Brian's life from infancy to the present time. The list was as much a palimpsest as Western Terrace.

The sumptuous menu reminded me of a gastronomical assault course. The north library is a small, intimate, room in the form of a cube. As the light faded the candles gleamed in the silver, and the company began to relax. Strands of Brian's conversation and laughter floated down the table. We noticed him rise and, accompanied by Martin, leave the room. I had a premonition that something was wrong and was not surprised when, on his return, he had to sit down near the door. His head fell forward. I knew he was on the point of death and went over to give him absolution. Some of the guests returned to the card room; others left immediately. An ambulance was called, a doctor was found in the club and pronounced Brian dead. I said a formal prayer of commendation, and the rump of the party assembled in one end of the drawing room. The paramedics had found movement in Brian's heart and he was taken to St Thomas's Hospital, accompanied by Peter Sheppard, Martin Taylor and Damian Thompson. A waiter brought in coffee, wine and fruit; but after an hour we were officially told, through a message from the hospital, that he had gone. 'He was a dear friend,' said Colin Anson.

Few deaths of relatively little-known people have attracted such celebrity as Brian's. Obituaries were published almost immediately, but it was Damian's account of the birthday dinner in the *Spectator* that started a chain reaction. The press was full of articles. Almost everywhere people would allude to it. When I went to Dublin for my holiday, people were talking about it there; and I was told of an evening in Donegal, held annually to read interesting obituaries in a country-house theatre, at which Brian's in the *Daily Telegraph* was the main feature. Details were circulated worldwide by the Associated Press.

In the immediate aftermath, my reactions were varied. I spent a troubled, sleepless, night and, in the small hours, the evening began to assume the dimensions of a dinner party of the damned where, one by one, the guests would come to realize that they were eternally trapped in hell. Next day it seemed more like the opening of a detective novel by P. D. James, in which a group of people were linked by a tenuous cord that unwound, through the host, in subtle connections that would eventually lead to the murderer. I said Mass for Brian as soon as possible.

Brian sometimes talked of his funeral, but he left no instructions, nor a current will. Peter Sheppard made the arrangements. St Etheldreda's is one of the most ancient and beautiful Catholic churches in London, noted for its good music and careful liturgy. The clergy attended in force, many reordained Catholic converts sat in choir, several rows of robed Anglicans sat in the nave, and the packed congregation reflected the same ecumenical amalgam. Brian's marblized coffin, with a wreath of white lilies, lay before the altar, flanked by candles of unbleached wax, his canon's hat placed on a stool in front. Fr Kit Cunningham, the Rosminian parish priest, provided a welcome note of grounded Catholic *pietas* as he celebrated the modern Latin Mass with effortless familiarity. I was given a heavy French preaching stole of black velvet, stiff with silver embroidery. The celebrant and deacons wore the black velvet Latin High Mass vestments from Holy Trinity that had once belonged to Beaumont College. The lessons were read by Brian's Oxford contemporaries, Alan Bennett and Ned Sherrin.

The choir was composed of professional singers, some of whom sang at Covent Garden. But there were few hints of the nineteenth-century Catholic 'shilling opera'. The plainsong proper of the Mass was complemented by Duruflé's *Messe des Morts*. At the offertory, one of Brian's musical confections from Reading, a Latin motet set to the music of 'Soave sia il vento', from *Così fan tutte*, added even more exquisite poignancy. But the moment that stopped my heart was the *Dies irae*, starkly sung by male voices, which spread from the organ gallery like a heavy velvet pall that enveloped the church.

'In the dignified liturgy,' wrote Edward Symon in *The Times*,

what Pugin once described as 'a slow dance of exquisite restraint', friends who had known Brindley extravaganzas of old found a distillation of all that had been important in his life and ministry. Perhaps, this once, plainsong spoke more eloquently than Berlioz, the canon's hat placed near the coffin more than the ostrich feathers which adorned bishops' thrones.

He awarded the service five stars and said it gave confidence in Christ's Resurrection and forgiveness. Many thought it was so evocative of Brian that they were surprised that he had not planned it. Afterwards, I could not help thinking that symbolically it was also a requiem for the style of Anglo-Catholicism that Brian had fought so zealously against the times to maintain, and which is now passing into transience.

Brian's coffin was carried to the hearse outside. The procession was preceded by Fr Cunningham, wearing a black velvet cope and biretta, walking as far as Hatton Garden. It sped through West London to the North Weald Cemetery at Stanmore, where I conducted the burial in the Brindley family plot. Nearly all Brian's closest friends were there. It was a beautiful summer afternoon, but when we returned to London it began to rain, and as we drove along an elevated motorway Paddington was suddenly irradiated by the broad span of a rainbow that framed the slate roofs of the terraces, the tops of the plane trees, and the steeples and tower blocks that pierced the skyline.

Brian's character was complex, shot through with inconsistencies and contradictions; he was as flawed as he was gifted. After his death, Andrew Brown, who was no friend as a religious correspondent on the *Independent* and never liked him, grasped the nettle in a *résumé* of Brian's obituaries in the press column of the *Church Times*. He made the point that

none of the obits faced squarely, any more than Brian did himself in public, the fact that he was gay but none the less trying to make a career in an organisation that officially reprehended this. Yet nothing about his life makes sense without this fact, not even his choice of career. The problem, for him and most of his generation, was simple camp, which became in time a troubling ambiguity about everything: was he a Catholic or an Anglican, drunk or sober, making a pass at a young man in the Athenaeum or merely 'fantasising'?

What was the point of emphasizing what was self-evident? From the beginning of Brian's clerical life, he would resent any criticism of his private life and would not admit that there was a problem. He guarded it closely. He never faced the question of moral probity, and the necessity of integrity of life, nor did he, as far as I know, examine his choices. He was unwilling to consider the expectations of the Church and his people. When McElwee knew that Brian was seeking holy orders, he observed to Colin Anson that choirboys would be his downfall. They weren't, but young men, as he freely admitted when I was interviewing him, were. They were his Achilles' heel. There is no point in whitewashing Brian's weaknesses: no portrait would be true without them.

Part of the ambiguity of an advanced Anglo-Catholic mentality is a tendency towards a schizophrenic style of life. There is, after all, something a little treasonable about it. It is a strand that has run through elements of the movement from the early days of nineteenth-century ritualism and has become a recognized canker. So strong is it that it has discouraged many from seeking reception into the Catholic Church because they cannot face its moral demands. The tragedy of Brian's career and achievements is that all he accomplished in the Church of England and in the General Synod will be judged by his downfall, and dismissed. By implication, the Anglo-Catholic position is likely to be damaged, and evaluated in purely psychopathological terms. Brian had many predecessors who shared his nature, and doubtless there are successors, but the mainstream of the movement was good, wholesome and productive. The problem flourished on the edge.

It is a crude analysis to assign the delicacy and complications of human nature to one cause. Sin is rarely confined to a simplistic definition of right and wrong: it is more subtle.

Responsibility for an action can be diminished, but not excused, by habit, inordinate attachments and other psychological or social factors. Brian was a man of his time and lived through a sexual revolution that has brought nothing but chaos, death and disorder. Many withstood it, but his fundamental flaw was that he never openly questioned the appropriateness of his behaviour. There is no justification for his divided life, but he was weak, and perhaps possessed by a compulsion he could not control. He lived in watertight compartments. The consequences of leading an esoteric existence lie in the damage that is done when it ceases to be secret, as much as in the life itself. For the Church at large, the ugly effects of clerical turpitude lie all around. The repercussions are best left to God.

In the last six years of Brian's life, he made his soul. The softening of his character enabled a fundamental goodness that had been buried beneath a carapace of sophistication to emerge. I, and others, saw it as a movement of grace. Grace forges human character. The stripping away of the competitiveness inspired by arrogance and insecurity brought out a depth of resignation and sympathy which was not, perhaps, so easily discerned in Brian's prime when he was enticed by the glamour of vanity and power. Brian longed for affection, and I wish he had known more of it, but I suspect he would not have known how to handle it. Barriers were a form of defence. He had always been generous, but these stronger virtues were latent and I suspect he would have seen it as weakness to show them freely. They were allowed to grow when the pressure was off. There was no trace of rancour in his final years, or of blame. Brian was rescued from the limbo of being a professional humorist, the clever fellow, the political fixer, the camp eccentric, and became true to himself. The huge amounts of money he had spent on Western Terrace left him straitened, and Brian came to an agreement with Peter Sheppard that he would buy the house and let him live in it for the rest of his life. 'I want to die penniless,' he said.

Not all moralize, and there are many whose eyes brighten when Brian is mentioned. He was one of the most stylish, intelligent, funny, learned and cultivated men I have known. His rare and unusual life enriched scores of people as much as it infuriated others. I saw his death as the end of a long line of Anglo-Catholic clergymen whose existence brought colour to a grey institution, and even greyer parishes, who served God through their imperfections. Part of the genius of the Church of England used to be that it could accommodate such priests, tucked away in small urban churches, brimming with taste, where they could combine service with class and *élan*. A memento survives in the form of a video recording of Brian's sacerdotal jubilee. It captures a fugitive moment of a brief and obscure period of church history that will, I suspect, come to be regarded with puzzled fascination by those who enjoy walking ecclesiastical byways. It has the attraction of an exquisitely delineated vignette. Brian Brindley was *fin de race*, one of the last of the high-kickers who knew the steps, and he was loved for it.

CHAPTER TEN

Charterhouse Chronicles

BRIAN BRINDLEY

Smoker's Paradise

I WAS BROUGHT UP in smoker's paradise, by which I mean that my father smoked heavily, my mother regularly, and my older sister with unnecessary enthusiasm for a young woman of her time; all their friends smoked, too. Social life was governed by a set of rules as complicated as any Japanese tea ceremony. No sooner had everyone settled themselves comfortably round the fire, or sat down at the dinner table, or on deckchairs in the garden, then out would come all their cigarette cases, and there would begin an elaborate ritual of denial – 'Have one of mine', 'No, have one of mine' – until at last one person's offer was accepted. I never discovered how that was settled; it was a bit like the game 'Mornington Crescent'. I suspect that a person who was ready to accept an offer without demur need never have carried any cigarettes at all, but would have lost caste; there were indeed one or two formalized jokes about moths coming out of cigarette cases.

They were really determined smokers. One apparent competition was to see how short a period of time that could elapse between the getting-out of cigarettes, lighting them, and stubbing them out in an ashtray; I think this was to demonstrate one's freedom from miserliness. The most important rule of the game was this: on no account must anyone see the cigarettes coming out of the cardboard packet in which they were sold in the shop. Everyone carried in coat pocket or handbag a cigarette case, of gold, silver, snakeskin or pigskin. These were always designed to hold fewer cigarettes than they were supposed to, secured in position by little elastic garters which perished and lost their elasticity, resulting in one or two squashed and battered cigarettes in every batch. On every coffee table in every sitting room there would be a rectangular silver box about the size of a brick; its outside was adorned with engine-turned ornament, and a panel with the owner's crest or initial engraved; the inside was made of cedar-wood. The rule was, the more airtight the box, the more squashed were the cigarettes; so, if they were undamaged, they were probably stale. Finally, little silver trinkets were collected that could be put on the dinner table, one between each pair of guests, each containing three or four cigarettes, so that they could help themselves without stretching.

Alongside the silver box was a table lighter, designed to look like something else. My father avoided the worst vulgarities: how I envied a neighbour who had a statuette of a knight in armour, whose helmet lifted up to reveal a lighter.

The smartest table lighter was the Ronson 'Queen Anne', which looked at first glance like a salt cellar; I still think they are rather nice. In the more masculine rooms there would be, instead or as well, a glass ball with a reeded exterior, full of red non-safety matches; it was a mark of one's macho qualities to be able to strike a match first time. (In later life I have discovered that the size of the glass ball is a mark of the owner's social standing.)

Smoker's novelties were an invaluable source of Christmas and birthday presents. My father had drawers full of unwanted cigarette accessories. Flat surfaces in spare bedrooms and inaccessible little ledges above staircases were always crammed with cigarette boxes that had proved their uselessness and been gradually shunted out of immediate sight: boxes that looked like the Parthenon, and boxes that looked like the Odeon, all delivering cigarettes in especially mangled condition. I used to play 'houses' with them; they were sold or given away long ago; now I see them in antique-shop windows, being sold as Art Deco. We never possessed one of those little Bakelite pagodas that, at the touch of a button, would slowly open their six sides to reveal a few sad ciggies, meanwhile playing 'Auf Wiedersehen' on a musical box; perhaps one came for my mother one Christmas, and was given away immediately.

My part in all this was a strange one. I was not allowed to smoke; but this prohibition was not policed. (I suspect that, if I had been caught smoking, which I wasn't because I didn't, I would have been punished for stealing, not for smoking.) As the years went by, his only son's non-smoking habit became something of an embarrassment to my father: he would say to his friends, 'I'm *afraid* he doesn't smoke.' (A bit like vegetarian children today, who are admired for their principles and cursed for their tiresomeness.) Bow-ties, suede shoes, China tea, reading Proust – and not smoking. Whatever next? I think it was adolescent rebellion on the part of me and my friends that made us the first non-smoking generation. We still don't smoke; and, in the meantime, British society has come over to our side.

I confess, I never thought that government exhortation could go so far as to turn smokers into a persecuted minority. Although I have never smoked myself, and have benefited from the change, I can't help feeling sorry for people brought up to smoke, and either disinclined or unable to give it up, who are driven into obscure corners, or even out into the open, to do something so natural, so necessary, to them. Besides which, what do you give nowadays as a Christmas or birthday present for the Man Who Has Everything? A computer game, I suppose; spare bedrooms and inaccessible ledges must be filling up with them.

Eating Whale

I have eaten whale. Before my conservationist readers get in a tizzy, I should explain that this was over 50 years ago, and in special circumstances. In wartime, steak (other than stewing steak) was not to be had in England, except by American servicemen, who were rumoured to feast on it every day. I came as a little boy to the absurd conclusion that a steak was in some way an especially American dish, like hominy or succotash. Before the war I had been too young for steaks, and it took me some years after the end of rationing to learn how to value them properly.

One day, whale meat appeared on the marble slab at Macfisheries, and my mother, rather daringly, bought some. It had the supreme recommendation, in her eyes, of not being rationed. Fish was not rationed, but meat was, severely, and whale counted as ... what, exactly? There was much learned debate in the Church in those days as to whether eating whale broke the strict rule of Friday abstinence: it must be meat, because it comes from a mammal; on the other hand, it swims in the sea. I doubt if the question was fully resolved by the end of the war; perhaps not even before the end of Friday abstinence.

When my mother got it home, there was nobody else in the family willing to sample it; so for my supper I had a large, thick, juicy whale-steak all to myself. *La recherche du temps perdu* is always difficult, and I had nothing in those days to compare it with: its colour was dark red, like mahogany; its texture was somewhat grainy; its taste, not at all fishy but somehow redolent of the ocean, a little oily like a duck. Perhaps the closest comparison nowadays is to the natural tunnyfish. I declared myself satisfied with it, and hoped there would be more. Whether my mother thought better of her daring, or whether Macfisheries' supply ran out, it never appeared on our table again.

I had been a child of rather precocious tastes in food, which my parents had indulged most generously. I do not mean to say that I did not enjoy all the traditional comfort foods of childhood, such as Nestlé's Condensed Milk, its label crammed with information about how to feed babies with it; Heinz's

Tomato Soup; H. P. Sauce, from the label of which (*'cette sauce de haute qualité . . .'*) one gained one's first, rather misleading, acquaintance with culinary French; Bird's Custard, which I fully believed was somehow produced by our feathered friends; and even salad cream.

But I also liked, and still do, things that children are reputed to hate: prunes; spinach; liver; even black treacle. For me, plainly boiled rice with warm black treacle is one of the best of puddings. My father, as I have explained before, liked expensive restaurants of a certain kind. For him, waiters rather than waitresses, starched white linen napkins, and, ideally, a small orchestra playing were the tests of gastronomy. Although he invariably called for cold, underdone roast beef, followed by a milk pudding, he encouraged me to sample the long printed menus boldly.

So it befell that, at the age of about 11, I started to eat oysters. It was my father's pleasant custom to alleviate the austerities of wartime rationing by meeting the rest of the family in London at midday every Sunday. (We none of us went to church, and he had to work for the war effort on Sunday mornings as well as Saturdays.) His chosen eating place was the vast basement Grill Room of the Trocadero, now converted into something quite different. We would join the long queue in Shaftesbury Avenue, for you had to queue for everything in those days, until they let us in at 12.45. My father was 'known' there – he liked to go where he was 'known' – and we would be shown invariably to the same table, which we called Our Own Table. Opposite sat Mrs Gluckstein, who more or less owned the place, being a principal shareholder in Lyons; and next to us sat Sir John and Lady French. Sir John

French was Permanent Secretary at the Ministry of Food. By the regulation of his department, in those days a meal in a restaurant could cost only five shillings and could consist of only three courses. Drinks were not regulated, but rather hard to come by. I am sure that the rules were strictly obeyed by the Trocadero – and by the Permanent Secretary; but somehow the food contrived to be luxurious, and fairly lavish.

The regulations were printed in full on the menu; among them was a provision (put in to save the oyster industry from ruin) that if the meal included not fewer than six oysters, the price was allowed to rise to seven shillings and sixpence. It seemed somehow like a way of avoiding the irksome restrictions of the times, so I, at that tender age, was allowed to eat half-a-dozen oysters every Sunday. Later, for a time, I allowed myself to be put off by the repugnance of my school friends; in those days they used to say 'Ugh!' where we would now say 'Yuk!' But, in the course of time, I returned to my original loyalties. There is no better way to start a meal (when there is an R in the month) than half-a-dozen English native oysters – unless it be a dozen. But I do not think you would get many oysters for seven shillings and sixpence nowadays.

Ever since, I have been adventurous with food, tackling cuttlefish stewed in its own ink, *baccalà con polenta*, and the various odd bits of animals that are the speciality of the *trattorie* in the Testaccio quarter of Rome. But I have never (knowingly) eaten whale again, and I do not suppose I ever shall.

A Norfolk Awakening

When I was a boy I spent a week or two of some summer holidays with a school friend of mine at the little old-world watering place of Sheringham, on the north coast of Norfolk. As far as I can remember, the big Edwardian hotel was still closed after the war; but, in any case, my friend and his family, though grandees in the city of Sheffield, preferred to stick to an old-fashioned north country way of taking a holiday, renting almost the whole of a little terraced house; the land-lady and her family retained the back kitchen, but otherwise moved out to a capacious hut at the end of the garden. We had all the bedrooms, and the front parlour where all our meals were served, and where we sat of an evening. We had books to read and the wireless to listen to; no television, of course.

It made for an easygoing and relaxing holiday; but there wasn't a great deal to do. John and I must have borrowed bikes from somewhere, for we explored the neighbouring villages, and I began a lifetime's habit of church-crawling. We visited many ancient parish churches, which even in those days did not seem to be very active: the strong winds of the North Sea had penetrated into them and seemed to have pickled them all in salt. At some time, 50 years earlier, they must have succumbed to a wave of enthusiasm for the Oxford Movement, for I remember lovely furnishings, big Italian sanctuary lamps (unlit) and sets of six baroque candlesticks. Their tract-cases seemed to have been last replenished in the 1920s, for there were little pamphlets with curling edges and rusty staples dating from the days of the Anglo-Catholic congresses: from them I learned that the Church of England was, really, Catholic – something I accepted and believed for a long time.

Of course, most of our days were spent on the beach. There we encountered the Children's Special Service Mission, a group of earnest evangelicals trying to convert young holiday-makers. I am afraid they did not appeal much to me, these spotty young men with spectacles, Adam's-apples prominent in the necks of their Aertex shirts, with dull khaki shorts and sandals, or the young women in dirndl skirts, with well-scrubbed faces and sunny smiles. In any case, John and I con-sidered ourselves too sophisticated for their hearty services and 'cocoa squashes'; we were, if not exactly men of the world, young aesthetes in the making. I am ashamed to say to say that I escaped from their attentions by telling a lie: 'You see, we're Catholics.' Truth is the daughter of time: John became a convert while still at Cambridge, and I too am now safely within the bosom of Holy Mother Church.

We should have been more artful, like my friend Francis and his sister, both card-carrying Anglo-Catholics. They encountered the CSSM at Lynmouth; each summer they would join in their activities and worm their way into their confidence, until eventually they were asked to 'build the pulpit' on the beach. This meant heaping together a sort of rostrum of sand, which was customarily decorated with improving texts in pebbles: JESUS SAVES or IN HIS SERVICE. When it came to their turn, Francis and his sister adorned their pulpit with HAIL MARY FULL OF GRACE or SACRED HEART OF JESUS; the evangelicals would smile and say how nice, and then try to cover up the shameful words with some of their own wholesome banners.

John and I would spend a lot of our time in the little Catholic church of Sheringham. This was the work of Sir Giles Gilbert Scott, an architect who has always given me a lot of difficulty. I acknowledge him as a genuine architect, unlike those charlatans Sir Hubert Worthington and Sir Edward Maufe: unfortunately, I simply cannot like anything he designed, from the Anglican cathedral in Liverpool to the new House of Commons: his new Bodleian Library in Oxford was a daily offence to me, and I should still love to see Battersea Power Station demolished. It is like the paintings of Van Gogh, the sculptures of Henry Moore, or the music of Benjamin Britten – the fact that I don't enjoy them doesn't mean that I cannot acknowledge them as works of art.

I do not know how the church at Sheringham has survived the aftermath of Vatican II, but in those days Giles Scott's rather precious style could be seen in all its perfection. Unlike the old village churches in the neighbourhood, that church was obviously well attended and well kept. It had a very efficiently run and generously stocked tract-case: here I bought my first Roman missal, a pocket Sunday missal in Latin and English, still in my possession. From studying this, I discovered that large parts of the Mass were similar in language to the service called Holy Communion in the Book of Common Prayer; thence I came to the conclusion (which I now see to be erroneous) that the eucharistic liturgy and doctrine of the two churches were identical.

But the best discovery by far was an American publication called *Father Peter Cut-Outs (with Paul the Altar-Boy)*. Father Peter was a cardboard doll in a cassock; he was provided with all the usual vestments, amice, alb, stole, maniple and chasuble, in paper, for colouring and cutting out; they had little tabs so that you could hang them on him. A second outfit included a cope, a humeral veil and a monstrance. Paul was a young lad in a cassock, whom you could dress in a cotta. There was also a three-dimensional cardboard altar, complete with six candlesticks, a tabernacle (over which you could put a paper veil) and an exposition throne. I should love to have illustrated this article with my Fr Peter doll; but alas, as is always the way with paper toys, it has long since perished. Trivial though these things may seem, they surely indicated the direction in which my religious development was likely to proceed.

Catholics at Oxford

I first encountered Catholics when I went up to Oxford as an undergraduate. My own school had a strong bias towards Cambridge, and so had not provided me with a large number of ready-made Oxford friends. For obvious reasons it was not easy to break into the tight circles of Old Etonians or Wykehamists; so I found myself moving naturally into the group of boys from Beaumont and Stonyhurst, Ampleforth and Downside, and the Oratory. They all had charming manners; and, if their religiosity was not quite so intense as mine, they at least knew what I was talking about.

One thing I noticed was that those who came from their public school with a recognized vocation to the priesthood (or the religious life) seemed to lose it during their three years at Oxford, while those who had no particular aim in life other than to hunt, shoot and entertain often developed vocations and have gone on to become distinguished priests. Similarly (though I am well aware that it is not quite the same thing), who would have predicted that the most fastidiously dressed and perfectly mannered of all my friends would have become by now His Eminent Highness Fra' Andrew, Grand Master of the Knights of Malta? It was exquisite manners for which the boys from the Catholic public schools were especially notable, and they were invariably friendly. They made no attempt to proselytize: it would, I suppose, have been deemed impolite.

Catholic life (for boys) centred on the Old Palace in St Aldates. This was a sixteenth-century building that took its name from the story that the first Bishop of Oxford had lived there. Over the centuries, it had been encroached upon by all sorts of shops and tenements; these Dickensian accretions were gradually eliminated during my time, and one day cards were sent out for a party, headed 'The Old Palace Restored'; the very useful Newman Bookshop was opened in their place. This had a snack-bar attached, which lured me away from the Welsh Pony, where I had for many months eaten bar lunches; I still possess a card identifying me as a member of The Recusants, which enabled me to buy glasses of wine.

The chaplain in those days was the courtly Mgr Valentine Elwes, scion of a large and patrician recusant family, son of Gervase Elwes, the tenor, and brother to Simon Elwes, the fashionable portrait painter. He was a man of exquisite taste. I much admired the shy way in which hints of his status as a domestic prelate to the Pope – a glimpse of a pair of violet socks, or a mere inch or two of violet stock – peeped out from beneath his faultless black suiting.

A little way down Rose Place was the old chaplaincy, two storeys, of which the upper had once been the chapel; but between this and the Old Palace was a new chapel. It could not be disguised, from the outside, that this was, frankly, a Nissen hut. It *could* be disguised from the inside, and was: the Nissen curves had been enthusiastically incorporated into a riot of baroque drapery. All the requirements for Catholic worship according to Fortescue and O'Connell had been provided in chaste cream and gold, in a rather plastic baroque style then very fashionable. It has since been demolished, and a new chaplaincy built.

I did not frequent the chaplaincy – I was still discovering the delights of Oxford Anglo-Catholicism – except when Mgr Ronald Knox was visiting, to deliver a 'Conference' (a sermon, really) at the principal Sunday Mass. A beautiful Hepplewhite armchair would be set at an angle in front of the altar and, seated in this (whether by some obscure monsignorial privilege, or because of his advancing years, or because it was only a 'Conference' I never found out), he would deliver an allocution delicious in its wit and faultless in its argument. But I was not ready to be converted.

The chaplaincy was, in those days – hard though you may find it to believe – for men only; the girls had their own Mass at Cherwell Edge, and much of the chaplain's time was given to stopping them from coming to the (more interesting, I suppose) Mass in Rose Place. A similar segregation was practised at the Anglican Pusey House. This made one's social life, based in summer on long cold drinks and late Sunday luncheons, rather difficult. My principal involvement was with the Candlelight Theatre Club, which had been founded to present improving plays about martyrdoms, but which had somehow been hijacked by my good friend Ned Sherrin (not a Catholic) and used for presenting revues, to the words of which I contributed enthusiastically. There was much earnest discussion as to whether Fr Elwes, who was forbidden by Canon Law from attending the theatre, could or could not go to a revue, and did it matter if we moved it from the chaplaincy to the Playhouse Theatre? I think we managed to convince him that it was an opera – not forbidden!

It was a world – *Brideshead Revived* – that no longer exists. Some might think that it should never have existed. But for me, at a formative stage, it produced an unconscious feeling that the Catholic Church was a good place to be: good not only because you were doing the right thing, but because you were doing it in such agreeable company.

A Spooky Story

This is a true story. It all happened some 30 years ago, so I think there can be no harm in putting it into print now. I was at that time the new and enthusiastic incumbent of a Church of England parish. It was a curious part of the town that had been laid out originally in the 1830s for genteel middle-class housing, but which had gone downhill suddenly with the coming of the railway, which ran through it. Just before I arrived, large swathes of it had been demolished, and the inhabitants rehoused on remote council estates, under the disastrous slum-clearance policy of those days.

There still stood, just opposite the municipal slaughter-house, and next door to the only good restaurant in town in those pre-gastronomic times, a pretty little late-Georgian villa, that had been degraded to a depot for the supply of motor-car spare parts, with an enormous warehouse built in its garden. One morning I received a telephone call from a friend, the incumbent of a country parish not far away, who had been consulted by a parishioner who was managing director of the spare-parts firm. The problem was that there was a poltergeist at work in the depot. Would I go and see to it?

It took me a little time to go into action. First, I discovered that the place was not actually in my parish, but just over the border in the parish of which the vicar was a highly respected evangelical, a powerful preacher, but not someone with much experience of exorcisms and suchlike. When I explained the situation, he was happy to leave the matter in my hands. There was not in those days anything like a Diocesan Exorcist – things are better now – so my next telephone call was to my area bishop. He was very bright and breezy about the whole thing. 'Do anything you like, dear boy,' he said. That was not at all the kind of advice I wanted, so I then telephoned my diocesan bishop, who was much more cautious: 'There can be no harm in saying prayers, but do not address words to any possible spirits.' I knew that danger, and was grateful for the restriction. 'May I use holy water?' I asked. 'Yes,' he replied.

So, armed with a *Ritual* and a vessel of holy water, off I set.

I should explain that my primary motive in going was to attempt to put a stop to the trouble, whatever it was. Any priest who is summoned to deal with a matter of this kind must take it seriously, and act in a businesslike manner – just like an employee of the Gas Board who is called to investigate a possible leak. There is no room for demythologizing the supernatural phenomena, which would have been a popular approach in some circles in those days. But I own to having a second motive: might I find out, in the process, whether the poltergeist in question was truly supernatural, or only a clever fake? I determined that only if I experienced something for which there could not possibly be a natural explanation – for example, an object leaving, in my sight, a static position and travelling through the air contrary to the law of gravity – could I be sure that it was genuine.

What I knew about poltergeists was that they are mischievous spirits who delight in throwing things about and knocking them over. They do not seem to be associated with the souls of the dead, but they generally manifest themselves only in the presence of adolescents, from whom it is presumed that they draw their energy. They seldom do any real harm. When I got to the place I found some very scared-looking and puzzled businessmen. Sure enough, there were two youths working for the firm, one of 16 and the other of about 18. I supposed that, if this was a true poltergeist, one of them was the source of its energy; and, if it was a hoax, they were the perpetrators.

For two days, I spent most of my time in the warehouse. Small things, mostly rivets, were flying about all the time. Boxes of nails and washers tumbled from their racks. At one point a pile of batteries was overturned; at another, a large motor-car exhaust system fell heavily to the ground. Nobody was injured, but I myself experienced a heavy claw-hammer whistling past my ear to bury itself in a plasterboard partition.

Watch as I might, I could never detect either of the two youths doing anything untoward. On the other hand, sadly, I never saw anything actually happen for which there could be no natural explanation. At closing time I recited Compline, with its prayer: 'Visit ... this place, and drive far from it all the snares of the enemy; let thy holy angels dwell herein to preserve us in peace.' I left behind a crucifix and an open vessel of holy water. Next morning, the crucifix was lying on the floor. I cannot say how it got there.

On the second day, there was a ludicrous interlude when reporters and photographers from the local paper appeared on the scene. The managing director was all for denying that anything at all was happening; but the press had already spotted me, attired in cassock and violet stole; I didn't look exactly like an industrial chaplain. I insisted on making a statement, referring to 'what appears to be a poltergeist'. During the course of that day, the phenomena gradually ceased, and that was the end of the episode. To what extent my prayers had been efficacious I cannot say; nor can I draw any conclusion as to the possible validity of my then Anglican Orders. It sufficed that peace was restored.

I have said this is a true story. A couple of years ago I told it, just as I have told it to you, to an acquaintance. At the end he said, baldly: 'You're a liar.' I am not much accustomed to being called a liar, and I particularly resent it when I have been at pains to tell the truth. I supposed he had caught me out in some inaccuracy of detail; but no, he disbelieved the whole story 'because things like that just don't happen'. This illustrates the difficulty of persuading people to believe in a supernatural religion: to the bigoted unbeliever, not even firsthand eyewitness accounts will carry any weight. If my friend would not believe me about a poltergeist, why should he believe Matthew, Mark, Luke and John about the Resurrection?

Walsingham

I first went to Walsingham in 1960. My friend and mentor Colin Stephenson had recently been appointed administrator of the Anglican shrine, after the death of Alfred Hope Patten, vicar for over 30 years and restorer of the shrine. I was invited to spend the whole of Lent there as a spiritual exercise and possibly to make myself useful in various ways.

I travelled by rail, taking a quaint little branch-line (abolished by Dr Beeching in his drastic reforms – the old station is now an Orthodox monastery) in a train that seemed to stop every few minutes at a series of tiny halts, with crowds of schoolchildren boarding and alighting; it was late afternoon. Eventually we got to Walsingham, where I was greeted by an apparition: a figure in a black cassock and a very bright royal-blue scapular, covered by a flowing cloak, and crowned with a mop of the reddest hair I ever did see. For a moment I thought I was being greeted by one of Miss Nightingale's nurses; but it was in fact a young man, a naughty boy who had been sent to become less naughty in the company of the little Augustinian community that in those days struggled to maintain an existence alongside the shrine, and who was exploiting to the full the possibilities of the monastic wardrobe.

I don't know that I actually made myself very useful. I laboured on a translation of the Akathist Hymn into English acrostics, which was typed out and bound and reposed for some time on a lectern in the Orthodox chapel; I put up, with cement, a panel of Dutch tiles over the door to the old refectory – tiles which, when I was last in Walsingham, had to my surprise and pride not fallen down; and I began to write a guidebook that I never finished. But my stay was very useful to me: not only did I learn something of the inwardness of Walsingham but I was able to experience the place before the great expansion of pilgrimage that has taken place in the past 40 years. It was then a sleepy little town, hardly more than a village, into which the shrine and its related buildings – college, hostel, convent – had been rather incongruously interpolated.

One of the great graces of English church life in the twentieth century (there have not been very many) has been the simultaneous and parallel revival of devotion to Our Lady of Walsingham by Catholics and Anglicans. In those far-off days, the Catholic presence was very small: a rather dull little church in the Friday Market; and, a mile or two away, the beautifully restored Slipper Chapel, containing the Catholic image of Our Lady, but set in the middle of nowhere. All the running had been made by the Anglicans, and Catholic pilgrims with time on their hands were more or less obliged to explore the C of E premises. I should make it clear that there was no hostility between the authorities of the two shrines – just a determination to ignore each other's existence. Among Catholic pilgrims four reactions could be observed: 'What a pathetic and unconvincing travesty of Catholic ways!';

'How *dare* they copy us and steal all our things?'; 'I didn't know Anglicans believed in Our Lady'; and 'I can't tell the difference – I just say my prayers.'

Hope Patten's achievement had indeed been remarkable. Soon after his arrival as vicar, he had set up a copy of the medieval image in the parish church; in those days the Catholic shrine was as far away as King's Lynn. As pilgrimages began to grow, so did episcopal disapproval, and he caused the image to be translated to a new chapel which he built on an old orchard in the village, which was intended to be a copy of the Holy House at Nazareth. This soon proved too small, and he added a big nave and choir, and contrived somehow to squeeze in no fewer than fifteen altars, one for each mystery of the rosary – a necessary facility in those days before the introduction, in 1963, of concelebration. Just before my arrival, the Holy House had been enriched by a magnificent reredos and altar-frontal designed in the best style by Sir Ninian Comper, all gleaming with gold leaf; this contrasted gloriously with the rest of the shrine, low and dark and crammed with devotional objects. To my mind, the shrine has since been spoiled by enlargements, which have been equipped with huge french windows, like those of an orangery, so that much of the old mystery has gone.

In 1978 I was one of the speakers at a conference at the shrine; another was the Bishop of St Albans, Dr Robert Runcie. I was present when he was invited to preach at the National Pilgrimage two years hence. By the time the engagement was due to be fulfilled, he was Archbishop of Canterbury; there was some speculation as to whether he would come or not. He came: well I remember his arrival, amid the plaudits of a great crowd of pilgrims. He was supported by two stalwarts of the Anglo-Catholic movement, the Bishops of London and Chichester. I look back on that occasion as the apogee of Anglo-Catholic triumphalism: ARCIC was still active, and we looked forward with confidence to corporate reunion with the Holy See; the divisive decision to ordain women to the priesthood had not been taken. *Tempora mutantur, nos et mutamur in illis.* Fr Graham Leonard is now a Catholic priest; Dr Runcie is enjoying a quiet retirement, sadly not in the best of health; Dr Eric Kemp is still, nineteen years on, Bishop of Chichester.

For over 30 years I visited Walsingham at least annually, often twice or thrice. Every year I took a coachload of pilgrims from my parish to the 'Grand National' – the National Pilgrimage at Whitsuntide; most years I led a weekend pilgrimage, often shared with adjoining parishes; and then there were conferences and retreats and the annual Priests' Pilgrimage. Some of the happiest hours of my life have been spent in Walsingham – as well as some of the most anxious, as any pilgrimage conductor will understand. But I shall not go back. I cannot sort out into anything like theological respectability the tangle of emotions and memories that I have of the place. To take part in a Catholic pilgrimage, as so many are doing this weekend, and make use of the splendid facilities that have been added to the Slipper Chapel, and to ignore the Anglican shrine would be impossible; to revisit that shrine, seeing what I now see and knowing what I now know and understanding what I now understand, would be just too painful. Our Lady of Walsingham, pray for us.

Clerical Errors

Language changes. John Wesley wrote an otherwise charming hymn, 'Lord, thou know'st my simpleness', which includes the alarming lines:

> Let the bowels of thy love
> Echo to a sinner's groan ...

I do not think it is much sung nowadays, even among the Methodists. And there is a lovely carol, 'Saint Joseph, meek and mild', which has to be avoided because the author (or translator) has solved the problem of finding rhymes for 'God' in a rather drastic way.

The clergy, who don't find it easy to keep up with the times, and perhaps especially those clergy who try to keep up with the times with limited success, are always at risk of being entangled by developments in everyday speech and imported slang. Such phrases as 'with it' and 'laid back' linger on in sermons long after they have been given up everywhere else. We frequently see on television a clip of a rather foolish C of E bishop, who says: 'I like to go down into the parishes and expose myself to them.' Just at the moment, the word that causes the most difficulty is the innocent little adjective 'gay', which has acquired in the past 50 years an almost official meaning quite different from what it had before. When I was young, the naïve little hymn 'Lord, for Tomorrow and its Needs' included the lines:

Let me in season, Lord, be grave,
In season gay . . .

But, in the modern hymnbook used in the church I attend, that verse is completely omitted. And I suppose that the clergyman (his mind presumably full of Edwardian music-hall songs) who told me with great gravitas that he was 'a bachelor gay' will by now have had second thoughts.

The clergy are always liable to be entangled by the tendency of harmless words to acquire scabrous sexual or anatomical meanings. This is not altogether a new problem: the Church of England's second *Book of Homilies*, published in 1573, contains two long addresses, intended to be read from the pulpit, in which it is explained that Hebrew words in the scriptures and liturgy did not mean what Elizabethan congregations supposed them to mean. There is much concentration on the word 'horn', used in the Old Testament as a sign of victory, but in the English vernacular provoking sniggers, being understood to refer to cuckold's horns — a usage now obsolete for centuries. These straightfaced homilies make quite hilarious reading today.

Of course, it is not only the clergy who are likely to make silly mistakes: the laity set traps for them. I have myself been handed a piece of paper asking me to give out as a notice: 'The preacher will be found pinned to the church noticeboard'. And on an ecumenical occasion I was asked to announce that the speaker would be 'The Very Reverend Archie Mandrite'.

Finally, I think of the well-intentioned clergyman who had some cards printed and pushed them through the letterboxes in his parish, reading: 'Fr Jennings called to see you and is sorry to have found you out' – and then wondered why he got such furtive looks from his parishioners.

Hot Religion

How was it that the tennis player Goran Ivanisevic won his way into the hearts of the British public, so that we cheered him on as one of our own, once Tim Henman was out of the running? Not, I think, by his habit of removing his clothes in moments of victory. No: what we found endearing was his transparently sincere and extrovert piety – or should one say superstitiousness?

Making the sign of the cross in such a forthright manner, kissing the ball before serving, falling to his knees on the grass to pray, ascribing both his successes and his setbacks unquestioningly to God – all obviously genuine, and not put on for effect. We envy someone whose faith is so bound up with his whole being that he is not afraid to express it. We approach our sports, as we approach most things, in a cold, Protestant way. We do not care to express our emotions, and we get embarrassed if we get caught up in a display of them.

For him, simple religion, what clever people call 'folk religion', is a central part of everyday life. He has the good fortune to come from a nation whose religion has never been called into question – persecuted from without, but never undermined from within. The impact of the Reformation on the English approach to God is a complicated one – caused partly by the heavy-handedness with which Mary I, and later James II, tried to restore the Old Faith. Now, even when we

Catholics try to be natural and exuberant in our piety, we do it in an awkward and hesitant way.

I have at home a videocassette of a lovely production of Mascagni's *Cavalleria rusticana*, filmed in a remote Sicilian village, with lots of the locals acting as extras. I watch it every Holy Week. The beautiful Easter Chorus is accompanied visually by a straggling procession, in which crucifixes, statues of Our Lady of Sorrows, effigies of the dead Christ, and so on, are carried along rough and winding paths by men in *sanbeitos*. How I wish we in England could do something like that! As far as I know, only the Italian Church in Clerkenwell can do it with sufficient bravura.

A few weeks ago, we were keeping the feast of the Sacred Heart. We finished the Mass with a jaunty rendering of 'To Jesus' Heart, All Burning'; and earlier we had sung 'O Sacred Heart!' to its swooning tune. I leaned over to my neighbour and said 'I do enjoy *hot* religion.' 'So do I,' she replied. I mean by 'hot religion' the religion of the heart, of the emotions; and by 'cold religion', the religion of the head, of the intellect. We need both. An invariable diet of hot religion would be indigestible, which is why I could not happily be a Pentecostalist; but a faith based exclusively on a careful and scholarly study of Scripture and the Fathers would be arid indeed.

Hot religion has been with us from the very beginning: the narrative of events on the day of Pentecost not only shows it in action but provides us with some thought-provoking symbolism. Throughout the Dark Ages and the Middle Ages, it came to the surface again and again, sometimes within the boundaries of the Church, sometimes giving birth to heretical sects. By contrast, in the late-seventeenth and eighteenth centuries, cold religion obtained all over Western Europe: Jansenism; the formal piety of the Hanoverian Church of England; and even dear Bishop Challoner erred a little on the cold side. The whole body of Christians was waiting for reinvigoration: and then the Curé d'Ars, John Wesley, William Booth of the Salvation Army and Fr Faber of the London Oratory came along. Religion heated up again.

But to return for a moment to Goran Ivanisevic. There is a dark side to his happy Christianity. Throughout history, the Croatians have been involved in religious violence and intolerance – sometimes as the persecuted, but sometimes as persecutors. The whole Balkan peninsula was and is shot through with interethnic rivalry that has managed to invoke (falsely, we would think) the name of religion. Somehow or other the Habsburg and Ottoman empires managed, until about 1913, to keep the lid on the seething pots of religious difference within their respective domains. Those pots boiled over in the Great War, and today we see the consequences in all their naked ferocity: Catholics, Orthodox of various kinds, and Muslims, all doing terrible things to each other.

I do not wish to fall for the facile assertion that 'Religion is responsible for three-quarters of the wars in the world.' But it is a sad fact that the Four Horsemen contrive, not only to wrap themselves in the tattered fragments of national flags, but also to brandish the sacred symbols of God-given religion. With the greatest possible irony, this is true in what used to be called the Holy Land: Muslim, Jew, Orthodox, Catholic squabble and murder and destroy in the very nexus of all our religions. We are adjured to 'pray for the peace of Jerusalem'; it is hard to think of any other way by which it might be secured. Nor can we in Britain afford to be complacent. Think of the horrible way in which beautiful Ireland, with its good and lovely people, is rent asunder and defiled by what are claimed to be religious differences: not the Catholicism and not the Protestantism that we have anything to do with. And recent riots in the streets of English cities, which are wicked and racial in origin, get all tangled up with inherited religious differences.

Oh dear! Never mind: three cheers (or three Hail Marys) for Goran Ivanisevic.

Poor Ibiza

'Where are you going on holiday?' they asked. 'Will you promise not to laugh?' said I.

'Of course we won't laugh', they promised.

Shyly, I admitted: 'Ibiza.'

Invariably, they burst into peals of laughter.

The little Balearic island of Ibiza has a bad reputation for Brits Behaving Badly, involving a vast consumption of lager and 'e', wild parties and vomit. I am told, though, that it is today the most prosperous part of Spain, thanks to the tourism industry, having been, until 40 years ago, a sleepy and seldom-visited island. In the ordinary way I wouldn't dream of going there, for I do not like to be shamed by my own compatriots abroad. I had, however, been offered the use of a villa on the extreme northern point of the little island (much the same in shape and size as the Isle of Wight), and I was assured that if I avoided the district of Sant' Antoni to the east, I should find it a very beautiful place – not unspoilt, indeed, for it is filled with postwar hotels and blocks of flats, but warm, relaxed and good to look at.

With the utmost misgivings I accepted the offer, got together a group of friends, and flew there early in July. We arrived in the middle of the night, at the rather bleak airport on the extreme south of the island, where we had some difficulty in finding our hired car. Undaunted, we drove off into the night, with only the aid of some rather imprecise written instructions. Fortunately San Miguel, our destination, was signposted. But when we got there we had some four miles of winding, steep and increasingly bumpy road to negotiate in darkness; somehow or other we managed to reach the spot – the road would become extremely familiar in the days to come – and found the villa. Aided by a torch, we just about made our way in, and tumbled into bed to sleep for what remained of the night.

When we awoke, it was to discover the principal attraction of the villa – the wonderful view, to the north, of pine-covered coastline, rocky bays and a dark blue sea broken by the whitest waves. The sea around Ibiza is sometimes a dark sapphire, sometimes almost indigo; not the brilliant azure that you would expect. It is very beautiful: I am not a great one for views, preferring architectural vistas, but this was lovely, especially in the evening when the sky was aflame with copper and gold, and the huge red disk of the sun slipped abruptly beneath the horizon.

From then on, every day followed the same pattern. We would sleep till ten, then, about midday get into the car and set off in any direction (except east!) along a main road until we came to the sea; there we would find a little cove with a bathing beach, sometimes very simple, sometimes disfigured by parasols of plastic raffia. Invariably there was a little shack where they would bring forth platters of freshly caught fish for you to choose from; there under the pine trees we would sit, with a dish of paella, or mussels, or huge succulent prawns. Afternoons were for sunbathing and swimming – beware of jellyfish and sea urchins – then we would head for home, to shower and change. At the Spanish hour of 10 p.m. (anything earlier would evoke derisive comment) we would set off for a recommended restaurant. Forty years ago, Spanish cookery was among the most disappointing in Europe, depending on tough old chickens, eggs and rice soaked in oil. With the coming of the tourists, Ibiza has acquired a number of first-class eating places: far into the night we would sit at candle-lit tables under groves of lemon trees, through which the full moon filtered.

It is not easy to find out how to go to Mass on Sundays in Ibiza, as the churches do not display lists of services. I was there for two Sundays: the first, I went down to a little town improbably called Jesus – all the towns, except the old town of Eivissa, are named after the dedication of their church – where I had been told there was a Mass at 12 noon. The churches (except for Sant' Eularia, perched dramatically on the edge of a cliff) are not impressive by our standards: square boxes, whitewashed, with only a little pyramidal bell-turret in the centre of the façade to mark their purpose.

Inside they are low, with a curious mixture of round and pointed arches.

Here at Jesus, the wall above the altar is covered by the most beautiful painted *retablo*. Alas, though, all the other furnishings have been cleared out, and replaced by poor-quality modern stuff, though round the walls there remain beautiful shrines of the saints, dressed up in copes and hung with jewellery. The Mass was preceded by orchestral music from a CD player; there was no ceremonial; lessons were read by a man and a woman who had been wandering in and out of the sanctuary, paying no attention whatever to the altar, or to the Blessed Sacrament in its beautiful Gothic tabernacle, which had been banished to a pedestal in the corner. Mass was in the local version of Catalan; the only words I could understand were 'Alleluia' and 'Amen'. There were about 30 people present, including just one adolescent youth.

The following Sunday I went to San Miguel, having found out the time of Mass by dint of going to the folk-dancing. Here it was much the same, only with no *retablo*; the old altar was still in position, with a cheap new one about eighteen inches in front of it. The tabernacle was on the gradine; so was a CD player. We had Schubert piano duets before Mass; before giving Communion from the tabernacle, the priest set going a whole movement of Vivaldi's *Gloria*. Once again there were about 30 people present, including just one adolescent youth. There was no ceremonial at all, and the priest read all the lessons himself. He had been wandering about in an open-necked shirt, looking just like a caretaker; after Mass he didn't speak to anybody, but made his way across the little plaza to the bar, pausing only for a massive expectoration of spittle. I suppose we can be thankful he didn't do it in the sanctuary.

Frankly, nothing but a very strong sense of obligation could attract anybody to these boring and slovenly Masses. Spain is a Catholic country, and I suppose the clergy still take it for granted that everyone will come to Mass every Sunday, so that there is no need to try to attract them in with beautiful ceremonies, music, and so on.

Poor Ibiza! Suddenly so rich, and so godless.

The Best Tunes

At the time of the Queen's Silver Jubilee in 1977 I was speaking on the telephone to a friend who was responsible for the music in a church in west London. 'What are you doing to mark the Jubilee?' I asked.

'Nothing in particular,' he replied. 'We're going to sing "God Save the Queen" after Mass.'

'Oh,' said I. 'To what tune?'

The question wasn't as silly as it sounds, for in that church they had the custom of singing hymns to all sorts of unexpected and extraordinary tunes, especially those drawn from the priest's vast knowledge of popular songs. (In fact, they drew the line at 'God Save the Queen'.)

There is, after all, a long tradition of singing sacred words to the tunes of secular songs. It was William Booth, founder of the Salvation Army, who posed the question: 'Why should the Devil have all the best tunes?' But older Catholics will remember singing 'This is the Image of our Queen' to the tune of 'Drink to me only with thine Eyes'; and Charles Wesley himself wrote 'Love Divine, all Loves excelling' with the intention that it should be sung to Purcell's 'Fairest Isle, all Isles Excelling'. The tune we all sing, every Palm Sunday, to 'All Glory, Laud and Honour' is related in some complicated way to the dance 'Sellenger's Round'; and recently a French Protestant hymn, 'A Toi la gloire, O Ressuscité', has become popular, sung in translation to the stirring melody of 'See, the Conqu'ring Hero Comes'.

In churches that I have been connected with, we sang a May carol, 'The Happy Birds *Te Deum* Sing', to the rollicking tune of 'The Lincolnshire Poacher' – sometimes sung to other profane words, and causing raised eyebrows in the street as we went by in the May procession. 'I'll Sing a Hymn to Mary' was always sung to the Eton Boating Song, which is a marvellous tune; and 'O Mother, Will it Ever Be' to one of the most beautiful melodies ever written, familiar from the Last Night of the Proms, 'Tom Bowling'. There must be something about the May devotions which encourages us to let our hair down.

Great impetus was given to the use of popular melodies for hymn-singing by Ralph Vaughan Williams and Lucy Broadwood in the preparation of the *English Hymnal* of 1806 – still, in my opinion, the best hymn book available. Those were the days when the English Folk Dance and Song Society was busy gathering up old melodies (and words) from aged country folk; how much easier their work would have been if the tape recorder had been invented, though there are a few phonographic cylinders. The tunes are, of course, eminently singable and catchy; but in some places, when they were introduced by innocent and enthusiastic parsons, they gave rise to unseemly giggling from parishioners familiar with the original words; the tune most usually sung nowadays to 'I Heard the Voice of Jesus Say' originally belonged to 'The Nut-Brown Maid', and so on. Vaughan Williams's original composition 'Linden Lea' is so successful in the folk-song idiom that it has the air of having been around for ever; it will carry the words of *O Salutaris Hostia* very well.

There are a whole lot of secular songs, popular between the wars, that seem to me ideally suited for religious use. Just pause and hum them to yourself: 'The Way You Look Tonight'; 'All the Things You Are'; 'Smoke Gets in your Eyes'; and, from an earlier period, 'Beautiful Dreamer' and 'After the Ball was Over'. Such lovely and memorable tunes, but they are not easy to fit to existing hymns; how I wish that somebody with the poetic gift would write religious words for them.

This is, of course, a two-way traffic: we are all familiar with the misuse of '*Adeste Fideles*' by those who are tired of waiting; with people wondering why was he born so beautiful to 'The Day of Resurrection'; and with the use of 'Onward, Christian Soldiers' by those who wish to emphasize their father's acquaintance with Lloyd George. There are dangers the other way: I once had to put up with an organist who, in an effort to annoy me, accompanied *O Salutaris Hostia* to the tune of 'The Red Flag'; he succeeded.

Nor need we stop there. Fragments of Masses, requiems and motets are regularly borrowed for commercials and signature tunes; we should return the compliment by freely raiding the repertoire of Classic FM. Two noble melodies by Wagner were incorporated into the *English Hymnal*, the opening chorale of *Die Meistersinger*, and the Grail motif from *Parsifal*; sadly, they have hardly been used in the Church of England, and they have never been adopted by Catholics; they should be. But what about such pieces as the aria 'Il mio tesoro intanto' from *Don Giovanni* and the duet from *The Pearl Fishers*? Would they not make beautiful motets if provided with sacred words?

After all, why *should* the Devil have all the best tunes?

Costume Dramas

Picture the scene: it is the day of the Anglican National Pilgrimage to Walsingham. Anglo-Catholic bishops, clergy and laity are assembled in great numbers. The concelebrants in their white chasubles are seated round the open-air altar in the priory ruins. About 1.30 p.m., one of them leans over to his neighbour and says: 'Just think, my dear Father' – for so it is that they speak to one another – 'in vicarages all over England the video-recorders are switching themselves on.' He was thinking of the Australian soap opera 'Neighbours', and the known devotion to it of the clergy of the Church of England. Let me confess that I have introduced the virus of 'Neighbours'-watching into a number of clergymen's homes, and it has invariably flourished.

Two soaps, 'Neighbours' and its barely distinguishable cousin 'Home and Away' have been astonishingly successful in promoting esteem for all things Australian. Before their coming, Dame Edna and *Crocodile Dundee* had introduced us to the kind of Aussie self-mockery to be found in books like *Let Stalk*

Strine by Afferbeck Lauder. It took the arrival of the soaps a decade ago to make that continent seem glamorous and its distinctive voice seductive. The soaps seem ordinary and accessible: their American equivalents, 'Dallas' and 'Dynasty', were set in opulent worlds that none of us could aspire to and few would wish to inhabit. The people of Ramsay Street and Summer Bay seem, on the other hand, very much like us. Despite their funny ways of talking about 'morning tea' and 'shooting through', despite the curious geography that enables them to go out for an ordinary picnic and encounter a ravine and fall down it and be killed, we can feel of them that 'next door is only a footstep away'.

Queen Elizabeth the Queen Mother has been most unfairly mocked for allegedly saying that she listened to 'Mrs Dale's Diary' because it was the only way to find out what the middle classes were thinking. Given her aristocratic background and the restrictions of her royal existence, it was commendable in her to wish to find out, and sensible to do so in such a painless way. The clergy cannot make the same excuse, that watching soaps is the only way to find out what ordinary people are thinking, for their lives are set among ordinary people, and they are often involved in the kind of crises that happen every other day in soap-land; it is perhaps consoling, from time to time, to be able to experience them at secondhand, to see how other people cope.

The soaps can make no deep demands upon the emotions. They do not require suspension of disbelief, willing or unwilling. Their plots are so over-the-top, the development of characters and storylines so perfunctory, the changes of cast and characterization so rapid, that even those who are completely hooked do not really believe. Forgotten grand-mothers, sons newly out of prison, ex-wives, unsuspected siblings, turn up out of nowhere as easily as in a Victorian melodrama or a Dickens novel, to both of which they have some affinity; but it is unlikely that the whole of England will weep over the death of Stephanie as they did over Little Nell. Perhaps this is because characters are subjected to sudden and violent changes: villains become loveable comedians, dependable grandmothers turn into alcoholics and back again, buffoons face heart-rending tragedies. And there is a constant coming and going of minor characters, usually played by actors who confuse things by having appeared, in other roles, in another soap. In Australia, as in Hollywood, an English accent is a sure sign of insincerity and unreliability.

So you don't have to believe: you merely watch. You can, with an easy conscience, wish that death or disaster will over-whelm a particular character. It is all part of what Arthur Marshall used to call Life's Rich Tapestry.

Within the richly woven plots the clergy often find themselves depicted. Births, marriages and deaths form an important element of the story, so christenings, weddings and funerals abound. There must be much grinding of teeth at the ignorance with which they are generally depicted. Only the other day, in 'EastEnders', Tiffany learned that the clergyman who was to officiate at her wedding had had a road accident, so 'I've got to find my own vicar.' That is simply not a thing that could happen, even in today's C of E. It reminded me of an episode of 'Brookside', a few years ago now, when the bride failed to turn up for her wedding; the bridegroom, unwilling to waste a reception, married her sister, then and there. (It was explained that he had had the banns called, as a precaution, some time before.) In the event, Tiffany was married by a personable young priest, whom we had earlier seen conducting the Veneration of the Cross along strict Roman lines. At the wedding he wore what I at first thought was a dalmatic, but later identified as a chasuble worn back to front. He has since baptized baby Courtenay wearing a 'Vatican' cotta and using the latest Church of England service.

Weddings are usually a bit of a muddle. I am not aware that the response 'I do' appears in any rite authorized in this country. It is certainly not in either the Catholic or Anglican services, yet it turns up with monotonous regularity in weddings on film and television, as does the ever-popular 'You may now kiss the bride.' The clergy wear all sorts of things: in dramas of the Jane Austen period they always seem to wear those huge lawn sleeves that have only ever been worn by bishops; as bishops were the ones who tended to get painted, the idea has got into the heads of the costume department that big sleeves were *de rigueur* for all.

I am amazed that the production companies do not find some tame clergymen to advise them on what the clergy actually say, how they dress and how they behave. In the film *Theatre of Blood* they hired a real clergyman to conduct a funeral; of course he was very convincing, but I believe his bishop disapproved. Sometimes nature imitates art: when Chris Braine, founder of the 'Nine o'Clock Service', was to be ordained, he fancied himself in a rochet and stole identical to those worn by Jeremy Irons in *The Mission*. His devoted followers went to much trouble and expense to secure them. Still, we do not turn to these programmes for accuracy but for fantasy, not for realism but for relaxation. Their absurdity is all part of the game.

A Real Catholic

'Of course, if you were a *real* Catholic, like us,' said the Catholic mother-in-law of one of the parishioners of my former Church of England parish. I had gone back for a family occasion, the golden wedding of two of my one-time flock. I had not encountered the opinionated old lady for about twenty years; it was the first time she had seen me in collar and tie. As we settled comfortably down after luncheon, she asked: 'And how do you like being a Catholic?'

'Very much,' I replied. 'Of course, I'm lucky: the church I go to has lovely services and lovely music.' It was then that she said: 'Oh, I knew you'd say that. Of course, if you were a *real* Catholic, like us, you wouldn't bother what the services were like; for us, the Mass is the Mass, however it's done.' She didn't mean to be insulting, she just spoke naturally what she was thinking. I'm afraid I exploded in anger: 'But I *am* a real Catholic; I'm as much a real Catholic as you are.' She was flustered by my reaction, and eventually I was able to guide her towards the phrase 'cradle Catholic' to describe herself and her family. But I bet she still doesn't feel that I am a real Catholic.

This attitude is all too common among those who have had the privilege of being born to Catholic families, baptized in the Catholic Church, and brought up as Catholics. They are a bit like the labourers in Our Lord's parable of the vineyard:

they have borne the burden and heat of the day and, though they theoretically welcome conversions, they half-pity, half-despise, latecomers like myself.

Over the years, the Catholic Church in England has received many converts, usually from among the practising and instructed members of the Church of England. I need only list the names of Newman, Manning, Knox, Chesterton, Waugh: without any need for comparisons, nobody will question that these became, in their own right, great ornaments to the Catholic Church.

In the past ten years, the Established Church has become so hopeless that there have been converts in larger number than ever before. Statistics are not kept or, if they are kept, are treated as secret. It is impossible to say how many lay people have left the Church of England to become Catholics. In the case of the clergy, the official number is 600. I suspect this is an underestimate, judging by the depletion of the circles in which I used to move, and by the numbers of former clergymen I meet as Catholics, whether ordained or not. For example, I had five curates during my 22 years as incumbent of a Church of England parish: of them, two are now Catholics (one a priest, the other pastoral assistant in a Catholic parish); one became a Catholic but has since died; and two are still in the Church of England as incumbents. Many of my very best friends have become Catholics, and are scattered all over England, so that I seldom see them.

I have, of course, been made very welcome in the Catholic parish where I was instructed and received, and where I now worship. For obvious reasons, as I am not ordained, I have no part in the closed society of the priests of the diocese. In the

Church of England I was on Christian-name terms with many bishops; as a Catholic I have met but one – my own – and him very briefly. Really, if you will forgive the jargon, it is as if one's whole support group of friends and colleagues had been snatched away.

I was, personally, very fortunate in my circumstances, in that I suffered no material hardship in following the dictates of conscience: the Church of England pays me a pension, all sorts of institutions for the Anglican clergy remain open to me, and I have, by inheritance, a nice house to live in. Many convert clergymen were not so lucky: in becoming Catholics they lost not only their vocation, their status and their income, but also their home. There are many instances, especially among those who are married and have children, of really heroic sacrifice. It is hard to think of any possible motive of personal advantage in their conversion; the same is true for those lay people who were often deeply and fulfillingly involved in the life of their Anglican parishes and now find themselves cut off from their friends and with no opportunity afforded them of serving the Church.

I have to admit that, after 30 years of striving for improvement and perfection in worship, both at the parish level and in the General Synod, it irks me to experience (not, I say again, in my own parish) the treasures of the Roman liturgy being squandered by the ineptitude and inefficiency of priests and musicians. In the same way, it is tedious to have to listen to homilies made up of pious clichés and ill-informed speculations by preachers whose imagination is as narrow as their education.

Not even God can make me a cradle Catholic; nor do I

claim to be a good Catholic. But to deny me the chance of being a real Catholic is to limit the power of God intolerably. I consider myself to be a true Roman Catholic: I believe in the power of the Roman Pontiff not only to teach doctrine, but also to regulate the liturgy and to define who is and is not, who may and may not be, in holy orders. I have not all my life been right about these matters, as 'real' Catholics have been; but I am right now.

Even ex-Anglicans are God's creatures: we want to be loved, and to be made use of. Love us, and use us.

.

CU00921619

Lucy lives in Kent with her family and includes amongst her hobbies: shopping, good times with good friends, sunshine holidays, handbags and shoes. Lucy has been writing for many years but has only recently secured a publishing contract. Lucy has written a children's book which is published under her real name.

For my Angus

Lucy Reece

THIS EXTRAORDINARY MAN

AUSTIN MACAULEY PUBLISHERS™

LONDON • CAMBRIDGE • NEW YORK • SHARJAH

A CIP catalogue record for this title is available from the British Library.

ISBN 9781528941204 (Paperback)
ISBN 9781528970648 (ePub e-book)

www.austinmacauley.com

First Published 2022
Austin Macauley Publishers Ltd®
1 Canada Square
Canary Wharf
London
E14 5AA

Thank you to everyone who reads this book—your support means the world. Thank you to my entire household for being just brilliant throughout this whole process. Leanne Smith, thank you for your pure brilliance. My roots are forever in your debt! My eternal thanks to my 'Lilac' colleagues for your creativity – I miss you all. Anita and Deborah, thank you for your support and inspiration. You put up with a lot! My thanks to all my dear, dear friends who have given me everything I've asked for including Prosecco, chocolate, a shoulder to cry on, and their honest opinion. Finally, my thanks to Austin Macauley who made this book possible too.

Although I reviewed and revised the text during lockdown, the story is set before Covid-19 was even a thing. I have omitted any mention of the reality in which we currently live in the hope that better times are ahead when we can look back on this pandemic and say 'Oh yes, I remember that. Thank goodness that's over!'.

This book makes reference to the very real experience of sexual abuse and although the main story is a work of fiction, it also includes subject matter that some readers may find triggering, including reference to coercive control, domestic abuse, violence and self-harm.

Further guidance can be found at the back of the novel.

Whatever your shape, size, colour, creed, gender or
background, live life to its fullest every day because you
never know when today will be your last.
Don't regret the things you've done, they can't be changed.
Learn from them, accept them and move on.
Don't let opportunity pass you by
and love whomever you want to love.
You are extraordinary.

For All of You

"It's cathartic," they said. "Put it down on paper, the relief will be immense," they said.

Okay then. I've been holding something inside my head for the past 30 years and I want to let it go. The hardest thing I've ever admitted is the next sentence, so here goes…

When I was 15 years old, I was sexually abused.

At the time, I thought I was just unlucky, and perhaps, as a developing teenager, I had given out the wrong signals, but now, years later, I realise that what he did to me was not acceptable. I was young, afraid, and I didn't know what the right thing to do was.

For the sake of anonymity, I will call him 'Mr J'. Mr J was a maths tutor, whom my parents had hired to give me private tuition for an hour a week every Tuesday from 4 pm to 5 pm. The time and day are forever etched into my memory. They thought I was getting invaluable guidance on how to pass my maths O-Level, as I was at a grammar school, at the bottom of the class and struggling terribly with maths. Maths tests caused me to feel anxious and intimidated because the result was always the same. I failed everyone. Private lessons were supposed to help me get a good understanding of the subject, to pull me from the depths of struggling with D grades to the dizzy heights of A grades. What I actually got, was a retired maths teacher, sitting with me at the desk in my bedroom, who took every opportunity to touch me inappropriately. I would be consumed with fear as each Tuesday rolled around and by 5.15pm, as his maroon Robin Reliant 3-wheeler trundled away, I would be dry-heaving into the toilet, sickened by the way he had managed to touch me again, despite my efforts to block his roving hands.

The lesson would start off innocent enough, he would arrive and chat politely to my mum about what we would be working on and she would show him to my bedroom where we'd sit at my desk, get my maths book out and the lesson would begin. A couple of minutes later, Mum would come in, put a glass of orange squash on the desk, that he requested every week, and would say, "Is there anything else you need before I leave you in peace?" and he'd reply "No thank you, oh could I just have a couple of tissues please?" and Mum would graciously provide them, and walk out and shut my bedroom door behind her. We would then turn to the books and he would talk me through the mathematical problem we were working on that week. How to show the workings out, how the example answers were reached, what might be on an exam paper etc. He'd then tell me to take on board what he'd explained and work on the next exercise. That was the point when it all changed.

While I was concentrating and working my way through the questions, he would start to fiddle with himself, through his trousers at first. Then he'd glance over at the book I was working on, unbuckle his belt, pop the button and zipper on his trousers, take out his penis and masturbate. Right in front of me. A 15-year-old girl. He'd start off keeping it concealed,

I think in case Mum came back in, but he soon realised that we wouldn't be disturbed so he'd pleasure himself on full display. There are no words to describe how afraid and disgusted I felt and how I prayed each week for my brother to be the naughty little shit he was and to rush in to my room to see what was going on, especially as Mum specifically told him to stay away. But he never did. Nobody ever disturbed us.

When Mr J had finished pleasuring himself, he would use the tissues to clean himself, drink the squash and then place the dirty tissue inside the empty glass for my mum to clear up. He would then ask how I was getting on with the exercise and check my answers. If I got the answers right, he would put his arm around my back as if he was going to hug me and then he would fondle my left breast while muttering words like 'aren't you a clever little girl' and 'that deserves a special cuddle'. So, I learnt pretty quickly to get the answers wrong, but he cottoned on and sure enough, by week 4, he was groping me whether I got the answers right or wrong. I used to pin my left arm as tight as I could to my side, using my right hand as extra leverage to hold it down, pulling it closer, but his bony fingers would always push and grope their way around for a fondle. I tried everything I could to put distance between us, moving away from him in my chair, leaning as far away as possible, but I was always pushed up against the wall with him sitting beside me, so I was, in effect, trapped. The winter was worse because it got dark so early and Mum would shut my curtains by 4pm and that made me feel more trapped, more afraid and more vulnerable in my own bedroom. I remember one particular time just after the lesson started, I pulled open the curtain beside me in the hope that the bright light from my room shining onto the front garden would draw some attention and someone would see what was going on, but he promptly closed it minutes before he commenced his masturbation session, and my heart sank. Once, when I wriggled and pulled away from him, he said he was only giving me a friendly hug as I needed it for encouragement. I told him that I didn't want a hug and would prefer words of encouragement but to no avail. Nothing stopped him. Sometimes, he would even try to fondle me while he was masturbating. Sick bastard. It was as though he felt he had a right to fondle and grope me. At the end of each torturous hour-long session, my mum would thank him and pay him £10 for the privilege. It didn't occur to her to leave my bedroom door open or to question why I was still struggling with my maths.

One particular Tuesday, about an hour before my lesson, I plucked up the courage to talk to my mum about it, so I sat her down and told her what he did to me every week. Afterwards, as tears of relief rolled down my cheeks, she looked at me very intently and I held my breath waiting for her soothing words, a protective hug and a promise that she would make it stop. But she told me with pure venom in her voice that I was a 'lying little bitch' and that I was 'only doing it to get out of math lessons'. She wouldn't hear of anything 'untoward' happening because he had been recommended to her and was very well thought of in the church circles he moved in. Oh, so he was churchy, well that was OK then. I asked her if I could please, please leave my bedroom door open, but that was refused as I had to have a quiet place to study. The compromise was that I could leave my door ajar, but about five minutes into the next lesson, my brother started to play-up, so Mum stealthily shut the door to keep out the noise. So that was that. The abuse continued.

It got so bad over the following months that I went to see my maths teacher at school and told her that my parents had got a private tutor in for me but that I felt it wasn't doing any good. I told her that what he was teaching me wasn't part of the maths lessons she taught me, and that I thought it was too advanced. She asked me to show her the book I was being taught from, which I did, and instead of showing her what I had been learning, I showed her the A-Level sections. She rang my parents immediately and told them that I was not being tutored appropriately and that she would give me extra work to do each week to help me through. I felt guilty that I had lied about the work, but I was desperate. I had been subjected to the same routine, every Tuesday, for that same hour, with no let up as he even came around during the school holidays. Of course he did – he was getting his rocks off groping a 15-year-old girl.

I remember very vividly, my mum telling me that she had cancelled my private lessons with Mr J. I wanted to scream with relief! She said I was better off with extra work from my teacher at school and that I was to promise to work harder at maths. Of course, I promised. Honestly, I would have made a deal with the devil – anything to make him stop.

After every lesson I would take a scalding hot shower. My skin would turn crimson with the heat from the water and I'd scrub myself with a soap-filled pad from the cupboard under the kitchen sink, the ones my mum used for cleaning pots and pans. I concentrated on my left arm, scrubbing and scrubbing until my skin bled because that was the arm that had let me down, hadn't been able to protect me. At least the sight of my red, bleeding skin meant I had cleansed myself of his touch, but my body soon became so unbearably sore. I then turned to the only thing that wouldn't judge me, that wouldn't hurt me, that would make me feel comforted and secure – food. I would take pleasure in eating sweet treats because they made me feel good, the very definition of 'comfort eating'. An open packet was an empty packet as far as I was concerned, and I couldn't save any, somebody might find them and they were all mine. I used to hide them under my mattress, in my wardrobe and I even stored bars of chocolate in boxes of tampons. Nobody was going to go there, right?

Forgive me for being pleased when I found out, just a few years ago, that he had died a slow, lingering death. My 15-year-old self would say it's what he deserved.

But the damage had already been done and I can never un-see what I saw or erase what I'd experienced. So, I developed the ability to detach myself from my emotions, lock my soul away so nobody could harm me. On the outside, people saw a hard bitch. On the inside, I was wrecked.

I've told you about my experience as a vulnerable teenage girl not because I want sympathy, I'm not sensationalising it, it happened exactly as I've described. I don't want you to feel sorry for me, I want you to understand why I am who I am.

Putting it down on paper has been very difficult but very cathartic. I won't let it define who I am. It hasn't destroyed me or deterred me; in fact, I'd like to think it's prepared me, perhaps in some way made me stronger. I've come to realise that we all need someone to talk to, we need to realise our hopes and dreams and to overcome our fears.

Many people now share every second of their lives virtually. They strive to be 'liked' or their posts 'shared', and they look for constant validation as they live vicariously through social media. Whether it's taking the perfect selfie (phone above head in outstretched arm, head down, eyes up, lips moist and pouting) or trying to portray that they have the perfect body/life/family/home/relationship/partner, they are still craving that validation. Moments and posts on social media are gone within 24 hours, replaced by other moments to be liked more and shared more, but the harsh reality is that our life is made up of sequences of moments that can't be erased, deleted or taken down. Some moments we block, some we forget, but they all shape the path we choose and the person we become. The only person you need to validate what you do, is you.

We are all flawed, and we all bear the scars of loss. Overcoming adversity is challenging, but I always have hope and that strengthens my soul so that I can deal with life's challenges. I hope that having shared my story with you, you will find the strength to let go of your demons, whatever they are. Above all, love yourself and do what feels right in your heart – it may not always be easy, but it will be worth it.

***

So, onto this story. It's dedicated to you, because you know that in real life, you won't ever bump into a gorgeous unattached billionaire, who can offer you the world and a career that money can't buy, can give you three 'earth-shattering' orgasms a day and has a huge…business empire!

The reality is that 99% of us are ordinary people, in debt for life, and possibly beyond, trying to juggle home life with a job. I could call it a career, but are you truly happy upcycling your job to a 'career'? Me neither!

Whether you are in a relationship, just coming out of a relationship, happy being single or looking for that significant other, this is your story.

It's real life (mostly), it's observational (definitely) and it's something everyone can relate to (undeniably). The names have been changed to protect the guilty!

It gives you a little glimpse into my life experiences, an ordinary woman of average height, with average looks and average intelligence. The only thing above average is my BMI and my passion for shopping! I have a body like a melted candle, a mind as sharp as a tack (or maybe I mean a tic-tac), and I desperately want to call time on the interminable ride that is the hormonal rollercoaster of middle age and menopause! I have a 'career' I hate, a salary of £4k, less than it was 20 years ago, and a healthcare plan that is the first aid kit which sits under my desk.

Yes, I am an ordinary woman, but when I least expected it…I met an extraordinary man….

Prologue
Present Day

Heathrow Airport, Terminal 2, Arrivals

Every time I'm at an airport, the chaos it generates never ceases to amaze me. Each person sharing these few moments in time, in this place. All of them glancing fleetingly at, but not seeing, the strangers who happen to be on the same journey through life at this precise time, all with very different end games, reaching very different destinations. Some are wandering aimlessly trying to remember where they'd arranged to meet loved ones, glancing at their watches and phones trying to work out the time difference now they're back in 'Blighty'. Some are lone travellers, with their clearly-too-big-for-the-cabin cases, who have flown Business Class and are looking refreshed, rested and ready to tackle the day in the office. No waiting at Baggage Reclaim for them, silently praying that the flimsy padlock they bought from WH Smith on the outward journey, has been strong enough to hold back the beast that is their undies and shoes, pummelling constantly from inside, trying to find any weak points to enable the contents to spew out for all to see. They are not the embarrassed soul standing distraught at the back of the crowd watching in horror as their bag takes its third turn around the conveyor, centre stage, having burst through the plastic curtain at the optimum time to reveal several pairs (clean and dirty) of comfortable but very tatty undies. Not forgetting skanky pants' very un-glamorous partner: the holey-heeled and peep toe socks. I know you know that panic time when the trickle of bags becomes a torrent, when everyone is rushing forward, or pushing through the crowd calling 'Janice, you grab it. It's coming towards you. Yes, that one there. No Janice, leave the kids with the other bag, they'll be fine.' We've all seen it. From tourists stopping without warning right in front of you so you clatter into their bags taking the skin off your nicely tanned shins; to couples returning from romantic getaways, still in that flush of 'just the two of us' love. Let's not forget the fraught families just thankful that 1. the flight was only delayed by two hours, 2. the kids behaved and 3. the in-laws had texted to say they'd watered the plants and turned on the hot water at home so you can wade through the five loads of washing your all-inclusive beach holiday has created. Let's not forget the damn good shower you need too to wash off that invisible film of grimy 'travel' that covers the body whenever you take a flight.

Some travellers are anxiously rummaging in the depths of bags and rucksacks wondering where they've left the car keys and parking ticket, whilst desperately trying to remember the location of said vehicle because nobody had a pen to write on the back of the ticket. (Was it car park 4 because we live at number 4, or car park 12 because we've been married 12 years?...) I smile as I remember how much better I feel when I'm reunited with my car – that trek through the long stay car park, spotting it in the distance exactly where I'd left it, and that first sense of 'being home'. You can almost feel that your big hunk of over-financed metal is attuned to your presence and like an over-excited puppy; you wait for it to wake up and welcome you back from your trip, ever so pleased to see you and ready to take you on the final leg of your homebound journey. No? Just me then.

Standing a short distance from the throng of people at the barriers, I chuckle to myself as I see holidaymakers and visitors emerging from the doors in the style of 'Tonight Matthew, I'm going to be…' ('90s game-show throwback – put it in your search engine) but nobody looks refreshed, gorgeous and 'Stars in Their Eyes' pop-star like. Once you've run the gauntlet of the longest short walk through the 'Nothing to Declare' lane of the UK Customs and Border Agency, the best you can look is elated. Take a close look next time – there's always a mixture of surprise and jubilation on everyone's faces. They've conquered the customs hall and come out victorious, if a little dumbfounded that they got through without the dreaded hand on shoulder and the sentence that makes all mortals blood freeze in their veins: 'Would you mind stepping this way please, I have a few questions for you…' Happens to me every time. I never bring back cigarettes or tobacco (don't know anyone who smokes), sometimes a bottle of rum (for personal consumption only) and always an oversized Toblerone, which I've already started and stroke lovingly, knowing that I will devour it during the evening with a few 'proper' cups of tea (it's never the same when you're abroad) whilst binge-watching two weeks back episodes of 'Neighbours'. Although the vast majority of people are well within their personal duty-free limits, there's always the worry that 800 cigarettes and six litres of moonshine have been secreted in your case by unscrupulous airport staff, using you as a mule for their bootleg operation. Isn't there? Just me again then.

I spent all day yesterday preparing myself to see him again. I've waxed, shaved and plucked every hair on my body (if it won't stay where it should, it's gone).

I've scrubbed, exfoliated and moisturised my skin until it glows (but that may be because I've removed about three layers) and my short 'do' is freshly washed and blow-dried. I'm wearing a killer outfit that's sexy yet sophisticated – dark pink Capri pants, black fitted top, which outlines two of my best features, and black open-toe wedge shoes. I've spritzed myself several times with my favourite fragrance (I call it 'layering'), my nails are painted a fresh, pale pink and I've managed to obtain a natural glow with my make-up, although it took two hours to achieve and I'm meant to look as though I have no make-up on! I've scrubbed up well if I do say so myself, and hopefully when he sees me, it will be well worth it. My God, I'm so nervous! My breakfast consisted of six Smint breath mints and I've only drunk a few sips of water. I don't want to run the risk of being in the toilet and missing him when he comes through those doors into Arrivals because I'm stuck in a cubicle with my knickers around my ankles (hmm, that reminds me of a whole other story!) and I've cleaned my teeth at least four times. It's been a hell of a journey these last 18 months and I want our first kiss to be memorable for all the right reasons and yes, I know he's just spent 23 hours on a plane, but at least I know that my breath is fresh and minty, and if his is a little on the stale side, I have that tin of breath mints in my bag…

This is it, I can see him! He's just about to come through the doors and as I step towards the barrier that separates the arriving passengers from the rest of the UK, my heart flutters in my chest, I can't swallow, and I think I might pass out. I take a couple of deep breaths, straighten up to my full 5'6", hold in my stomach and wait for him to notice me as he glances at the sea of waiting faces. He turns momentarily and takes his children by the hand, gently encouraging them to hold on to the baggage trolley. I gasp as I see them again; I was hoping he'd bring them, but I wasn't sure he would. All three of them look thoroughly worn out and very dishevelled; his eyes are red rimmed with fatigue, and are glazed and slightly sunken. I can see he has black bags under them that would give Samsonite a run for their money, but other than that… Oh, his hair has got a bit long and could do with a good cut, and I notice that he's lost weight but is still wearing the same old clothes he had before. Actually, they are a bit shapeless and the black trousers and black polo shirt he has on make him look quite skinny. I shrug all this off and remind myself that he's travelled a long way over the last two days and I should really be grateful that he's here. This man, whom I love with every fibre of my being.

Chapter One
February 2016

The day he walked into my life, he knocked me sideways – quite literally. As he walked out of the office, I walked past the office, and our worlds collided. He was not a stunning man. No chiselled jaw sporting designer stubble, or perfectly coiffed just-the-right-length hair. He wasn't wearing a designer suit with handmade Italian brogues and he definitely didn't smell of sandalwood and citrus. Seriously, what sort of combination is that anyway? And why do rich, successful, impossibly-sexy-but-fake men in erotic novels smell like that? Back in the day, sandalwood and citrus was also known as Pledge polish. They never smell of Right Guard, sweat and sheer hard work. But he did. This man.

This man, who grabbed my hand when I extended it for him to shake in greeting, pulled me into a bear hug that was so strong it squeezed the air from my lungs. This man, who was so charismatic and confident, showed the briefest glimpse of anguish in his eyes for a nano-second as he pulled me close. It was so brief I could've been mistaken, but his smile definitely didn't quite reach his eyes. But I lost the thought as a moment later this man then slapped me on the back in that rather awkward way that heterosexual men do when they greet each other. (All that backslapping and joviality, whilst trying to keep a modest distance between their nether regions to stop them from accidentally touching.) The words that then left this man's mouth were not sweet nothings tinged with toothpaste, organic goji berry compote and finest Columbian richly roasted. They were tinged with Nescafe, Weetabix and an Australia accent. In fact, the words that left this man's mouth still make me shudder to this day, although now they make me laugh. A bit. When I've consumed the best part of a bottle of Prosecco and eaten my body weight in Pringles (believe me, when I pop that top I don't stop until I hit dust!).

He said, "Oh mate, hello! It's so good to finally put a face to the email. You must be Louisa. Mate, it's so great to meet you. I'm Angus. Angus Pewk." I know – mate? Seriously! And Pewk – what the fuck?

All I could respond with was, "Ha, ha, Angus, hi. Ha, ha, ha, ha." I had nothing else. No other words formed in my head. None whatsoever. As he pulled away from our 'mate' hug, smiled, nodded and walked off down the corridor, I turned to the ladies in the office who were both shaking with laughter, enjoying my awkwardness a little too much.

"There's that look, Vickie. You were right, it's priceless," said Kay, pointing a well-manicured finger at me.

To which Vickie replied, "Told you! Same reaction – I win again. That means the first round's on you tonight."

I looked from them, still giggling and 'high fiving' each other, to him and back to them. All I could say was, "Pewk? Really?"

But whilst my brain was still processing my encounter with this man called Angus Pewk, my body was zinging and fizzing. My nipples were erect and so hard they hurt, and there was a fire in my loins that I hadn't felt since 16th June 2014.

I put both these down to the following facts: 1: The window in the office was open and the particularly chilly breeze was making my nipples stiff, and 2: I was wearing polyester 'granny pants' and standing on a nylon carpet – a combination of man-made heat sources any fire department would have trouble extinguishing!

As I watched him disappear down the corridor towards his office with all the swagger of a three-legged donkey at the Melbourne Cup, in his wool blend off-the-peg suit and the sun reflecting gently off of his bald patch (I am aware that I'm not portraying him in a very good light here), I knew I wanted to get to know this man much, much, much better. Oh, and in case you were wondering, he had a fantastic gluteus maximus!

I made myself a coffee and took it back to my office slightly short of breath, very red in the face and with the warmth of his touch still resonating through my back. Or maybe I'm just making something out of nothing; after all, he did slap me quite hard several times. And call me 'mate'.

16th June 2014 is a day I remember vividly. There was definitely something stirring in my loins that day, but sadly it turned out to be nothing more than a solitary stray spark even though it was the day I met the man of my dreams. Now, he was tall with just-the-right-length dark hair, Italian, sexy as hell and smelt of sandalwood and citrus, and he had very dark brown, almost black, eyes. As I looked down slowly, taking in every inch of this Italian hunk, I didn't get as far as his shoes, if you know what I mean. I was sitting very demurely on the edge of my seat in the waiting room with lip gloss on (thankfully), eyes all dewy and sparkly (thanks to the old boy sitting next to me who had doused himself in 'Old Spice') when in he walked. Boom! Fire lit. Stand back behind the barrier, this is going to get hot. Our eyes met and after a moment he looked down at his notes, looked back up at me and said "Louisa? Is there a Louisa Scott here?" Fire immediately extinguished as realisation dawned on me. This gorgeous, sexy man was the doctor who was about to take me into a consulting room, tell me to take my knickers off and lay on the bed and check my swollen and throbbing haemorrhoids! So close, and yet, so far.

Chapter Two

The rest of the day passed in a blur of telephone calls, meetings, emails, meetings, pointless conversations, meetings and a very rushed lunch of strong black coffee and one-and-a-half packets of Jaffa cakes. (What? I could've eaten two packets and aren't they part of my 'five-a-day?) Oh, and did I mention meetings? I didn't see any more of Angus, although I heard him a few times, and at 5:45 pm, I shut down my computer, grabbed my phone and bag, and walked out of the building. Kay and Vickie had already left; they were no doubt in the pub reaping the benefits of their little wager. It was February and there was dampness in the air; it was dark, and I had a 45-minute journey home. I climbed into my car, threw my bag behind me, spilling the contents onto the back seat (half a packet of pocket tissues, an almost empty tube of hand cream, a bent safety pin, a lipstick that was worn down to the barrel, a tin of Vaseline lip balm, 3 tampons and 2 sachets of Cystitis granules) and slipped off my high heels. I put my head on the cold steering wheel, shut my eyes and as my body heat started to huff up the windscreen, I felt relief throb through my feet. They were killing me – I'd been tottering around all day trying to look confident and sexy, and it was damn hard work. My feet were swollen and there was no sign of my ankles. They'd vacated my legs by mid-afternoon and were last seen running for the hills.

Damn! I'd forgotten to get my 'driving shoes' out of the boot first. There was no way I could drive without shoes and even less chance of getting my heels back on, so I clambered out of my cobalt blue (my favourite colour) Toyota Yaris (not my favourite car) and walked in my tights round to the boot to retrieve my hideous yet undeniably comfortable driving shoes. They were stored in a bag for life in a shoebox in the boot. I never let anyone see me in them; they were light brown, lace-up, and they absolutely stank (I had to drive to and from work in them every day, of course they did).

I remember very vividly the day I bought them. I had run into the first shoe shop I came to in Bluewater, picked up the first pair of women's shoes that didn't have a heel, waited an age for the woman to find them in my size and when she asked if I wanted to try them on, I'd replied, "Oh no, they're not for me, they're for my aged auntie," paid for them and ran back out of the shop. Really, what possessed me to buy them in light brown is beyond me, I think it was blind panic. In fact, I often have dreams that my car has been stolen and all that's left in the parking space is my stinky shoes in their equally stinky bag, hanging out of the shoebox in full view for everyone to see because no self-respecting car thief would take them along for the ride.

I slipped one shoe on, hitched my dress up to my thigh to allow free movement of my other leg and just as I'd got my other foot up on the bumper lacing up said aged auntie shoe number 2, I heard a voice beside me. "Louisa, mate, it was really lovely to meet you finally today. Thank you for all the help you gave me before we moved over here, it's much appreciated and I…"

Fuck! He'd looked down at my shoes. Do I explain or just ignore? I was waiting for my brain to help me out but all it came up with was 'leave me out of it – you bought the shoes, you silly bitch, you explain them!' So, I did what any self-respecting woman would do. I stood up straight, smoothed down my dress and pushed my boobs out as far as I could by squeezing my arms at my side. Bingo! Attention averted from hideous shoes to cleavage. His eyes widened and for a few seconds he just stared at my boobs. The girls had done well, and as I looked down at my impressive cleavage and my boobs straining at the 'V' neck of my dress, I could feel my nipples start to harden again. It must be the cold air.

"Oh, don't mention it," I responded, still with maximum cleavage on display to divert from hideous footwear, "It was no problem, I'm always happy to help. I hope your relocation from Australia went well, it's great to have you on the team." He was still staring at my boobs and I wasn't sure on protocol now. Did I carry on talking to a man who was more interested in making eye contact with my nipples than with me? How long do I stand here for? What happens if he talks to them? I glanced down again and there were my nipples standing to full attention, sticking out just as if they were coat hooks, teasing Angus. I could almost hear them screaming 'look at us, we are so hard, and we want you to wrap your tongue around us,' or maybe that was just wishful thinking on my part?

I didn't need to worry. The silence was broken as Angus' phone rang out a piercing, shrill tone and I caught a brief glimpse of the word 'Joanna' on the screen. So, wife or girlfriend? He nodded his goodbye to me with a smile, looked down at my shoes (mortifying), did a 'thumbs up' (even more mortifying) and swiped at the screen of this phone. As he walked to his car, which was parked a couple of spaces away from mine, I just caught the tone of a rather irate voice coming from 'Joanna'. He blipped his car alarm and as he climbed into the driver's seat, I heard him responding with, "Yes, I am on my way. I'm sorry. I just got held up…"

On the drive home, all I could think about was 'Pewk'. I wondered why I didn't already know his surname and then realised that while we had been emailing each other across the globe, he had only ever signed off as 'Angus'. Even his email address was AngusJ@some-random-provider.com and I had just assumed that his surname began with an 'J'. But I could totally understand why he wouldn't want to broadcast his surname. What about Mrs Pewk? God, you'd really have to love a man to take on that name.

Once I'd waited an eternity for the condensation to clear from my windscreen, I drove for over an hour through the rush-hour traffic. Utterly exhausted (I know it's bad when the bags under my eyes hang down lower than my boobs!) and longing for a long hot soak in the bath, I turned into my road and saw my neighbours' houses glowing with the warmth of lamplight as it seeped through the sides of drawn curtains and I imagined couples replaying their day to each other over a glass of red and a foot rub. There was one house tucked away in the corner, looking like an afterthought that had been built on a postage stamp sized piece of land, its curtains open, lights off and a handful of leaflets poking out of the letterbox. Looking as empty and unloved as I felt, it was a 2-bed-but-really-a-1-bed-with-a-large-cupboard, and it was where I called home. I pulled onto my drive and switched off the engine. As I sat there, staring at my dark and empty house, I longed again for a significant other to be waiting inside for my return, with dinner on the hob, a bubbly bath run, the wine open, big strong arms to pull me into a bear hug and slap me on the back…

No! I shook my head to scatter the thought and reached behind for my bag (I didn't bother scooping up the detritus, it could stay on the back seat) gathered up my heels and my phone and climbed very unladylike from my car. Fumbling in the dark with my keys (I really must remember to put the outside light on), I unlocked my front door, ripped the 'to the occupier' crap from my letterbox and stepped into the cold hallway. My shoulders dropped in despondency as I turned up the thermostat and made my way through the house flicking on lights and closing curtains. All alone.

That evening I sat on the sofa in my favourite faded pyjamas, my skin red from the too-hot bath – I'd lay in for too long – with my boobs free range and resting gently on my stomach, my legs tucked under me, watching that day's episode of *Neighbours*. I was just about to take a sip from my wine glass, which contained the remains of a bottle of cooking wine, when the doorbell rang.

I wonder – does wine actually have a use-by date? I found the open bottle at the back of the cupboard with some Worcestershire sauce three years out of date and extra virgin olive oil that clearly was no longer 'virginal' and had seen more action than I had. I call it 'cooking wine' because I must have opened it to use in a recipe – I can't imagine opening it and then not finishing it. Either that or I'd tried it and didn't like it and couldn't bear to throw it away. Yep, just tasted it. Second option.

I huffed my distain at being interrupted, stood up and reached for my dressing gown with the red pepper humus stain down the front (What? Honestly, you can't ever get that stuff out) and slipped my feet into my comfy but very old slippers. It was probably the window cleaner; I don't think I'd paid him for a while for the privilege of his soapy wet chamois being thrown at my windows every six weeks and being charged £10 for the pleasure. I pulled my dressing gown tight around me (whoever it was, I couldn't subject them to my 'spaniel ears' boobs), opened the front door and there stood… Angus!

My mouth dropped open in astonishment, I stared at him, then glanced past him over his shoulder and out to the road where his car was parked. I don't know what I was expecting to see – Mrs Pewk sitting in the car tapping talon-like manicured nails on the dashboard while trying to frown at me with a paralysed-by-Botox face perhaps? But no, there was nobody around.

"Angus? What? How did you…?" I was stunned. It was bloody freezing outside too; my nipples were standing to attention for the third time that day and were actually chafing against my pyjamas. I pulled my dressing gown tighter around me and folded my arms at my waist (remember, I had no bra on) in an attempt to cover up said nipples.

"Louisa, I'm so sorry, I had to see you. I know you felt it too when we met. We had a connection, a moment, and I can't stop thinking about you. I've been sitting in my car for hours trying to pluck up the courage to knock on your door and speak to you. Plus, I really need to pee so is it OK if I come in and use your bathroom?" Seriously? I stepped to one side, speechless, and motioned for Angus to come in. I was mentally trying to recall what state my bathroom was in. There was undoubtedly a bubble line all around the inside of the bath and as I'd finally got my razor to my legs and pits, there was probably a cut hair ring around it too (I hadn't bothered with the bikini line – nobody saw it these days anyway and it was still winter, so I needed the extra layer for warmth.) There may also be a box of tampons on full display on the shelf, along with my 'For skin over 40' face serum. Luckily though, the toilet was clean (I lived on my own with no men around, of course it was clean) and there was a fresh set of towels on the rail so maybe it wasn't all bad.

"Go ahead, up the stairs, second door on the left," I replied as I waved him over the threshold and past me. Angus and I held each other's gaze for a second longer than necessary and then he touched my arm gently and very briefly as he walked past. It was undeniable that time, I definitely felt something, and as I was wearing cotton knickers and my carpet was woollen, could it be that he had just turned me on?

I sat on the sofa trying to make some sort of sense of this man being in my house. This man, who I had only met THAT DAY. I heard the toilet flush and two minutes later (good to know he washed his hands), he strolled down the stairs and came and sat next to me on the sofa. I stared at him, unable to speak or move. I could feel the heat from his leg as he rested it against mine and it radiated up my body, stopping to crank the thermostat up to maximum between my legs. We looked into each other's eyes for what seemed like minutes but was probably just a few seconds then without breaking the gaze he took my hands in his, leant forwards and kissed me gently on the lips. It was the softest, most tender kiss I have ever, EVER had, and I instantly felt all my nerve endings firing as endorphins surged around my body. He broke our kiss and stood up. My eyes were now level with his groin and as he tried to pull me to my feet, I could see his cock straining at the zip of his trousers. My God, he was hard! I could distinctly see the outline of it and I licked my lips in anticipation – I couldn't help it, it was almost instinct. I let go of his hands and slowly reached for the button of his trousers, then as my hands moved to the zip and slid it down, I could see his cock twitching with anticipation. I slid his trousers down his thighs and swallowed hard as I sprang him free from his boxer shorts. Then, I took a few moments to admire the mass of black hair that surrounded his incredibly hard cock as I used my fingers to trace the thick line that reached up towards his belly button and beyond. As I fanned them out over the curve of his stomach and grasped his hips, I dropped to the floor on my knees, opened my mouth and took him in. He gasped, and as I shut my eyes, I worked my mouth slowly from the tip to the root, taking my time and taking in all of him.

As I worked my tongue around his tip and licked along the length of his cock, I massaged his balls with one hand while holding his shaft with the other. He started to tremble and push himself further into my mouth. I smiled to myself, I hadn't lost my touch, and as I flattened my tongue and rolled it around the tip, he said, "Louisa, I'm going to come. Stop if you want to, but I'm almost there." I released him and stood and as I did, I looked down at his cock, wet with my saliva, then his lips were on mine and his tongue was frantically darting around my mouth. He was driven by desire and it took me by surprise. It had been a long, long time since I'd been kissed like that and I slowed him gently with my own tongue until he calmed and held my face in his hands. Fuck, it was so good! There was so much sexual chemistry between us and as we finished our kiss, he rested his forehead against mine and said, "God, Louisa, I can taste me on your tongue." I put my arms around his neck and he started to caress my erect nipples, rolling them gently between his finger and thumb. I started to kiss him again, with great urgency, and I could feel his cock pushing against my pyjama bottoms, seeking out my very wet and ready opening. Now, I am usually a strict 'lights off' girl as I have a body that should carry the warning label 'Contents may have settled in transit', but I didn't care that the lights were on. I didn't care what he saw or even what he thought of what he saw. I just knew I had to have this man.

"Angus, I want you," I said with a throaty husk, hardly able to speak. "NOW!" I added, just in case he thought I meant not immediately, but perhaps we could pencil it in for next week! As he pushed me gently back onto the sofa and started to pull at my pyjama bottoms, I closed my eyes in anticipation and heard my alarm clock going off upstairs in my bedroom…?

Fuck! Fucking fuck, bollocks! It was my alarm clock and it had just woken me up from the best sex I hadn't had and as I looked around, I realised I had spent the night on the sofa. The TV was still on and the message on the blue screen informed me that I had reached the end of my programme. No kidding! My dressing gown was on the chair and I was still wearing my pyjamas, although there was an incredibly damp patch between my legs. I had just had a very graphic, very erotic dream about a work colleague, a man I had only just met. How wrong was that?

Chapter Three

I showered and dressed conservatively for work that day. No sexy heels or black pencil dress. My erotic dream about Angus had thrown me and I felt at odds with all my senses and emotions. I put on a pair of wide leg black trousers, flat ballerina-style shoes, a grey 'interview' blouse I found in my wardrobe, which still had the price tag on it, and a longline black cardigan. My make-up was quite muted, reflecting my mood, and as I placed my driving shoes back in the bag for life, back in the box, back in my car and slammed the boot, the heavy 'thunk' noise mirrored how I felt. With a burning throat and inexplicable tears bubbling up to my eyes, I set off for work and the usual routine of sitting in three lanes of solid traffic as I joined the daily grind of commuting. The local radio station was my only company and the two presenters were far too cheery than should be allowed at this time of the morning. I switched off. Completely.

As I pulled into the car park, I noticed that Angus was already at work so in some sort of defiance, I parked as far away from him as I could to avoid a repeat of the shoe scenario (even though I was wearing flats and didn't need to change footwear but still, better safe than very, very sorry) and as I walked towards the car park barrier, I found myself drifting towards his car. Well, as I was there, I might as well take a sneaky peak inside; you can tell a lot about someone by the state of their car. I felt a bit awkward, as if I was violating his privacy even though he was nowhere around, and I could hear the engine ticking and clicking under the bonnet as it cooled down, so he must have only just arrived. I looked through the front passenger window and saw a chocolate bar wrapper on the centre console and a mobile phone charger plugged into the cigarette lighter. So, nothing to give away who this man was or anything about his personal life in that little stash.

Then I saw it and it knocked the breath from my lungs, the evidence that he had a beautiful, sexy wife-slash-girlfriend who didn't have a body like a melted candle and who catered to his every whim. Someone who cooked him his favourite dinner every night and who served it as he walked through the front door. Someone who was always immaculately dressed and radiated vitality without even trying. Someone who applied only tinted moisturiser, bronzer and lip-gloss in the morning and still looked flawless when Angus came home from work. Someone who gently 'glowed' after a workout with her personal trainer, unlike me, who broke into a heavy sweat at the mere façade of a gymnasium. The evidence wasn't a photograph of her pinned to the dashboard or even a G-string hanging from the rear-view mirror, it wasn't that obvious, but it was evidence nonetheless. There in the cup holder, was an empty energy drink can. What? Of course it was evidence! It proved that he's up late every night servicing his wife-slash-girlfriend in every conceivable sexual position and he needs the energy drink to get him through the day. He was obviously doing with her all the things he was going to do to me in my dream last night, and why wouldn't he? She was gorgeous and sexy after all.

Suddenly, I felt incredibly upset and my eyes filled with tears. But what worried me more was the other feeling I had which started as a knot in my stomach and worked its way up to my chest where it took up residence around my broken heart. Yep, I was jealous. What the fuck was all that about? I had no right to be, I didn't even know this man. I may have been emailing him for the last two months sorting out his system access, payroll and visa checks but in reality, I have only actually known him for a day. Oh my god! I met this man less than 24 hours ago and already I've slept with him (in my dreams, literally) and I'm going all *Fatal Attraction* on him! I'll have to ask him if he's ever had a pet rabbit!

I pushed the bizarre feelings of jealousy to one side – I'd have to deal with them later – and as I made my way from the car park to the office, my mind turned to what that day had in store for me. I was mentally ticking off my 'to-do' list as I pushed open the front door and was immediately greeted by the sound of Angus' laugh ringing through the office corridors. That's the thing about Angus, you can hear him before you see him, so I took a wild guess at which corridor he was in and walked along the opposite one. I didn't want to see him, I would only start imagining him with his nympho wife-slash-girlfriend, and all the time I wasn't getting any, I sure as hell didn't want to waste my energy imagining anyone else enjoying sexual shenanigans.

As I turned towards my office, I couldn't help looking towards the sound of his voice. Damn! I knew as soon as I did that, I'd regret it. He was standing very close to Kelli, Mr Williams' PA, and he had obviously just said something very funny to her in his sexy Australian accent because she was all giggly and coy, tucking a strand of her long hair behind her ear and…no way! Now she was pushing her boobs out as far as possible by squeezing her arms at her side. Bitch! That was my trick. She didn't need to emphasise them, she had that certain something that had men quivering and drooling over her. Angus touched her briefly on her arm in a very intimate way and as he turned, he caught my eye. Shit! He saw me looking at him. He raised his hand in greeting and smiled warmly at me. I gave him a weak, nonchalant smile, a sort of 'Oh it's you, I think I met you very briefly yesterday, but I can't remember your name' sort of smile, and quickened my step. I was now being followed along the corridor and it wasn't Angus, it was the green-eyed monster and he was hot on my heels and biting at my ankles. I mentally kicked him in the nuts to halt his stampede and as I flung open my office door, I literally launched my handbag at the space under my desk and leant down to jab viscously at the power button on my computer.

Just as I was giving my printer an equal dose of hatred, in walked Angus. Fucking hell, this was all I needed. I straightened myself to full height (all 5 feet and 6 inches), smoothed down my blouse (it was non-iron and meant to be creased) and tried to appear aloof in a 'we are work colleagues, we will always be professional' look. It was water off a duck's back.

"Well, hello, Louisa," he said flirtatiously, looking me up and down.

Oh God, that accent.

"Good morning, Angus," I replied in a clipped tone. Fuck! He knew about my dream last night. He must do, he was giving me a really strange look. But how could he possibly know? Maybe he was a mind reader in his spare time. I could feel my cheeks starting to colour just as the cheeky git started laughing at me! He was looking down at the floor and laughing and pointing. And as I followed his gaze to my feet, I just about heard him say, "Louisa, that's gold! Mate, you're hilarious!" before the blood rushed to my ears deafening me and with a whole new level of embarrassment I never knew existed, I too noticed what he had. I WAS WEARING ODD FUCKING SHOES!

"Mate, what it is about you and shoes?" he said as his laugh resonated through every fibre in my body and every brick in the building. His mouth smiled and this time it reached his eyes, and I was mesmerised and mortified in equal measure. It was all I could do to turn away from him. He was laughing and shaking his head as he turned and walked out of my office. I could still hear him laughing as he made his way to his office on the other side of the building and although it was getting quieter, it still cut just as deep. I, however, was rooted to the spot and apoplectic with a burning rage. This couldn't be happening. Maybe this was a dream too and I was going to wake up on my sofa with the credits to *Neighbours* rolling. I pinched myself. Shit, that really hurt. Not a dream then. I swallowed hard, looked down again at my shoes just in case they had miraculously transformed into a MATCHING PAIR, and when I saw that they hadn't I jerked my head up and shut my eyes, all the time mumbling 'Oh my God' over and over. Yeah right, as if He'd help.

How had I done it? How had I left the house wearing odd shoes? One was black, and the other was dark grey. As if that wasn't bad enough, the black one was shiny and the grey one was… well, the grey one wasn't. What a monumental fuck-up. This was the fuck-up to end all fuck-ups. I'm surprised Gok Wan didn't show up at that moment with the fashion police and drag me straight to jail. Do not pass 'Go', do not collect £200.

I had no choice but to wear the odd shoes all day. Well, I say no choice. The other choice was to get the driving shoes out of the car, but you already know my thoughts on wearing those. I stayed in my office as much as I could and when I needed to go and make a coffee or visit the toilet, I did a quick reccy first to ensure minimum witnesses.

I left the office late that evening when only the cleaner was left on site. She was so busy with her mop and bucket, singing tunelessly to something indecipherable and tinny on her phone with the volume up loud and her ear buds rammed in, that I managed to walk out un-noticed.

At least I would have an Angus-free rest of the week. He was off to Birmingham for a few days to visit one of our sites so wouldn't be around (hmm, I wonder what wife-slash-girlfriend thinks about that?) which gave me a bit of time to think about how and why I was feeling so overwhelmed and sexually drawn to this man.

Chapter Four

The week passed slowly, and I was surprised to find myself missing Angus. My thoughts frequently wandered, and I imagined us in different scenarios, like sitting in a little café somewhere enjoying a latte. He'd be holding my hand across the table and telling me how much he loves and adores me. Or, meeting for dinner in a fancy restaurant and I'd arrive (a few minutes late, obviously) in a stunning red dress, long and sleek, with perfect hair and sultry makeup, and he'd be sitting at the table waiting for me and he'd turn as I walked in and gasp when he saw me. He'd smile at me, stand up and kiss me and say in that sexy voice, "My God, Louisa, you look stunning." Or, we'd be in a kitchen, open plan, with white worktops, modern gadgets everywhere and a centre island you could sit at, sink in the middle with one of those funky taps that looks like a coiled spring. I'd be cooking dinner wearing sexy lace knickers, one of his shirts and a smile. He'd arrive home from work, throw his bag and keys on the floor, walk over to me with purpose and without saying a word, he'd spin me around to face him, kiss me long and hard then scoop me up (note to self: must go on a diet before this scenario can come to life) and carry me off to the bedroom, where we'd make love for hours. The dinner would be ruined but we'd sit together on the sofa afterwards, languishing in the glow of post-sex euphoria, and we'd share a bottle of wine and a pizza. I have no idea where this house is, whose it is or how we even came to be there, but ooh, the endless possibilities… Not that I've thought about any of this for any length of time, you understand. It's all just random thoughts that pop in and out of my head. Honestly!

Anyway, Friday came around eventually and as I delivered a whole stack of cakes to the staffroom that morning, Kay came in with a massive bouquet of flowers, a bottle of Prosecco, a huge bar of chocolate and a card. "Happy birthday, lovely Louisa," she said giving me a great big hug, "These are from all of us." The flowers were beautiful and all my favourites, and as they filled my head with fragrance, I smiled. Happy Birthday me!

Note: Isn't it strange how, even though we are always grateful to receive a lovely bouquet of flowers, wherever they are from, nothing beats the feeling of a proper bouquet from a proper flower shop? Professionally arranged and wrapped in crinkly paper with a little pod of water at the bottom of the stems to keep them alive, encased in a beautiful box tied up with proper ribbon (not just parcel ribbon that you run through the edge of the scissors to curl!). It's even better when they are delivered to work! That anticipation as everyone admires them and 'ooh' and 'aah' at their beauty, everyone guessing who sent them while they wait for you to open the tiny, handwritten-by-a-four-year-old-child card that came with them. You know what I mean, when the writing starts off big but then whoever has written it realises they can't fit it all on, so it gets smaller and sort of drops off the line? And there's always a spelling mistake in it too! The only proper flower shop flowers I received came with a card that said 'Happy Anniversary love, from Steve'. I know it was only a comma in the wrong place and it wasn't his fault, but it sort of changed the whole context. Maybe it was a sign, and that's why Steve is now my ex-husband!

I enjoyed work that day. Colleagues were dropping by my office all day to wish me a happy birthday and to thank me for the cakes, my boss gave me a bottle of Moët (it's been under his desk since Christmas but who am I to turn down real Champagne?) and after an extended lunch with Kay and Vickie, I left work early to get ready for my night of cocktails and dancing with Dee. Dee and I were long overdue a catchup and combining it with my birthday meant it was going to be a night to remember. I might even tell her about Angus…

That evening, I sat on the sofa with my bottle of Prosecco, bar of chocolate and the card from work. I was gutted, not only because I was all alone on my birthday because Dee had cried off from an evening of cocktails and dancing as she'd found out her boyfriend was cheating on her, and I had made no other plans for the entire weekend having anticipated recovering from a serious session. But also because I had read every single comment and analysed every scrawled signature on that card and there was absolutely nothing from Angus. Not even a squiggle. I refilled my wine glass (should have just put a straw in the bottle) and heard the microwave 'ping' signalling that my birthday meal for one was ready. I grabbed a plastic fork from the drawer (no washing up) and sat sipping my wine and eating my moussaka out of the foil container (again, no washing up) when suddenly my eyes filled with tears. Before I could stop them, they were leaking out of the corners and pouring down my face. My chin was wobbling and I was properly sobbing. Wracking sobs that shook my whole body and I didn't bother to stop them, I just let them flow.

I am such an ugly crier and I don't know how long I sat there but when I had no more tears left, I wiped my face with the sleeve of my dressing gown, drained the last of the Prosecco into my glass, stood up from the sofa and sloped off up the stairs, trusty wine glass in hand. I was going to see Bob and as he was waiting for me in my room I needed to prepare. Did I not explain about Bob? Oh sorry, yes, Bob. I've known him for a while; he's dependable, doesn't answer back, is strong and solid with four different speed settings, rotating beads for my pleasure and is about six feet tall. Sorry, sorry, I mean six inches tall. 'Bob' – my 'Battery operated boyfriend'!

I've had a 'Bob' for a while, he's been different shapes, sizes and guises – my ex was not gifted in sexual prowess and foreplay included him removing his socks and pants. I bought myself a Bob after I tried to give him some pointers following one particularly lack-lustre performance. He said he'd rather watch Match of the Day and if I was so clued up on my own pleasure, I should take matters into my own hands. So I did, quite literally. I looked online and ordered what I though was an innocuous, sleek 'bullet' vibrator, but what actually arrived was a huge rechargeable beast that looked nothing like that on the website. I opened the box and was faced with packaging sporting a picture of a monstrous vibrator with considerable girth and 'veins', the combination of which brought tears to my eyes and not in a good way. I popped open the plastic hoping that the picture was a sort of 'you bought blah, blah, and this is what our other customers who also brought blah blah have recommended'. A sort of 'serving suggestion' if you will! But no, this was the actual thing itself. It fell out with a heavy thud and at that point I saw the important notice printed on the pack of the packaging. 'Once opened, due to hygiene reasons this item CANNOT be returned unless faulty'. WHAT? So now I had to keep the ugly veiny bastard? As if it couldn't get any worse, it had different speeds, it pulsed and it lit up like the batons aircraft marshals wave around to guide planes into stands at airports. Oh yes, and it needed to be charged, as in, plugged into the mains! But I resolved to give it a go because even this huge hunk of pulsating flashing plastic would have more skill than Steve, so I started to hunt around for a suitably hidden socket that would bring Bob to life. Damn! All the plug sockets upstairs had extension leads plugged into extension leads so I couldn't risk adding more fuel to a potential fire, and I certainly couldn't leave this huge phallus charging on the sideboard next to my phone/laptop. All the sockets by the TV were taken up with cable, broadband, DVD player, stereo etc., which left the only other option, the double socket behind the microwave in the kitchen. I plugged in the veiny beast and the red light illuminated to show that it was charging. Phew! At least the socket worked. I pulled the microwave forwards and angled it slightly away from the back of the kitchen worktop and dropped the vibrator down behind with a thud. It fitted in the gap nicely and more importantly it couldn't be seen. I decided that the next time Steve put football first, I'd make a date with my new Bob.

Over the coming weeks the opportunity didn't really present itself and if Steve binned me off for football, I invariably arranged to meet various girlfriends to drink Prosecco and slag off men. Bob was forgotten about until one evening, while I was attending a late project meeting for work, I got a text message from Steve. It was a picture of my vibrator on charge with the caption 'Microwave Surprise' underneath. I didn't reply, I was hoping it would give him time to realise that I really wasn't satisfied in the bedroom department and as a strong woman, I was prepared to take my pleasure seriously. However, when I got home, Steve had placed Bob on his side of the bed poking out from the leg of a pair of his pants. Eew! And in his dreams! Bob sadly never lost his virginity, I released him from his shackles and dumped him in the bottom of the bin, wrapped in several black bags as a precaution just in case he sprung to life and started buzzing, flashing and grinding as the dustmen collected the rubbish. I couldn't risk a 747 diverting to our back garden, so now he sees out his days singlehandedly plugging a methane shaft at the nearest landfill site. RIP Bob number 1.

Chapter Five

Over the coming weeks, work was manic with late nights and early mornings in the office, and I was thankful that I had no further shoe-tastrophies. I was very careful with my footwear choices, and I even went as far as purchasing a brand-new pair of driving shoes. They were plain black brogues, nothing fancy, understated yet comfortable. I still kept them in a bag for life in the boot of my car, but at least it was a new bag for life. You should have seen the cashier at Tesco when I gave her the old one in exchange for a new one (that is how the 'bag for life' scheme works after all). She took the old bag off me with a smile and a, "Certainly, madam, I'll get rid of that for you," but before I had the chance to warn her not to open it, she opened it. I have never actually seen anyone turn green before but the pong that burst forth from that bag for life when she looked in it was nothing short of toxic. The poor woman was gagging as she breathed in my stinky foot-funk; it was like a giant fart-in-a-bag!

Angus and I formed a solid friendship. We became really comfortable in each other's company and the banter flowed at work. I got over the shoe incident, eventually, although he told everyone in the building, which meant for two weeks I was subjected to every shoe related joke or story imaginable. Vickie even had a shoe brooch made for me! He still called me 'mate' and as he now knew it wound me up it meant he could win every argument just by saying "you're right, mate" because I would huff, shake my head and walk away. We were work colleagues, but we had a connection, and every time he gave me a hug, or came into my office to talk to me (again, that accent), I felt it. Oh God, how I felt it. I tried to feign indifference whenever he walked into a room, so I'd walk out, but the pretence wasn't working. I was fooling nobody, least of all myself. The truth of it was the harder I tried to cool it, the deeper I fell. I had an ache inside. There wasn't one thing about him I didn't like. Oh, I know I hadn't spent any time with him properly and I had no idea what he was like to live with, whether he left the toilet seat up, what his annoying habits were etc., but I was beginning to realise that, based on the evidence I had seen, I could happily spend my every waking hour with this man.

He knew that I was a divorcee, and therefore, a lonely old spinster (his words, not mine. Although he did say "So you're a lonely old spinster then? Oh, mate") but I knew hardly anything about him. I knew he was planning on living here for a couple of years while he completed his Law degree and upon his return to Australia, he wanted to start up his own company, but other than that his life was very secret. He didn't talk about his wife-slash-girlfriend, although there had been numerous occasions when I had been in his office filing case notes (no, that's not a euphemism) and his phone would vibrate. I would have a sneaky glance over his shoulder, just to see, and it would always be her. He would either dismiss the call and turn his phone face down, or leave the office with a "Sorry, Louisa, I just need to take this." We never socialised outside of work and I did find myself missing his company at the weekend, but I was happy with us being friends. Of course, I would have loved more and I still really, really, REALLY wanted to kiss this man every time I saw him, but I knew he didn't feel the same way. To be perfectly honest, I would rather have him in my life as a friend than not in my life at all. He flirted outrageously with every woman and yet he still made me feel as though I was more special to him, and that gave me a spring in my step and a smile on my face. This man was different. This man 'got me'. This man took my breath away and made my pulse race every time I saw him. This man was like nobody I had ever met before and quite frankly, the feelings I was having for him were scaring the shit out of me.

But all this became totally irrelevant one day when two things happened in very quick succession...

I was asked by my boss to post some important paperwork, recorded delivery, to a client, and as Angus was in my office when the request came in, he offered to drive me to the Post Office. Of course, I wasn't going to turn down a little one-on-one time with him, so I accepted. As he signed us both out of the building, I quickly nipped into the toilet, where I powdered my nose, bronzed my cheeks and glossed my lips. Then just in case, I sprayed some breath-spray and popped a Smint into my mouth. Like I say, just in case! With a quick sniff of the pits (oh come on, you do it too) and a quick check of the teeth (never eaten spinach so how the hell does it get stuck in them?), I was ready to go. Angus and me. In his car. Alone. Together.

We walked out of building, chatting about work stuff, and as we approached his car, he blipped his key fob to unlock it. He climbed in the driver's side and I yanked the door handle on the passenger's side, but it was still locked. As I stumbled backwards, I noticed – 1: Him reach across to unlock my door with his left hand, which sported a gold wedding band on his ring finger, and 2: Two kids booster seats in the back. I was floored. How had I not noticed the wedding ring before? Our entire friendship was in jeopardy because he had left out some pretty important and fundamental points. This man was married. This man had children. This man had never once mentioned specific members of his family when I was helping him arrange his visa and accommodation. But his emails had been really sickly-sweet and almost grovelling I had taken the piss out of his overly enthusiastic comments. Thinking he was a bit of an arsehole I had only sent him links to sites and let him sort things out for himself. He was a grown man after all so how hard could it really be to move to the other side of the world, uproot your entire family, start a new job, arrange a work visa, sort out somewhere to live... Yeah, come to think of it, that was really mean of me, and I deserve to not know.

The drive to the Post Office was, for me, strange to say the least. He was really chatty but it was all innocuous stuff and varied from what he had for lunch (prawn sandwich, seeded bread, a handful of rocket, just a scrape of butter, no avocado) to why petrol is cheap in Australia (something to do with Saudi Arabia I think, but I wasn't really listening). He looked across at me every now and then while he chatted and I listened (OK, I gave the impression that I was listening). All I could think about was how down and dirty I wanted to get with this married man. I wanted him to be very unfaithful to his wife, and I mean seriously unfaithful. I wanted him to do things to me that made me blush at the mere thought of them. To convince myself how wrong it was I tried to focus on his left hand and the wedding band that practically screamed 'keep away, he's MINE' but what I envisioned were his strong hands (with a smattering of hairs) and long fingers (oooh) as they caressed and stroked my neck. Then they were moving down and caressing my breasts (I wish) and I could feel my nipples hardening to his imaginary touch. With my eyes closed I leant back against the headrest and imagined him kissing my neck as I slowly rolled my head. It was just as well my hands were gripping the A4 envelope otherwise I would not have been responsible for their actions!

"Are you OK, Louisa? Have you got a stiff neck?" he asked, cutting into the foreplay that was playing out deliciously in my head.

'It's my nipples that are stiff, not my bloody neck,' was what I wanted to say. What I actually said was, "Can you pull in just here, the Post Office is down the road a bit but the parking is a nightmare," as I was brought back to reality with a jolt.

There was a queue in the Post Office, but Angus waited in his car for me. Of course he did, he was kind and considerate. He wouldn't have dropped me off and made me walk back although I had half expected him to. When I emerged from the Post Office 15 minutes later and made my way towards his car, I saw he was on his mobile phone. He was looking out of his window and the conversation seemed tense. He was flinging his hand around as if he was trying to emphasise something and shrugging his shoulders. Frowning as he ended the conversation, I opened the car door and as he sighed heavily, he threw the phone into the centre console and shook his head.

"Everything OK?" I asked casually. Fucking hell, Louisa, why do you do it? You know you don't want to know, yet you still ask!

"Oh, it's just Joanna," he replied. "She's got the hump because she's running late and hasn't picked the kids up from the childminders yet. She's just asked me to do it but it's going to take me at least half an hour to get there. I just feel bad that it looks like they've been forgotten. I imagine them sitting on their own with the childminder as she drums her fingers on the table huffing and looking at her watch every few seconds."

"Oh, right" was all I could say as it was now confirmed. He definitely had a wife. He definitely had children. He was definitely off limits.

We drove back to the office in silence. He sighed occasionally, I sighed occasionally, we both sighed for very different reasons.

Chapter Six

I left the office on time for once as my feeling of desolation hadn't passed and I couldn't concentrate on my work. I'd typed and re-typed the same paragraphs so many times in the lease agreement and I'd monumentally fucked up the copying and pasting until I didn't know which one was the original and which one was the revised version. I hit 'save' and logged off my computer. As I flicked the 'off' switch on my printer, it sighed at me despairingly before the screen went black and it shut down. I felt complete empathy with it. What I wouldn't give to shut down after the Post Office revelation. Nonetheless, I put on my smile and cheerfully waved goodbye to whichever colleagues I happened to bump into in the corridor. As I walked past the big boss's office, I noticed his door was open slightly so out of courtesy I popped my head round and said, "See you tomorrow Mr...oh! I'm so sorry to interrupt." Christ, everyone was getting some except me. He was just pulling away from a very intimate embrace with his PA, Kelli. Eew! There's no accounting for taste and I know beauty is in the eye of the beholder, but she could have her pick of men. As I back out of his office, I'm wondering if all the rumours I've heard are true...

Mr Williams looks like a meercat and every time I see him in his brown cords, white shirt and pale green tank top, I'm reminded of the well-known price comparison site advertisement. Supposedly he has four children – two with his wife and one with each of his ex-PA's. That's going some and I can only imagine that all his charm must be in his underpants!

As I scurried down the corridor, I literally shook my head to try to rid myself of the image of the two of them, but it's permanently burnt into my retinas – you can never un-see or un-hear things – and as I push open the front door and step into the fading weak sunlight, the cold air fills my chest. I took a few deep restorative breaths and walked to my car where a quick glance around the car park revealed that Angus has already left for the day. He must have gone to collect his children from the childminder and as I thought morosely about their perfect family unit, the perfectly balanced organic meal that's waiting for him on his return and his perfectly perfect fucking perfect wife, I feel the emotions catch in the back of my throat. I wish they'd choke me and put me out of my misery.

On the way home, I stopped at the local co-op and bought two bottles of their cheapest chardonnay. It flowed freely that evening, along with the tears. I didn't even bother with a glass; I just swigged from the bottle. Not even Bob could console me. He stayed well out of the way. I fell asleep on the sofa very late into the evening and only woke when I heard myself snort. A tentative glace at the clock on the TV told me it was 3:10 am. I felt like shit. My top lip was stuck to my dry teeth, I had a banging headache, and my eyes were red and swollen from the tears I'd cried. My alcohol-steeped dreams had been peppered with images of Mr Williams and Kelli, and Kelli and Angus. Both scenarios were equally disturbing, and I could tell from my damp face that I'd been crying in my sleep too. I was shrouded in an overwhelming feeling of loss and loneliness, and I was angry with myself because I had no right to feel those things. Angus wasn't mine to lose and I was alone before I met him and discovered he was married with children. I wasn't even having a relationship with him. It still hurt like hell though.

I picked up the phone and rang in sick. The answerphone at Williams & Bowman Solicitors was very unsympathetic.

Chapter Seven

I didn't go to work for a few days; my personal torment knew no bounds. I did the old 'I've got sickness and diarrhoea' routine. It's never questioned as nobody wants to talk about someone else's poo! Angus, Kay and Vickie all texted me at various times asking if I was all right and each time I just replied with 'Feeling a bit better, just drained', which is the blanket response to any non-serious illness recovery. When I missed three calls from my parents and two from my boss, I just switched my phone off. I went from the sofa to my bedroom and occasionally into the kitchen. There was a strange funky smell in my house that followed me around and after spending a few minutes inspecting the bottom of my slippers and the contents of my bin, I realised it was me!

After three days of wallowing in self-pity and self-loathing, I finally went back to work. Everyone was genuinely pleased to see me and even my boss made me a cup of tea (always a sign that he'd missed me and was struggling to cope without me). At 10 am., we were all called to a staff meeting, told that the company was going through a restructure and that we would probably all have to apply for our own jobs.

Somebody up there really didn't like me.

Chapter Eight
June 2016

The next two months really took their toll on everyone as the restructuring got underway with gusto and the friendly banter and flirtatious behaviour we all enjoyed, disappeared as we knuckled down and tried to prove our worth. Angus and I were still good friends but like our colleagues, we had lost our mojo. He was very stressed as he'd given up his life in Australia to join our UK company and now his position at the firm was in serious jeopardy. He really didn't know whether his job was safe or whether his relocation had been a huge waste of time and money. I was devastated when I found out he was married and had children, which was stupid because we were only ever friends, and he had no idea how I felt about him. I think it was the finality of it. In my eyes where we were once a 'could have been', we were now a 'never will be'. I was going to have to force myself to move on, but that was easier said than done seeing as I worked with this man.

It turns out that grieving for something you never had with someone you also never had, and having a really shit time at work, are great appetite suppressants although I wouldn't recommend them. Just like my colleagues, I'd gone through weeks of anguish not knowing about my job and all I wanted

59

to do was talk to Angus about it, but not only was he going through it too, he was also the reason why I couldn't eat or sleep. One minute I was feeling really positive, looking to the future and meeting a man (I'd even got Dee to help me sign up to online dating), the next I was sobbing uncontrollably into my cup-a-soup (the only thing I seemed to be able to keep in my stomach lately). I was losing weight rapidly and should have been really pleased, but I was just really, really sad. All I wanted was Angus.

Chapter Nine
September 2016

With a few voluntary redundancies from the more senior members of staff, us minions came through the restructure with our jobs intact and as the office banter returned and we basked in the summer weather that was still with us, the boss announced that he was going to throw a party to say 'thank you' for pulling together, and also to celebrate the close of a very lucrative deal which Angus had been an integral part of. Now, when I heard the words 'office party', I imagined lukewarm Lambrini, cans of Fosters, a selection of stale sandwiches with indeterminable fillings and enough peanuts, crisps and snacks to see Mr KP and Mr Walker enjoy a very comfortable retirement. You can imagine my sheer joy (something I hadn't had much of lately) when he asked me to find a hotel that would cater for a "fucking brilliant night out with enough booze to sink a battleship. Dinner, rooms, entertainment, the lot, whatever you like." As if that couldn't be topped, when I asked what the budget was, he replied, "Just get them to send an invoice." Bring it on!

A wonderful evening was spent with a bottle of Prosecco and my laptop, carefully researching venues. I even let Bob have an input (wink, wink).

I booked a fantastic boutique hotel in London that had just had a cancellation for two weeks' time and we basically stepped in and took the entire booking! It promised to be a stonkingly good night. The food was being prepared by the trendy up-and-coming protégé of a celebrity chef so would undoubtedly be phenomenal; there was a promising new stand-up comedian booked to perform to an intimate crowd (i.e. us); there was a disco until the wee small hours. I had lost three stone in weight in the last two months; oh, and Angus was going to be there.

I pinned a notice on the board in the staffroom for everyone to sign up to this grand night out and asked them all to confirm their room requirements. Don't get me wrong, I wasn't encouraging promiscuity and infidelity in the workplace, we do have a couple of husband-and-wife teams at Williams & Bowman, and I just wanted to know who wanted double and who wanted single rooms. Although why you'd want to work with your spouse is beyond me. I couldn't think of anything worse! Of course, Kelli claimed that she was getting picked up by her (fictitious) boyfriend and wouldn't need a room, and Mr Williams wanted a double suite – aye aye! Everyone else arranged to share with colleagues so I booked five twin rooms for all the secretaries and admin staff to share, and eight double rooms for all the partners and senior staff members. As Williams & Bowman was footing the bill, everyone would be making good use of the facilities and no doubt the mini-bars would be bled dry and the grossly overpriced salty snacks would be consumed by the bucket full. But God help anyone who had porn added to their room bill!

I arranged for all the girls to be on one floor, with me at the end by the stairs, and all the men to be on the floor above. It was purely coincidental that I could nip up the fire exit staircase just outside my room and be outside Angus' room without being spotted. My over-zealous thoughts of spending a night with him had somewhat blurred the lines of reality and I had almost, almost, convinced myself that Angus and I would end up in his bed at the end of the night. I drew on all the times I'd heard those words 'never say never' so just in case the opportunity arose, and to be on the safe side, I'd taken a trip to Bluewater where I'd hung around outside the Anne Summers shop for nearly 20 minutes, pretending to be on my phone, waiting for the window of opportunity when I could get through the doors without anyone on the concourse seeing me go in. Once inside the den of iniquity (as my dear old Nanna would call it), I'd spent an enjoyable couple of hours buying some very sexy but completely impractical lingerie, a starter kit of aromatherapy oils and a 'quick guide to erotic and sensual massage' (not sure if the 'quick' related to the massage or the outcome). Bizarrely, the guide also came with a silky eye mask and a tickling stick! Oh, and I decided to upgrade Bob too while I was there (ahem).

Whilst browsing the accessories area at the back of the shop and having a good old laugh at the names and shapes of the 'erotic massagers', I became fascinated by the clientele that were coming and going (pardon the pun). Women came in with friends, some made purchases, some just came to look, whereas the men seemed to 'grab and run'. The only men I saw had clearly been told what to buy and whereabouts in the shop said items were located as they rushed in, almost blinkered, grabbed their items, paid and rushed from the store.

Done in about 40 seconds (hmmm, reminds me of my ex-husband!), I was just trying to decide on whether I should buy some chocolate willies or jelly boobs (hilarious 'Secret Santa' presents – you should see the recipient's face!) when I heard a voice I vaguely recognised.

As I peeped around the screen, I saw a short, stocky woman with long, straight, severely dyed black hair and what I can only describe as a unique sense of style. She had a large nose (not her fault, I know) which dominated her face and she could do with a few lessons in how to apply makeup. I may be being bitchy, but the clever use of makeup can really enhance your best features and play down your less good ones, but she was drawing attention to her nose by tightly scraping her hair back into a ponytail and wearing jammy-looking red lipstick. Her foundation was completely the wrong shade causing a pancake line and giving her a 'mask' effect. Her eyebrows needed a damn good pluck and I was tempted to pin her down, get my travel tweezers out of my bag and start yanking those buggers out. She was wearing faded black trousers with a broken zipper (the fly was undone) and a strappy top that she kept yanking down the hem of as it didn't meet the waistband of her trousers. She had on a dirty coloured bra, the straps of which were wider than her strappy top, and she was wearing clumpy looking sandals on her feet that were covered in plasters where the broken straps of her shoes rubbed. Her toenails had been painted fuchsia pink – about three months ago! She had terrible dandruff too and the white flakes showed up against the jet-black of her hair. She kept making comments about how 'disgusting' the shop was as she browsed, and tutted loudly at the accessories on offer as she stepped behind the screen, where I was hiding my face in mortification. Too late, she saw me.

"Louisa, hi," she said in her naturally loud voice.

"Oh, hi, Angela," I said as I stepped away from the willies and boobs, "fancy seeing you here. Ha ha ha, I've just come to pick up some bits for a err, friend's, um, hen night." Oh God, she knew I was lying! Thank fuck my purchases were tucked away in the bottom of my 'Shuh' shopping bag with a strategically placed three pack of 60 Denier XL 'shape enhancing' reinforced gusset tights resting on top (believe me, if you rummage through a bag and come across these bad boys, you don't carry on rummaging).

Angela was a dot com picker at our local Tesco and I'd literally bumped into her one evening after work when I was browsing the chocolate aisle. She was crouching down by the chocolate wafers, unseen behind her cart, and I had just spotted large share bags of Maltesers (yeah right, like I would actually share) when I rammed her cart with my trolley and knocked her over. She was really lovely about it and we got chatting; she was married with two teenage children and they had moved here from Dubai to give the kids an opportunity to study in England and for them to travel. She was a qualified logistics manager but doing the dot com picking four days a week meant she had plenty of time to arrange fantastic trips to Europe for them all. Her husband had been offered a job as a solicitor in Singapore, which he'd postponed for a year, so we naturally got chatting about my job at Williams & Bowman. Whenever I saw her during my grocery shop, she would always stop her picking to talk to me and she'd lean on her trolley and laugh as I regaled her with stories about awful clients and what the partners in the firm got up to, and she seemed so intrigued and interested it was genuinely nice chatting to her.

But now outside of her customer-service based work role, Angela had a very abrupt manner verging on plain rude, and if that wasn't her then she was being unfairly judged, and as wrong as that may be, first impressions do last. As the sales assistants were whispering about her, I decided to do the decent thing.

"Shall we get out of here and go for a coffee?" I asked Angela, crossing my fingers behind my back in the hope that she'd say no, she had somewhere to be.

"Oh, thanks, Louisa," she replied, "but no. I've got a bit of shopping to do and then I must get back to cook tea. I always like to have a meal on the table when hubby and the kids come home."

"OK then, I'll let you get on," I said, trying to hide my relief.

As we made our way to the exit, with Angela still tutting and muttering 'disgraceful' as she fingered the material of a particularly revealing S & M outfit, one of the sales assistants mouthed 'thank you' to me and wrung her hands. I had a feeling this wasn't the first time Angela had been into the shop to 'take offense'!

We emerged onto the concourse where she immediately tossed her head back, said 'disgraceful' far too loudly at the window display, and walked off.

"Right. Bye then," I said as she walked away.

"Yeah, see ya," she responded without even turning around. Rude!

She was last seen diving into the pick and mix sweets in the shop opposite, leaving me staring after her in astonishment. Maybe if she had a 'Bob' in her life, she wouldn't be so uptight!

Pleased with my purchases but still rattled by Angela's attitude, I decided to reward myself with a little refreshment. I took my seat in a coffee shop with my decaf skinny wet cappuccino and a raspberry and white chocolate muffin, and watched the world go by, smiling saucily to myself as I fantasised about Angus relieving me of my gorgeous new undies.

Chapter Ten

The big day finally arrived. The 'fucking brilliant night out' was all anyone could talk about all day. The coach was picking us all up at 3 pm and we were travelling in luxury. I had bought six bottles of Prosecco (to share, not just for me) and plastic flutes (I know, how classy is that?) for the journey up and the evening promised to be just what the boss requested. We all stacked our overnight bags in the luggage hold of the coach and as the driver took his seat, there was a chorus of cheers and whoops led by Angus who was pacing up and down the aisle high-fiving everyone. I stood at the front and counted the people on board to make sure we hadn't left anyone behind and was pleased to see so many smiling faces. All present and correct, I did a 'thumbs up' to the driver and took my seat by the window at the very front (I have to sit at the front when I travel on a coach as I suffer from terrible travel sickness). I was just about to spread out and make full use of the empty seat beside me when Angus sat there. Oh my, this day was getting better and better!

All the way to London, we drank Prosecco and sang cheesy '80s pop songs. Nobody minded when we got held up in traffic, it just meant we had longer for drinking and singing. Pre-dinner drinks were at 7 pm so we had plenty of time.

However, I wasn't thinking that far ahead. All I could think about was the heat radiating from Angus' leg as it rested comfortably against mine, and the several occasions when he touched my hand, not by accident, but in a very purposeful and intimate way. Something had been lit and was gently smouldering between us, but having been there before, I was trying to stamp it out. However, by the time we reached the city and he turned to me, smiled and winked, it became an all-consuming bush fire!

Chapter Eleven

The coach stopped in front of the hotel and we disembarked. The mood was electric, mainly because most of my colleagues were already sozzled, relishing an evening of unlimited booze and a night away from their respective partners/spouses. There were lots of people drinking and smoking in the pretty courtyard of the hotel and as the parade of secretaries and admin staff trooped off the coach, you could feel the eyes of the city slickers mentally undressing them, ogling them. But as the men filed off the coach, it was like watching an Animal Planet documentary. The males pulled themselves up to their full height, sat up straight and jutted their jaws forwards, looking like a pride of resident lions whose territory had just been invaded by a younger group looking for the lionesses to mate with. A roar from one of the pack leaders wouldn't have been out of place! But all I could think about was having some bubbles in my bath and some bubbles in my glass while I prepared myself for the evening ahead. If he wanted to, I would have no objection to Angus unwrapping me, layer by layer, like a very sexy, sassy, kiss my assy present! I'd selected a very simple red bodycon dress, nude heels and, of course, the Anne Summers underwear. I'd practised my 'smokey eyes' make up and had got up extra early this morning to ensure my hair was coiffed to perfection. A quick conversation with the driver confirmed that he was booked to pick us up at 10 am. the next day (Mr Williams had allowed us all the morning off), and with a cheeky flick of my hips and a 'whoop whoop' as I jumped down from the coach, I led the troops into the hotel to check in. Ladies and gentlemen, let the fun begin...

Chapter Twelve

The evening was absolutely spectacular! The food was indeed phenomenal but not quite what I had expected. Each course was a taste extravaganza with mini portions of every item on the menu served on large white circular plates as we mingled and drank. It was a very social way to eat. My colleagues thanked me throughout the evening for organising such a 'top notch shin dig' and as I circulated, I kept glancing across at Angus, who was constantly holding court and had a gaggle of women around him most of the time. He would occasionally look over at me, wink and raise his glass, and every time I caught the sound of his voice or his laugh, I literally went weak at the knees. That man had an effect on my body that I had never experienced before.

The comedian was very good but very blue, and I'm no prude but I did find myself blushing at a good few of his observations, especially when he said that women won't need men once they can make a vibrator able to cut the grass and take out the bins. I thought about poor Bob languishing in the bottom of my underwear drawer!

I made my way to the ladies' restroom, which was at the end of the corridor to the right of the 'Garden Room', where our do was being held. The gents' was at the end of the corridor to the left and it looked a bit like a catwalk show if you timed it wrong as you'd easily find yourself walking towards a colleague after exiting the loo and then having to turn into the room together. The restrooms were amazing – we had proper thick paper napkins to dry our hands on, the most divine smelling handwash and hand cream, hairspray to touch up the glossy locks and even miniatures of all the hotel products to take with us. There was also a hairdryer, straighteners and – oh God – a wall of full-length mirrors you had no choice but to walk past if you wanted to pee. They were either side too, so no escaping! As I put my head down and rushed past my kryptonite, I caught a teeny tiny glimpse of myself in one of the full HD effect (so it seemed) gargantuan mirrors. I actually stopped to look. No, really, I did. I couldn't believe that the person looking back at me was me. She was sexy and slim in a gorgeous red dress, her legs looked long and lean in a pair of killer nude heels, and her hair was a great mix of blonde and caramel highlights. Fucking hell, I scrubbed up well! I rushed into the cubicle, shut the door and let my head fall back against it. I closed my eyes and took a few deep breaths. Then I had a pee, pulled up my knickers so they sat just so on the hips (you've done it too – making sure none of the love handle bulge squidges over the top), adjusted the girls in their lacy restraint and smoothed down my dress. I'd been very diligent at dinner and hadn't eaten anything that might make my stomach bloat or give me wind, so had had pretty much no food. The bubbles had taken the edge off my anxiety of 'will it/won't it' with Angus and I had alcohol-induced confidence, so I strutted out of the ladies'. As I made my way back towards the throng of the disco, which was well and truly underway, I saw Angus hanging around on the outskirts, whiskey and diet coke in his hand, looking around for someone. I approached and he turned, gave me his killer smile, took hold of my hand and led me onto the dancefloor. In one swift movement, he placed his glass on a table and turned to face me, his hands holding mine, just as *Love Me Now* blasted from the speakers.

Now, I don't know if you've ever heard the song, but the words evoked such emotion in me that I fought to hold back the tears. The lyrics go something like this…

Pulling me further, further than I've been before. Making me stronger, shaking me right to the core. The lyrics were powerful and as I heard them loud and clear, I felt violated, as if the singer was revealing my deepest thoughts and feelings in his song.

I don't know who's gonna kiss you when I'm gone, so I'm going to love you now like it's all I have, I know it will kill me when it's over, I don't want to think about it, I want you to love me now. The rhythm thrummed through my body and the words resonated in my very core. My stomach somersaulted, and I thought I was going to throw up. What the hell was I doing? Wanting to get involved with a man who was so unavailable in so many ways, not least of all going back to live in a country that was as far away as you could possibly get without coming back! Just as I was about to pull out of his grasp and make a dash for the ladies' again, he pulled me in close, wrapped his arms around me and enveloped me in a wonderful, strong embrace. A few of the secretaries throwing shapes on the dancefloor grinned at me and did the 'thumbs-up' sign but other than that nobody took a blind bit of notice of us. My whole body reacted to his embrace – my head rested in the crook of his neck, my cheek on his shoulder, and I inhaled his masculine scent. He smelt of deodorant, clean washing and a very subtle citrusy aftershave. It was divine, and as my arms gripped around his strong back, our bodies melted into one. There was literally no space between us, our legs worked in unison in time with the beat, no stepping on toes, no awkwardness. I could feel his cock through his trousers, hard and ready as it strained against the zipper. My naughty area was awake and ready for action, and if I'd had my way, we would have given our colleagues an X-rated floor show right there and then, such was the longing I felt for this man.

The song finished, and we grudgingly pulled apart. The tunes became very upbeat and dance-y, and as we stood unmoving, Angus looked into my eyes, his hands gripping the tops of my arms, and I could see something troubling him. Was it guilt? Had we gone too far and he was regretting the intimacy we'd shared at work and on the dancefloor?

"You don't get it, do you, Louisa?" he said.

"Get what, Angus?" I responded as my shoulders slumped. "Please, tell me what's wrong."

"It's you," he said a little too forcefully, "You really don't know do you? I'm in love with you."

And he turned and strode purposefully to the bar, leaving me utterly dumbfounded standing in the middle of the dancefloor.

Chapter Thirteen

I approached Angus at the bar as he slumped over neat whiskey. I touched his back lightly and he turned and smiled at me, but it was a smile tinged with sadness. I tilted my head onto his shoulder, looked into his eyes and said, "Angus, you have no idea how you've made me feel these last few months. You've made me laugh, you've made me cry, you've made me feel I can conquer anything. The only reason I get up in the morning and drag myself to work is because I want to see you, my crazy Aussie Tim-Tam. But…."

"Jesus, Louisa, you call me a fucking Tim-Tam?" He interrupted before I could finish. "You are a nutter!" And he turned to me, took my face in his hands and kissed me in a way I have never been kissed before. I am smitten…

Chapter Fourteen

We were tearing at each other's clothes by the time he'd finally located his room key. We snogged passionately several times before we actually got to his door and our kisses were so intense that our mouths banged heavily on one another, almost painfully but very deliciously, and I was worried he'd give me stubble rash. As we burst through the door, I kicked my shoes off, threw my clutch bag to the floor and flung myself at him. There were lots of 'mmmmm' noises and plenty of slurp-y sounds as we kissed and groped and kissed some more. Finally, he pulled the zipper of my dress down and the whole thing fell to the floor. He stood back and looked me up and down, and I suddenly felt very self-conscious. What do I do? Do I stand in a sort of 'ta-da' pose? Do I do the 'show pony'? (One leg bent, bum out, chest out, stomach in) So I just stood there, waiting for him to make the next move. Which he did.

He stepped towards me, muttering, "Christ, Louisa, you turn me on so much. You are so sexy, I only have to be near you and I'm instantly aroused. Feel," and he took my hand and held it against his crotch. Holy fuck! I swear it was actually throbbing. I licked my lips and started to undo the button on his trousers as we kissed passionately. I was fumbling a bit as there was a clasp to undo, and he had a belt on. "Fuck!" he mumbled, losing patience, "I can't bear it, let me do it." And he released the belt buckle, popped the button, slid the zipper down and dropped his trousers and boxers to the floor.

My God, he was a magnificent beast! His cock stood very erect and ready for action, and although it wasn't what I'd call 'girth-y', it did have an impressive length. All I could think about was him inside me but if I thought too much, it would all be over there and then. He just kept muttering "Fuck, Louisa" and "God, I want you so much" over and over, and then, with one swift movement, he released the girls! They were free range once more and before I had time to worry about them swinging around by my stomach, he reached for them. He gently pushed me down onto the bed and I fell flat on my back, my mouth and legs slightly open, inviting him. He rolled one nipple gently between his finger and thumb and teased the other one with his tongue, sending sparks of sexual electricity through my body. I automatically tilted my body towards him and as he manoeuvred me up the bed with a swift and practised confidence, he dragged my expensive and very impractical lace panties down my legs where they stayed hooked around my right ankle. He spread my legs wide and lying between them he kissed and nipped me gently from my very swollen breasts, with nipples so hard they were almost painful, down to my stomach. I giggled a few times as it had been a very, very long time since a man had tantalised me like that and it did tickle a bit. He worked his way down my body while I gasped in anticipation and as he mumbled, "Fuck, Louisa" for the umpteenth time, he plunged his tongue deep inside me. I did the only thing I could – I closed my eyes and had my fill of this man.

Chapter Fifteen

As I slowly opened first one eye, then the other, I realised I wasn't in my own bedroom at home. My skull pounded, and my eyes were sore. I don't remember taking my make-up off and I certainly don't remember raiding the mini-bar but the detritus was scattered all over the floor. It took me a few seconds to remember that we had had the works do the night before and I had consumed far, far too much Prosecco. As I looked around in the semi-darkness, I could just make out the outline of a figure under the covers next to me. What the fuck? With a rising panic, I remembered that Angus and I had ended up in his room and from the damp patch between my legs, I knew that we had got up to some pretty naughty stuff. But I couldn't remember it! All I remembered was getting to his room, clothes coming off and… Oh yes, his very skilled tongue. But what did we do after that? I seriously had no recollection.

In the half-light, I frantically scanned the floor for evidence of our sexual exploits but there were no condom wrappers, only an empty Pringle tube, half a packet of chocolate buttons, a half-eaten Mars bar and a Skittles packet. There was an open bottle of water on my side of the bed and I drank gratefully from it, letting the tepid liquid soothe my dry throat. As my eyes adjusted, I saw that we had emptied the mini-bar of its entire contents. Hell, that was going to cost a pretty penny; how on earth could I hide that expense from the Williams & Bowman accountants?

I pushed myself up onto my elbows and scanned the room. I could make out my underwear in a heap on the floor and my dress lying crumpled by the TV stand. As Angus snored gently beside me, I sat up and planned the quickest way to gather/dress/exit. I pushed the covers off, being careful not to disturb him, slid to the edge of the bed and stood up. As I turned to fold the covers back over the bed, what I saw next makes me flame with embarrassment to this day.

The sheets were crisp and white apart from the long, brown stripe that ran from the indentation left by my bum, right to the edge. As bile rose in my throat, I realised with disgust that I had been so pissed last night, I appeared to have actually shit the bed during the night. I would never, ever be able to look at Angus again. I would hand in my notice as soon as we got back to the office at lunchtime and I would go now. Today. As hot tears rolled down my face, I stepped forward to gather up my clothes and noticed in the mirror a brown lump on my left bum cheek. What fresh hell was my mortification taking me to? The offending faecal nugget WAS STILL ATTACHED TO MY ARSE! If I went into the bathroom to remove the offending poo pimple, that meant I would still be in the vicinity of Angus and the chance of him waking up and seeing the skidder on the bed and the evidence stuck to my arse was not one I was prepared to take. I grabbed my lacey knickers and did the only thing I could – I used them to wipe the poo off my bum cheek. They were definitely going straight in the bin after this. In fact, I may even burn them! I stepped into my dress, grabbed my shoes and bra, which I stuffed into my clutch bag, and as I fumbled with the door lock, I heard Angus mumble, "Louisa, please don't go. Stay and…"

But I didn't wait to hear the rest of the sentence. With hot tears of shame streaming down my face, I raced through the fire doors, down the stairs and into my room.

Chapter Sixteen

I lay on my hotel bed and sobbed as though my heart was breaking. What had I done? Forget the fact that I'd spent the night in a married man's bed with no recollection of our sexploits, which paled into insignificance compared to the mortification I felt at having let my bodily functions ruin possibly the best thing that had happened to me. How ironic that the best sex I don't remember having is now the worst experience of my life. I must have been really, really bad in a previous life and karma had come back to bite me – on the arse.

My plan was to get showered and dressed and be on the coach before anyone else. I would sit at the very back in the very corner and if I didn't have breakfast, I would have nothing to bring up if the travel sickness kicked in. With a mediocre plan in place, I stepped out of my dress and walked into the bathroom to grab a sanitary bag to put the offending panties in. As I rolled them into a tight ball and shoved them into the bag, I caught a faint waft of something emanating from said undies. It was sweet, like – chocolate to be precise. Could it be? With some trepidation, I held my knickers to my nose and inhaled tentatively in the general area of the brown stain (I'm aware this sounds very, very grim). I thought I would lose control of all my bodily functions at that point as I realised that yes, the offending brown blob was in fact a chocolate button! My elation was short-lived however, when having remembered seeing the half-eaten packet of chocolate buttons on the floor, I remembered Angus placing them on (and in) various part of my body and trying to get them out with his tongue. He had clearly missed one! Well, at least I hadn't poo'd in the bed, but Angus was still going to see the skid mark. As I turned on the shower, I heard a frantic knocking on the room door. I slipped on a towelling robe and crept over to the spy hole but all I could see was someone's eyeball. Damn! I was going to have to answer. I put the chain on and opened the door a crack.

"Louisa, it's me," came an urgent whisper from the corridor. "Please, let me in."

I sighed and released the lock. As I opened the door, Angus rushed in, his face pale and grey. He must have seen the skid on the bed.

I took a deep breath and at the same time as I said, "It was chocolate…"

He said, "She knows about us…"

"WHAT?" we both said at the same time.

"Louisa," he interrupted, "she knows that we got cosy on the dancefloor. I'm done for. She's already been on the phone and told me that she's booked flights back to Australia and if I don't go back, she's going to take the kids away from me. Louisa, I can't lose my children." He slumped down on the bed in a state of shock and I could see tears in his eyes.

"Angus, I'm… I don't know what to say. I'm so sorry," I said as I sat next to him. Should I hold his hand or rub his back? It was all very awkward.

"Louisa, last night was amazing," he said, turning to me. "I feel as though we've connected on every level. We are so good together, you are my equal. But you have no idea what goes on at home and the state of my marriage. You'd tell me to grow a pair, and I know I need to, but right now, I need to get back to try and talk Joanna out of it. It's a case of damage limitation."

"But who the fuck would have told her?" I exclaimed. I didn't think anyone at Williams & Bowman knew his wife.

"I have absolutely no idea," he replied. "But she knew all the details. What you were wearing, the song we were dancing to and the time we left the party. Together."

"Oh, Angus, I'm so, so sorry," I said as I gave his hand a squeeze while stupidly, selfishly thinking I was so glad this had overshadowed chocolate-button-gate. No need to mention chocolate skid marks now.

"It's not your fault," he said, snorting a little derisively. "You're single; I'm the married man with a family and responsibilities." Ouch! That hurt. Reminding me cut deep.

I was not ready for what he said next.

"At least we didn't actually have sex," he said, taking my hand and rubbing his thumb along my knuckles. He looked at me and smiled, but it didn't reach his eyes and I could see his pain.

Whaaaaaaat??????

"Oh, did we not?" I questioned, recoiling in shock. Seriously, 'did we not' – what the fuck!

"Believe me. I really wanted to have sex with you," he continued, "but you fell asleep."

85

"I did what? I fell asleep?" my voice raised several octaves in disbelief. Oh my God! Could this get any worse? Clearly it could.

"Yeah," he said, with a small smile, "after our little game of 'Sweet hide-and-seek', you asked for a glass of water and when I got back into bed, you were spark out, snoring. I watched you for a while and then when it became clear you were not to be roused, I took a long, cold shower to dampen down my ardour!"

I was completely taken aback and pulled away from him. So, we hadn't had actual penetrative sex, but we had done pretty much everything else. I clearly remember him pumping away in and out of my mouth and grunting. "Oh my God, I have never had a blowjob as good as this!" I also found it a little unsettling that he had watched me sleeping. But at least I had clarification about the chocolate button incident. Every cloud and all that…

"Anyway," he said, as he suddenly remembered why he was there, "I'm going to take a few days off to try and sort this out. I have to tell her that nothing happened between us, Louisa. I can't let her find out that we spent the night together. The thing about my wife is that she's manipulative, controlling and narcissistic, and I thought that moving over here would save our marriage, but it was clear from day one that she wasn't prepared to work with me. You wouldn't believe what she does," he continues without pausing for me to even guess "she befriends the same people as me on social media so she can stalk them and question them. She logs onto my emails and reads them, deleting the ones she doesn't want me to read, and she constantly accuses me of having affairs with EVERY woman I meet. I've never been unfaithful, until last night with you, but believe me the thought has crossed my mind over the last few years, as her obsessive behaviours have got worse. What have I got to lose really? I only have to look in the general direction of a woman and I'm accused of fancying them. Joanna likes to play the victim; she makes out to friends and family that I'm a terrible husband and father and she's sacrificing her happiness by putting up with me for the sake of the kids. I've become immune to all her viscous lies and comments now, all I really want is someone to love me and to be loved. My future doesn't lie with Joanna, I think we both know that, but for now, here in another country and so far away from home, I need to make an effort to put things right. For the kids."

I stared at him, dumbfounded. None of this was right.

He sighed as his phone rang and I saw the word 'Joanna' appear. If he answered it, that was bringing her into the room with us. He pressed 'Decline'.

"Are you sure you should be doing that?" I questioned, casually removing my hand from his grasp.

"Nothing I say will make a difference, she's apoplectic with rage. I can't talk to her on the phone; it needs to be face to face."

I had a feeling he wanted to tell me more.

"Angus, I'm here for you anytime," I said. "Please, you can't go through this alone, and we may have seen every inch of each other's naked body, but I'm still your friend."

"You have no idea what that means to me," he replied taking my hand again, "Thank you. I don't regret what we did last night, not one bit. Please, please don't think for one second that I do. I was so afraid that I'd lose your friendship once we crossed the line, and I want you in my life, I really do. But right now, I need to try and sort this out and Joanna is not easy to reconcile with. One day, when it's all over, I promise I will tell you everything."

I just nodded and put my hand on his arm. He was bracing himself for the mother of all rows with Joanna. He'd tell me more when he was ready.

Chapter Seventeen

We all travelled back on the coach in silence. The atmosphere was nothing like the heady excitement from yesterday afternoon; everyone was a bit jaded and nursing intense hangovers. We'd all had a fantastic time, and everyone was thanking me for organising it. The only one who ignored me was Kelli; she kept out of the way and sat by herself at the back of the coach. I took my place at the front, sitting in the window seat trying to shrink into the upholstery, staring unseeing out of the window. Angus didn't even look for a different seat, he smiled and sat down next to me, giving my leg a little touch with his finger as he did so, but he didn't talk. He was constantly checking his phone or texting. He would occasionally rest back against the headrest and sigh or rub his eyes. My heart went out to him. His wife clearly had a lot of issues and whilst he had cheated on her with me (gulp), it sounded like he'd gone through years of unhappiness and for his family's sake, he needed to get it sorted.

The traffic was light coming out of London so we made good time getting back to work. As we pulled into the carpark at Williams & Bowman Solicitors, he craned his neck to look over the tops of the other seats to see if Joanna was there and with a barely audible, "Oh fuck, I thought so. She's here" he jumped out of his seat like a scalded cat. He turned to me as the coach juddered to a halt and with a desperate look on his face he said, "Bye, Louisa, we'll talk soon. Joanna's here." And he jerked his head to where a figure was standing at the office doorway.

I couldn't see Joanna, the perfectly groomed and aloof wife of Angus Pewk, but I could see Angela, the dot com picker I knew from my local Tesco. What was she doing at my work and why did she have a face like a dropped trifle? Where was Joanna? As Angus approached the office doorway, his body language completely changed. Gone was the confident, strutting Angus that I knew, to be replaced by a somewhat lesser version of himself with the look of a frightened child. As Angela started yelling at him and waving her arms around, I thought I was going to black out. I couldn't quite comprehend that this woman, whom I'd thought was 'Angela', was in fact his wife Joanna and who, only days previously, had been in a sex shop with me where I'd purchased saucy undies, which I wore last night TO SEDUCE HER HUSBAND!

WHAT. THE. ACTUAL. FUCK.

Chapter Eighteen

Understandably, Angus took some time off work; he clearly had a lot to work through. I was struggling to get my head around Angela and Joanna being the same person and I spent each evening after work curled up on my sofa crying and replaying every single one of my conversations with her. Had I told her that I was in lust with Angus? Had she assumed that all my exaggerated stories about the Williams & Bowman partners' extra-curricular activities meant that Angus was playing away too? Had I told her in Ann Summers that I was buying underwear to seduce someone? But mostly I was devastated that I had been so cruelly and catastrophically deceived. Why would somebody do that? What would drive someone to such deception?

Angus' revelations simmered away in the realms of my consciousness as I came to the conclusion that she was indeed a manipulative, controlling, narcissistic evil bitch.

Almost a week passed, and the work do wasn't mentioned while I was around. Everyone kept their distance, which suited me fine as I was still smarting from the whole betrayal and certainly didn't need the added pressure of defending myself to my work colleagues. I stayed in my office as much as I could, sat at my desk to have lunch and left after everyone else at the end of the day. I let the gossips have their time.

My mobile phone rang one lunchtime while I was sitting at my desk scrolling through the world news online. It was face down and I automatically answered it without taking much notice of the caller. It wasn't until the connection had been made that I realised the screen was announcing the call was from Angus. I scowled as I answered, anticipating perhaps Angela/Joanna on the other end about to recall her version of our night together, using me as a pawn in her sick games. "Hello?" I said tentatively. Angus's voice came at me in urgent, hushed tones, and I knew from the echo that he'd probably shut himself in the toilet to make the call. At the sound of his voice, I found myself smiling and my tense shoulders relax slightly. It was nice to hear his voice; I'd missed that Australian accent. He wanted us to meet for a drink in the pub that evening, it was more of an order than a request, he said he wanted to talk to me about 'everything' and that Joanna was taking the children to a swimming party, which meant he had a couple of hours. He said he would have to leave after her, so she didn't get suspicious, so we arranged to meet in a quiet pub near the river at 5 pm. At 4:35 pm, having done next to nothing at work since he rang, I shut down my computer and spent half an hour in the ladies' touching up my make-up and trying to hold down the acrid bile that kept rising in my throat, I was that nervous about seeing him again.

Chapter Nineteen

I reversed my car into a parking space right against the hedge in a dark corner of the pub car park. It was well away from the glaring pub lights and couldn't be seen from the road. I didn't want to risk being spotted although I was confident that Joanna didn't know what car I had, but I still didn't want to risk being caught, as much for Angus' sake as mine. I got out of my car shivering, although it was a mild night, and walked an indirect route hugging the edge of the carpark, keeping to the shadows. As I nipped in through the pub front door, I went straight to the ladies' toilets. The bile was rising and burning my throat, I was pretty sure I was going to be sick.

As I stood at the basin running my hands and wrists under cold water, I took deep deliberate breaths to calm me down, and slowly the feeling of wanting to vomit abated. I dabbed my clammy face with a paper towel, took one more deep breath and walked out of the ladies'. As I approached the bar, I glanced around at the few patrons dotted around the quiet pub. I wanted to grab a seat in a corner out of the way but there was an old man sitting there, hunched over and nursing a glass of amber liquid. He was deep in thought and as he swirled his glass he looked up and... Fucking hell! It was Angus. I smiled at him, but I couldn't hide my shock. He stood as I approached, and I noticed he had big dark circles under his eyes, he was unshaven and unkempt. We kissed each other on the cheek in greeting and he pulled me in for a hug. His eyes glistened with unshed tears and as my own rolled down my cheeks, my heart broke for this man as he prepared to bare his soul.

Angus' Story

My mates warned me. From the very start they said I shouldn't get involved. She was a friend of a friend of a friend and the talk in our extended group was that she'd had a series of unreliable and troublesome men, with one boyfriend clearing out of her apartment and moving in with another woman while she was at work; and another maxing out her credit cards to fund his thirst for recreational drugs, leaving her heavily in debt. She was unlucky in love, but she was everything I wanted in a woman – sexy, kind-hearted, self-assured, attractive, and she wanted a family as much as I did.

***

We got together in a nightclub in Caloundra. My mates and I had been on a bender and we were very drunk. All the bars in the town were closing and, adamant that we weren't going home until the sun came up, we fell into the first club we came across. The music was thumping, the bass so loud, I felt it reverberating in my throat, The beer was watered down and the clientele less than desirable, but I was well on the way to annihilation and needed alcohol, in large quantities and quickly. It was my round so I forced my way through the throng of hot bodies to the bar and ordered the drinks. As I handed over my dollars and gathered up 6 beers precariously between my fingers, I turned to navigate a path back through the clubbers to where my mates were waiting at a sticky table with questionable stains, when she sidled up to me and with a full-on smile and a sassy attitude said, "Hi Angus, you probably don't remember me? I'm Joanna, we met last year at Henry's party. I can give you everything you need. I'll be a great wife and I'll give you beautiful kids!" Talk about forward. Her forthright attitude shocked me but we chatted easily and got on so well that evening, it was almost as if we'd known each other for years. The conversation was flirty, she was very touchy-feely and she melted my heart. From that day on, we were inseparable and in love, and she moved into my apartment two weeks later. Within a year, we were married. The alarm bells had started to ring in my head intermittently during that year especially as she'd hinted after about three months of us dating that we shouldn't hang around; we should sell the apartment and find a family home. When I hesitated, she said that if I loved her, I'd propose. She was right, there was no need to delay. I silenced the alarm bells and pushed any doubts to the back of my mind; I just needed to live for the moment, be less 'plan' and more 'just do'.

I thought long and hard about the way I wanted to pop the question. I wanted it to be romantic, memorable but also intimate, and a guided walk to the top of Sydney Harbour Bridge with a glass of champagne at the summit was just perfect. It took some planning, with lots of secret emails and phone calls but the day finally arrived. We had a late lunch in a bistro on the harbour front and there was lots of hand holding, arm touching and talk of 'the future'. We walked arm in arm from the restaurant to the base of the bridge where I turned to her and said, "Come on, let's climb it."

"What?" she gasped, looking up at the bridge towering above us.

"It's all arranged," I said, chuffed with myself that I'd kept it secret and it really was a complete surprise to her.

She was laughing and shaking her head as we pulled on our climbing suits and our guide clipped our lines to the safety rail. With much trepidation, and not just about the climb, and the ring I'd purchased (I knew what she wanted, she'd accidentally left the computer open on the jewellers page – one brilliant cut diamond, at least one carat, platinum band) secreted in my inside pocket, we made the steep and dizzying climb to the top of the bridge. As we both stood in our all-in-one climbing suits, tethered to the safety rail, with champagne glass in hand and the wind whistling around us, the safety team moved slightly to one side and I got down on one knee (well, as much as I could on a 134m high bridge) and proposed to her just as the sun was setting. I thought it was incredibly romantic – we were (almost) alone and high above one of the most beautiful cities in the world with an incredible view across the harbour. Her response was "Of course I'll marry you, but I didn't think you were going to do it here." She seemed almost disappointed, but we kissed and toasted our happiness, and by the time we'd climbed down to the base of the bridge, the reservations that had formed in my head from her initial reaction were forgotten. It wasn't until years later that I found out she'd told her best friend that she would've preferred to arrange the proposal herself, so she could have exactly what she wanted! She didn't want a romantic gesture at all, she wanted an audience.

But I was easy-going and happily went along with all her suggestions for a life together. I sold the apartment (made a killing on it), paid off her debts, paid for a lavish wedding and had enough left for a deposit on a small house in the suburbs. It started to go wrong as soon as we left our wedding reception when she questioned me about a woman I had been talking to. We had an almighty row because she thought I was flirting, she even suggested that I'd asked the woman for her number as apparently she'd seen her pass me a piece of paper. Seriously? On my wedding day? The woman was the assistant to the registrar, who had just married us, and the piece of paper was our Marriage Certificate! Looking back now, I should have seen the warning signs, especially when I was approached by her best friend and chief bridesmaid on the morning of our wedding and told that "Joanna is great but she's fake. Are you sure you know what you're doing? She'll change as soon as you put that ring on her finger."

Unfortunately, she wasn't wrong…

By the time we'd celebrated our fourth wedding anniversary, I was trapped in a world of emotional torture. I wanted her to be happy, so when she suggested us activating the tracking option on our mobile phones in case we were ever in a situation where we couldn't get hold of each other; I agreed. But it just gave her the freedom to use it 24 hours a day to track my every movement. The second I walked through the door, I'd be subjected to an interrogation – why had I left work so late? Why did I need to go to the petrol station? If I'd only bought a couple of items from the grocery store, why was I there for 45 minutes? Why had I made a detour on the way home? It was relentless and at first I thought she was just being overly protective but it soon became possessive, I began to feel suffocated by the depth of the control, almost trapped. I foolishly turned off the tracking option when I got to work one day but was subjected to such abuse when I got home, I had no choice but to reactivate it. She threw my dinner in the bin as 'punishment' because I had caused her a great deal of emotional stress. She said I was a 'worthless piece of shit' and if I had nothing to hide, why was I making such a fuss about being tracked. I suppose she did have a point.

Her possessive nature didn't change and our invites out with friends got less and less until eventually we only socialised with her friends; we'd fallen out with all of mine. There'd been many occasions previously where we'd gone to a party or out for dinner and she'd spectacularly fallen out with every one of the female partners of my mates. She would always storm off crying, accusing them of insulting her, and I'd have to smooth things over, follow her down the street and ultimately ring my mates and say that if their partners didn't apologise to Joanna then we wouldn't be able to meet up with them again. It didn't take long for me to lose all my friends. I was starting to feel as if there were invisible tethers binding me to her. It was her way or no way and she was slowly but surely manipulating and controlling every aspect of my life. It was dawning on me that all she wanted from me was my money and my genes, as the only thing that was good in our relationship was the sex (albeit very vanilla and very clinical) – we both wanted children and, of course, I was happy to indulge in as much baby making as possible, which paid off because she was pregnant within two months. I was ecstatic, as was Joanna, and if I thought this would make our relationship stronger, I couldn't have been more wrong. Our sex life became non-existent, we grew more distant and she grew needier. As her belly swelled, she became paranoid that I didn't desire her anymore and rows would ensue. I couldn't tell her that it wasn't her size that made her undesirable, it was her character. If I instigated any form of sexual activity, she claimed I was being selfish, that she was growing a baby and therefore needed her rest, but some nights, all I wanted was to fall asleep in my wife's arms. I lay next to her every night, feeling very alone.

The day Charlotte was born was one of the happiest days of my life and I was brimming with love for this tiny person we had grown together. She was our little bundle of hope and the bond I share with my daughter is immeasurable to this day.

Joanna became very jealous of Charlotte and I worried about post-natal depression. How could she be jealous of a tiny baby? When I mentioned it, she said I looked at Charlotte with love and affection, but I looked at her with only contempt. It was entirely untrue, I loved Joanna with all my heart but I had no idea how to make things right.

I did as much around the house as and when I could in an attempt to make Joanna's life a little easier. I knew she was finding it tough being in the house with a demanding new-born and I didn't put any pressure on her or make any demands. I would come home from work at around 6 pm where I'd always find Joanna sitting on the sofa eating snacks and watching TV so at least she was relaxing and putting her feet up. Charlotte would be sitting happily in her rocker, arms and legs flailing around in joyous un-coordination, and Joanna would stand and say, "Your turn to take over now. I've had her all day; I'm done in and need sleep. I've already eaten so if you want something, you'll have to sort it out yourself," and without so much as a peck on the cheek, she'd take herself off to bed. Most nights she'd spend an hour on her phone FaceTiming her mum and by the time I'd settled Charlotte, showered and hauled myself, exhausted, upstairs to bed, Joanna would be snoring.

I loved those evenings when it was just Charlotte and me, but the hardest was night-time. Joanna would stay in bed, sleeping through it all, and I'd get up to do every feed, every nappy change and deal with every whimper until my alarm went off at 6 am. when I'd get up and go to work leaving Joanna and Charlotte sleeping peacefully. Most days, I'd barely get three hours sleep, but I didn't complain. Joanna was the mother of my child and I wanted to give her the world.

For the next 18 months, my routine remained unchanged. My health suffered as I was constantly exhausted and most days I didn't bother with dinner. I mentioned a couple of times that perhaps I needed to speak to our GP about my health concerns but Joanna just called me a sook, saying I needed to 'grow a pair' and how it would be so embarrassing for her if I went to the GP because I was feeling run down and tired when she's the one who was looking after the baby. But Charlotte was thriving and Joanna looked a picture of health, so it was all good and although I barely remembered what I did at work for those 18 months, I do remember all the precious moments I spent with Charlotte. Imagine my delight when Joanna fell pregnant again, although God knows how that happened! By now the only romantic gesture was me removing my socks when I thought we were in for a bit of between-the-sheets action. She gave me very clear signs when

I was allowed to make love to her – a damp soapy flannel and a towel were always placed on my bedside table. No spontaneity. I had to get her in the mood and whilst I was very happy to oblige, she was never willing to participate in the act of arousal. She never touched me and when I suggested she might like to use her tongue on me, as I did on her, she was disgusted and said I was 'depraved'. Our foreplay consisted of me pleasuring her, whilst I stroked and caressed myself so that I was hard enough to enter her when she decided she was ready. She always criticised at least one aspect of our love-making – whether it went on too long, or she didn't feel particularly aroused or she thought I was too noisy, she always had something to complain about. I even had to clean her up afterwards (that's the reason for the damp flannel and towel) so she didn't have to get out of bed. But I indulged her every whim. I turned her into a spoilt princess. I created a monster.

By the time Charlotte turned two years old, we welcomed a brand-new addition to our family, our son Ethan. I couldn't believe how lucky we were, a daughter and a son – our family was complete.

Unfortunately, the same problems with Joanna and my relationship were still there, and I remained on the merry-go-round of sleep deprivation, ill health and Joanna's constant criticisms and accusations that I was 'cranky' and 'giving her shit'. I don't remember 'giving her shit', I remember looking after two young children while she took every opportunity to rest. I booked to see my GP one afternoon so I mentioned it to Joanna and said that I was leaving work early for the appointment and would be back at the usual time, I wouldn't expect to be late home. On my way to the medical centre, she rang me to say she needed me at home because Ethan had the sniffles and she was feeling under the weather too and needed to go to bed. She'd taken the liberty of cancelling my GP appointment because she felt it was unnecessary and a waste of Dr Davos' time, so I was to go straight home so she could sleep. While my wife and children were going from strength to strength, my well-being was at rock bottom and when my mum mentioned her concerns over my health, I broke down.

I told Mum everything – how I felt about my relationship with Joanna, how I felt like I was living on the edge of a precipice just waiting for the slightest thing to tip me over into the abyss of self-doubt and self-loathing. I was wrecked, and she knew it.

My mum was so supportive. She moved in with us for a month, so she could help out, and she did absolutely everything, from cooking and cleaning to washing and ironing. She even picked the children up from day care (Joanna needed 'me time' so Charlotte and Ethan went three times a week to give her a break) and she was my rock.

The relationship between Joanna and my mum had always been strained at best. Mum could see Joanna for who she really was, and Joanna hated that Mum and I were so close. In fact, Joanna hated that I had a life before I met her. Her jealousy knew no bounds, something which I became painfully aware of early one morning…

***

Mum was still staying with us, and unbeknown to me, she'd had a 'quiet word' with Joanna about my health, constant exhaustion and how nice it was that she had 'me time', but that after a long day at work trying to bring in a decent wage to give our family a good life, maybe I needed some 'me time' too. Joanna had turned on Mum like a rabid dog! Shouting, screaming, accusing her of trying to come between Joanna and me and refusing to see that maybe she'd been a little bit selfish.

One night at around 1 am, I crept into our bedroom and quietly clicked the door shut so as not to wake Joanna, my mum and my kids. I slipped out of my joggers and t-shirt, leaving them in a heap on the floor, and climbed exhausted into bed beside a sleeping Joanna. I let the soothing coolness of the sheets envelop me, felt myself relax completely ready for sleep to take me, when a sudden bright flash assaulted my eyes. Within a nanosecond, Joanna started with the accusations and insults and as I dragged myself back from the brink of sleep and opened my eyes, I knew I was in for a rough night. She laid into me good and proper, accusing me of getting drunk and falling asleep on the sofa until the early hours (I'd actually tidied away the kids' toys, folded the washing, emptied the dishwasher and put another load on but I didn't have the energy to correct her). I've never heard such malice in her voice as she informed me that she'd told my mum in no uncertain terms that she wasn't welcome in our house anymore and that she was to leave in the morning. She told her to stop interfering in our marriage and if she ever questioned our relationship, she would never be able to see her grandchildren. Joanna felt 'betrayed' by her. What a crock of shit!

I lay in bed in an absolute daze, barely able to process what she was saying. She was hurling insult after insult at me and her swansong was to throw my mobile phone at me, which I hadn't been able to find all evening, which she produced from under her pillow, as she spat the words "I know you've had affairs, Angus, I'm not taking it anymore. I will take you for everything you've got – the house, the kids, EVERYTHING. I've seen it all on your phone, your social media, emails, everything. All the evidence is there, phone numbers, text messages, flirty comments, all of it. Don't try and deny it or delete them, I've got screenshots of them all." She was actually admitting to a gross invasion of my privacy, and she thought she had the right.

Joanna would frequently log into my emails; she said because she often gave out my email address instead of hers as I checked mine more often through my phone, whereas she had to log in to her iPad for hers. She knew my email login information, but I had nothing to hide so I had no problem with her checking occasionally. I didn't realise she was so thoroughly going through emails and social media accounts on our home computer and I recalled many times when I'd see an email in my inbox marked as 'Read' yet I hadn't opened it. She was trying to control and manipulate every aspect of my life, from my real friends to my social media contacts, and nothing got past her. In fact, I remember one particular time I was checking the settings on my Facebook account and discovered that she'd deleted every woman I was friends with; she'd wiped WhatsApp conversations and blocked contacts on my phone.

I grew weary of her need to control every aspect of my life and frequently changed the passcode on my phone, even though I had absolutely nothing to hide, but there was a principle involved. I couldn't help it if she perceived messages I received as flirtatious or suggestive, I certainly wasn't sending any like that and so I, naively, left them all there. She constantly monitored my phone, she'd rush to read any messages that popped in before I got to it and I'd often find it not where I'd left it. She was logging into my social media accounts from her iPad so she could monitor my online activity while I was out. Infuriatingly, she would always 'check in' with me wherever we went – restaurants, cinema, supermarket (??) and even home; then upload a selfie of the two of us, neither of us looking particularly happy it has to be said, with comments like 'Date night with hubby' or 'Can't beat snuggles on the sofa with my man' which we NEVER did! It was always 'Joanna Pewk is with Angus Pewk….' One of my mates commented on my page once that Joanna may as well have pissed on me as she was clearly marking her territory! I thought it was funny, Joanna didn't; she logged into my phone and deleted his contact information. Change of passcode again.

I remember one particular Friday, I'd had a shitty week at work and a few too many whiskeys that night. I was fiddling around with my phone as I lay on the sofa watching a film and I must've nodded off because the next thing I remember is rousing from an alcohol-induced sleep with the feeling that my right arm was not my own, it was literally flailing around in the semi-darkness of its own accord, I had no control over it. I opened my eyes to see Joanna kneeling beside me manipulating my arm and touching my hand; she had my mobile phone in her other hand and she was trying to place my thumb on the touch button to activate the screen unlock, no doubt in an attempt to uncover my non-existent infidelity. As I'd changed my passcode I can only assume that she had tried logging in with the old one and when she couldn't access it, she got desperate. I was shocked that she'd stooped this low but again tried to reassure her that I wasn't having and never had had an affair. She apologised for being so underhand but I think that was only because she'd been caught and she promised to talk to me instead of trying to catch me out. As a compromise, I agreed to stay off all social media for a while and promised that I wouldn't contact friends or respond to work colleagues' messages. I even had to agree to all phone calls with my mum being on speakerphone, so she could listen.

So that's how she kept control over me, by monitoring everything, and in turn that's what she based her assumptions and judgements on – the fake cyber world of social media. She was demanding, critical, always snooping and checking up on me, she guilt-tripped me constantly and attached conditions to love and affection, even once telling the kids that "Daddy won't let Mummy have a night off from cooking and buy us all a takeaway because he doesn't love us very much!" She was always putting me down and making me feel inadequate and I knew that this wasn't just a quirky side to her personality, or a bad patch in our relationship, this was cold, calculating emotional abuse. End of.

I was very fearful of Joanna's manipulation and the lengths she would go to to get me disengaged and disconnected with everyone and everything around me, and I couldn't begin to figure out how to fix it. When the offer came up at work to move to England for a two-year placement, I jumped at it, seeing it as an opportunity to get away from the negative influences and sycophants she seemed to surround herself with.

I poured us a glass of wine that evening and pitched the overseas move to her and her eyes lit up. I was so relieved. She immediately started planning – the children could go to a school in England, we could travel around Europe, see snow at Christmas (unlikely in London but I didn't have the heart to tell her), but for me it was the chance that we might bond again and rekindle our relationship as husband and wife.

She immediately posted the move on social media and waited for the avalanche of 'Likes', 'You're so lucky' and 'I'm so jealous' comments. As she revealed every detail of our plans on Facebook with hourly updates, I felt as though I had to ask permission from the virtual community before finalising anything. She was constantly posting on social media asking everything from recommendations for cleaners, to 'What is zucchini called in England?' (it's courgette by the way). She even 'checked in' to a storage facility when she dropped off packing boxes! She had constant attention from people who commented on and liked absolutely anything she posted and as she revelled in her one-upmanship, our relationship sunk to new lows and all the time she was still monitoring my every move.

A particularly tough part of the move for me was leaving my mum behind, but she was incredibly supportive and even offered to come over with us to help us settle. I politely declined her offer, there was no way Joanna would agree to that without her mother coming too, and it was going to be hard enough moving our little family unit without the added stress of mothers/mothers-in-law. Mum and I did agree that we would FaceTime and email each other at least once a week and with the promise of her visiting in a few months sitting heavy in my heart, I bid her an emotional farewell. She hugged me tight and told me that no matter what happened in my life, she would be there for me, that she always had room in her home for me and that she would support whatever decisions I made. It was a very poignant moment and strengthened the bond I had with her, which is still strong to this day.

The day of the move was upon us in no time and having packed up everything we owned, put it all into storage and made sure the tenants for our house were settled, we boarded the Singapore Airlines flight bound for Dubai, in 26-degree heat, final destination London Heathrow which was currently basking in thick fog and 5-degree chill. As I watched the kids on their iPads and Joanna sleeping soundly while cabin service got underway, I wondered for the thousandth time how my life had got to this point and whether I was making the right decision for my family. On paper I had everything – a family, a bit of money put aside, great work prospects and the opportunity to travel. But I felt far from happy, far from loved and far from home.

It took us a few weeks to settle into some sort of normality. In England, the weather was cold and damp with interminable rain and the kids suffered from terrible jetlag. They were awake every morning in the early hours so I'd nap on the sofa while they watched cartoons, then I'd get up and start work while they went back to bed and slept until late morning, just like Joanna. I arranged to work from home for a month before joining the team properly to make the transition easier for my clients on the other side of the world, but the time difference took its toll and I longed for the normality of an office.

We signed a two-year lease on a house, a new build very close to my work and after a while we got into a steady routine. The kids got a place at a local school which got them out of the house and making friends, and Joanna started to talk about looking for work. Life was okay, and I buried my head in the sand, ignoring all the warning signs that our relationship was not faring well. I spoke to Mum every week on speakerphone and every week I told her that yes, we were fine and yes, Joanna and I were getting on just great, but deep down she knew that nothing had changed, we had just taken all our problems to another country.

Joanna became more hostile towards me, she complained that the weather was too cold, the house was too small, the kids were too noisy, and she couldn't talk to her mum or her cyber friends because they were in entirely different time zones. Our sex life was non-existent and the shower was the only space I had where I wasn't watched (because I didn't have my phone with me so couldn't contact all the women I was having affairs with I suppose!) so was able to escape and lose myself in my thoughts. Self-gratification became part of my morning routine.

A month later, I walked into the office of Williams & Bowman, excited by the opportunity to learn about English law, meet new people, expand my client base and be able to take my experience back to Australia where I ultimately planned on opening my own practice. Joanna got a job as a dot com picker at the local Tesco, which meant we had a little bit of extra money coming in for holidays and treats, and that took a bit of pressure off me. I was pleased for her as she'd be able to get back to being Joanna, not just Charlotte and

Ethan's mum. She really enjoyed her four hours, three times a week and seemed really happy. She made lots of friends at work and had a good social life but for all her confidence, she was very easily led. She was now back in daily contact with her mum and friends in Australia (either she or they stayed up to talk most nights) and it became a routine that I would get home from work and hear her slagging me off to them as I walked through the door. The kids would be running around the house because she'd be on the couch all afternoon with a bag full of snacks and sweets that she'd dish out if they complained they were hungry, and it was always up to me to cook dinner. I love cooking, but when I've had a full 12 hours at work and I get home to a chaotic house and starving children, I cook for convenience. She'd sit and eat her dinner in front of the TV and I'd sort the kids, get them bathed and in bed and invariably fall asleep myself whilst waiting for them to nod off. I'd often wake in the early hours on top of the duvet, still dressed in yesterday's clothes and absolutely famished because I'd missed dinner. I feared that our relocation was not the fresh start I'd hoped it would be.

I drank every evening when I got home from work. Only one drink usually, sometimes two. A double measure of whiskey, lots of ice and a splash of cola. I drank partly due to the stress at work, mostly due to the stress at home. Alcohol was my friend, it enveloped me in its warmth and made my thoughts less decisive. I felt calm when I'd had a drink and the edges of my life were less sharp and spiky. I'd go to bed feeling fuzzy and relaxed and sleep would be instantaneous. Joanna became a little more understanding and used to make silly jokes about the amount of alcohol I'd consumed and how

111

much I snored, but surprisingly she never moaned even when I'd be semi-comatose for the entire night.

I didn't realise how much damage my drinking was causing until I caught her on my phone one night, texting female friends on Facebook pretending to be me and trying to incite them into admitting infidelity with me. The light from a phone had woken me up and as I focussed on the bedside clock, worried I'd missed my alarm call, I saw it was only 3 am. I turned to Joanna and saw she was on my phone, angrily typing something on the screen. I sat up in bed and through the fug of last night's whiskey, I asked her what she was doing on my phone. She screamed at me that it was my fault that she had to be deceitful and that she didn't trust me using social media. She showed me my phone, she was logged in to my Facebook page and using Messenger. There were many messages of bewilderment from my female friends as they responded to 'my' IMs of 'we must meet for a drink when I get back but don't mention it to Joanna' and 'I've always liked you'. I asked her why she was doing it; I told her again that I had nothing to hide and as calmly as I could, told her that she'd really crossed the line this time. She actually gloated that she still logged in to my accounts every night to snoop. Apparently because I always have at least one drink, it's easy for her, she just waits until I'm sleeping deeply and holds my phone under my thumb, just like she did before. Hey presto! My phone again gives her full access to all my social media accounts. I was dumbstruck that she was doing it again, I had hoped we'd turned a corner but realisation dawned as to why she wasn't complaining about my drinking – she could take her time perusing everything on my phone because I was too pissed to realise. I grabbed angrily at the notebook on the floor beside the bed and wrote down all my passwords. I slammed it down on the bed and struggling to keep my voice calm, I informed her yet again that I had nothing to hide but she could have access to my phone, email accounts and everything else and was welcome to look at whatever she liked, using the passwords I provided. I felt it was easier that way, the alternative was unthinkable.

Chapter Twenty

"So, that's me. The rest, they say, is history," Angus said, shrugging and leaning back in his chair.

I was breathing fast and my head was spinning. It was three hours later, and he'd done pretty much all the talking while I'd tried to process his revelations. I knew I'd seen something in his eyes the day I met him, it was anguish.

"Uh huh" was all I could find to say.

"I hope you can understand why we need to um…" Angus hesitated.

I stared at him, waiting for the rest of the sentence.

"Why you need to…?" I questioned.

"Why we need to um… go back to Australia. To sort things out?" he questioned.

And there it was. As quick as he came into my life, he was leaving.

"Yes, yes, of course, yes of course I do. Absolutely. 100%. Completely understand," I gabbled out my reply, my throat burning.

"Look, Louisa," he continued, "I know this is a lot to take in but it's important to me that you have the facts. If I've hurt you, I am so, so sorry. It was never my intention to and I certainly hope you don't feel as though I've led you on. I can't make any promises, Louisa. I have so much shit to sort out and it's not going to be easy. If I divorce Joanna, she's not going to go quietly. She will fight me every step of the way for our children, money and my integrity. Divorce laws in Aus are different to England; we must separate for at least 12 months before we can file for divorce, we have to have counselling, we need lawyers involved at every stage. The first thing I need to do is get an injunction in place, so she can't take my children more than 60 kilometres away. Her family has money, and they will stop at nothing until I have nothing. The thing with Joanna is that she constantly feeds her family lies; they all think she's perfect, and because they live so far away, they rely on social media and daily conversations with her and she can hide behind a façade. It makes me sick when I see their posts saying how wonderful she is, how lucky they are to know her because she has a 'heart so full of love'. She has a heart of stone, Louisa, and I can't take it anymore."

I placed my hands gently over Angus's hands, he was wringing them anxiously and I could feel his whole body shaking.

"Oh, my gorgeous, wonderful Tim-Tam," I said as I looked into his troubled eyes, "I will always, always be here for you. I have no expectations of you; all I want is for you to be happy. You're so unhappy in your marriage but only you can decide what you want out of your relationship. If you and I have the remotest possibility of a future together, that would be amazing, but if we don't, then that's okay. I love you, Angus, and because I love you, I only want what will make you happy. You are a broken, shell of a man compared to the vibrant, confident one that first knocked me off my feet. Go back to Australia, sort out your life and decide what you want from it. Don't wait for someone to make the decisions for you and take away the control you have."

"God, Louisa, I love you so much," he said, looking straight at me, "please, promise me one thing," he continued.

"Anything," I said, leaning forward.

"Don't ever call me your Tim-Tam again!" and as he laughed, he pulled me in and kissed me deeply.

We pulled away and smiled at each other. I was choking back tears now.

"Your mum will be pleased to see you back in Aus," I said, stroking his hand.

"Yes, she will," he replied, his mood lifting slightly, "and she would've loved to have met you. Especially as I've told her all about you, she knows how much I love you!"

WHAT??? I am going to throw up, I can feel it rising from the pit of my stomach.

Angus laughed, "Don't worry, Louisa, it's fine. Mum and I are really close, I have no secrets from her. She's an amazing woman, she knows everything about mine and Joanna's relationship, she knows about you and me at the party and… you don't look well, Louisa, are you alright?"

The feeling that I was about to puke dissipated as I took a few long, slow breaths.

"Fine" I replied, nodding and swallowing several times, "but what if your mum tells Joanna? Oh my God, what have I done? I…"

"She won't," interrupted Angus in soothing tones, "I promise you, Mum is no fool."

All I could do was nod. My brain couldn't process this information and I couldn't find the words to express any concern. I literally had nothing, so I was going to have to park this information for now, but before Angus went back to Australia, I would come back to the revelation that his mum knew about me.

"One thing I don't get," I said quickly changing the subject, "is how Joanna knew about us, that night at the party?"

"Oh, yes," Angus recalled, rolling is yes, "that was down to Kelli. Joanna befriended her at an exercise class. They got chatting and she told Kelli that she was writing an erotic novel about people having affairs in the workplace."

"But?... How did she?..." I stammered.

"Joanna likes to familiarise herself with people I work with by looking them up on the company website. It's another form of control," he shrugged noncommittally, as if it's all perfectly normal, "she can see who I work with, whether they are male or female, young or old, whatever. Kelli listed one of her interests as 'donning my legwarmers and shaking my glow stick with fellow keep fit clubbers at the community hall every Tuesday night'. It didn't take a genius to work out where she was going so of course Joanna started the same class and they got talking. Kelli used to regale her with stories of the partners and their mistresses, and she asked if she could use her stories."

I was stunned. How could Joanna not only think it was okay to lie and deceive people, but admit all this to Angus? The woman was practically a stalker. Did she have any morals?

"Kelli being Kelli," he continued, "she was only too happy to oblige and took great delight in recalling all the sordid details of the affairs that have taken place at work, whether they are true or not, and embellishing the stories along the way. Apparently, she mentioned the work party to Joanna, who immediately suggested that she contact her during the evening and tell her first-hand what was going on. She said she could get it all into her book and she'd make it funny, but she needed to know as it happened, so she could capture the atmosphere. She promised that she'd change the names and Kelli was not to worry about revealing all her colleagues' secrets. Kelli, not knowing the connection, was only too pleased to admit to Joanna that she and I had flirted every day at work and how I was 'desperate to get into her pants'," and he did the air quote bunny ears thing. "And, that if we ended up shagging," he said, opening his arms wide to exaggerate the point, "she'd tell Joanna all about it." And he pah'ed as he shook his head in disbelief.

I just opened and closed my mouth in astonishment, like a gasping cod!

He continued, "Joanna must've found it unbelievably difficult to keep quiet about the party. She'd obviously plotted every last detail and I'm shocked that someone I thought I knew could do this, it verges on insanity. She's always been devious, but this is just so wrong. She was almost gloating when she recalled the night of the party, in the minutest detail. It was so accurate it felt as if Joanna had been there on the dancefloor, watching us. Kelli had phoned her, can you believe that? She was jealous when she saw us kiss at the bar and couldn't wait to spill the beans to Joanna. It didn't quite play out how Joanna expected, but nevertheless, she got what she needed."

I could feel the blood thrumming in my ears. Kelli was so fucking gullible. Seriously, an erotic novelist? I've never heard such shit in my life!

"Now, I have to deal with the consequences," he said standing up, glancing at his phone and frowning. "I guess I'd better go. Joanna's been home hours and I've got 8 missed calls from her and 6 irate text messages, she'll be mad that I haven't been there to bath the kids, put them to bed and cook dinner. She'll get up me for leaving her to do everything. I'm over it now, nothing I do will make a difference." He shrugged nonchalantly as he stood up.

"Come on," he said as he collected up our empty glasses and placed them on the bar, "I'll walk you to your car."

As we stepped out into the darkness, I was just thinking about awkward goodbyes when he took my hand and said, "One day I hope we can walk down the street like this, without looking around to see who's watching. I want to be able to do this," and he held up our entwined hands, "and this, in broad daylight." And he turned to me, put his hand up to my face and tucked a stray piece of hair behind my ear, but he didn't need an excuse to get close. I closed my eyes and leant into his hand. He leant forwards and as our lips touched, he pulled me in for an intense and frantic kiss. I responded and gripped his shoulders as we kissed passionately in the middle of the pub carpark. He kissed around my jaw and down my neck, and I knew that I was going to have severe stubble rash. My lips were already tingling from the intensity of his beardy kiss!

"Louisa, let's get into your car, please," he begged, while still kissing and nibbling. My heart was hammering so loudly in my chest, I thought he could hear it and I desperately wanted this man inside me. But not in a pub carpark.

"Angus, we're not going to do it in the back of my car in a car park," I said.

"God, no," he answered as he pulled back and looked at me, "I just want to kiss you and touch you. This is not lust, Louisa, this is love. I don't want our first time together to be in a carpark; when I do have you, it's going to be special and I want you to feel cherished. This is not a sex thing for me, Louisa; this is about being with a person I love and respect and knowing that those feelings are returned."

"Good to know," I responded with a cheeky grin, "but get in the car now, I'm going to give you something that will blow your mind!"

Clearly, he didn't need asking twice. I could see his cock spring to attention and strain against his zipper, desperate to be released, and I was only too happy to oblige. He practically fell into the front seat and with ragged breaths he very quickly undid his trousers and sprang his cock free. He leaned back and looked at me with such sadness in his eyes, I almost couldn't do it. Almost…

I leant forwards and kissed him on the mouth, gently biting his lip, teasing his tongue with mine, and as he kissed me back, I reached over and took a hold of his cock. He groaned in pleasure as I gently moved my hand up and down his shaft, slowly, slowly. He groaned again and gasped, "Please, Louisa, take me in your mouth…please!"

"All in good time, Angus, all in good time," I teased as I slowly increased the speed of my strokes.

He moved his hips up and down in time and closed his eyes. I gave him one last soft kiss and then I leant down and took him in my mouth. He jolted his hips up which pushed his cock further in and as I gently gripped him with my lips and moved him in and out of my mouth, his groans turned into

"Fuck! That feels so good" and "Oh God, Louisa, take me all the way in!"

I smiled to myself; it was good knowing I was giving him such pleasure.

I felt his head lift off the back of the headrest and knew he was looking at me bobbing up and down between his legs, so I moved position slightly and let his hard cock slip out of my mouth so that he could see as well as feel it. I grasped him and continued the up and down rhythm with my hand, then I swirled my tongue over the very end of him and kissed his tip. As I took all of him in my mouth, I rolled my tongue down his shaft and he gasped in pleasure. He put his hand on the back of my head and I could feel his hips rising and falling as he eased himself in and out and pushed gently down on the back of my head. It was very erotic. Even though the gearstick was stabbing me in one side and the handbrake was gouging into my stomach. But it was worth it because I began to feel Angus' cock harden and swell as he reached a shuddering climax, so I gently eased off the pressure and let him pump into my mouth.

The immediate aftermath of a sexual encounter such as this is not pleasant and there was lots of fumbling around for tissues, pulling up and straightening of clothes. Not to mention the awkwardness that a confined space brings in itself! Luckily, I located a bottle of water and although it was luke-warm, I drank gratefully, washing away his salty residue.

"Well, I suppose I'd better go," Angus said, turning to me as I screwed the lid back on. "Louisa, I meant what I said," he continued, stroking my neck with light touches, sincerity in his voice, "I love you with all my heart. Nothing will change that, no matter what happens. I want you to know that."

"I know that, Angus," I replied, as tears inexplicably sprang to my eyes. I squeezed them tight shut and leaned against his arm, kissing his wrist.

"Thank you," he said, "and I don't just mean for that," he continued, smiling. "Thank you for everything, Louisa. I couldn't have got through the last few months without you. Just knowing that you're there for me is enough to get me through the heartache and the shit storm to come."

"Well," I said, "I know you'll do whatever you need to and I'm not going anywhere, I'll be here for you, Angus, always."

He stopped stroking my neck and reached his hands to my face where he wiped away my tears with his thumbs and then he looked me deep in the eyes and said, "Louisa, I love you."

"I love you too, Angus," I replied.

He opened the car door and as he stepped out, he said, "I'll contact you soon and let you know what's happening. It will all be OK, Louisa, trust me."

He slammed the door, blew me a kiss, waved and walked to his car. I waited until he drove away then I rested my head back on my seat and sobbed. I had never before cried as I did then. Great wracking sobs that shook my whole body and burnt the back of my throat like acid.

I was mourning the death of what very nearly was with this extraordinary man.

Chapter Twenty-One
October 2016

I kept myself busy at work, each day much the same as the last, each night spent alone in my house with my microwave meal for one, watching mind-numbing reality TV shows until exhaustion overcame me and I stumbled upstairs to bed falling into a fitful sleep plagued by unsettling dreams. There were times when I longed to get to the end of the day without thinking of Angus and times when I could only get to the end of the day by thinking of him. I was glad he was going back to Australia to sort his shit out, but the selfish me wanted him to stay because I had no idea how I would cope without his physical presence in my life.

He didn't come back to work and the partners announced that he had taken indefinite leave for personal reasons. The hum-drum of office life continued as if he was never there and at times I wanted to scream out, to stop this merry-go-round of life and get off, take a breather for a few minutes, and get back on again. It broke my heart every time I walked past his office and he wasn't in there. There was always that little glimmer of hope that one day I would glance in and he'd be sitting at his desk – he'd look up, smile cheekily at me and wave. But his office always remained in darkness, as did my heart.

One particular afternoon, I took my usual route back from the staffroom with my coffee cup in hand, past Angus' office, but instead of glancing through the window, I opened the door and walked right in. I could smell him immediately! It was the scent of Angus – his deodorant, his laundered clothes, that citrusy aftershave he wore. I breathed deeply and closed my eyes as memories of us together flooded my head. Behind the door I noticed his akubra hat and stockman coat hanging on the hook and so out of sight. I slipped them both on. It felt just like he was hugging me as my senses fizzed and I was enveloped in everything Angus.

From then on, whenever I was having a bad day or just needed a bit of time with Angus, I'd pop into his darkened office and slip into his hat and coat. The safety and comfort I felt being back in his 'arms' got me through some pretty tough times. Not least of all when he rang me late one Friday when I was just finishing up for the day to tell me that he and his family were flying back to Australia in three weeks' time.

You can imagine how the conversation went – lots of crying and declarations of love, and that was from Angus. Shocked, I thanked him for letting me know and suggested that we meet up one last time, as friends, to say goodbye. He said he'd see what he could do. That's what our relationship boiled down to – "I'll see what I can do." I immediately reverted to my way of dealing with trauma and upset, and I withdrew inside myself. I vowed there and then that I would never let anyone in, ever again, because I could not put myself through that sort of pain again. I pulled up the drawbridge on my emotional fortress and locked my feelings away in the metaphorical tower, far away from harm and the outside world. I could not put myself through that sort of pain anymore. It was torturous.

Chapter Twenty-Two

That night, after a long soak in a hot bath, I sat on the sofa in my favourite faded pyjamas, with my boobs free range and resting gently on my stomach, my legs tucked under me. The TV was off. I had drunk the best part of a bottle of Prosecco and having finished a whole tube of Pringles, I was now eating dry cornflakes straight from the box (food has always been an emotional crutch for me). I was surrounded by the remains of yet another crying session; scrunched up dirty tissues were on the sofa and piled up on the floor around the bin where I'd made a half-hearted attempt to throw them in and missed. My emotions were all over the place; one minute I was pleased that Angus was going back to Australia so soon because it meant that he could get the process (whatever that was) started, and the next I was plagued with the unsettling feeling that as soon as he got on that plane, I would never see him again.

I was just tipping the last crumbs of cornflakes from the upturned box, straight into my mouth, when the doorbell rang.

I stood up, huffing my disdain at being interrupted, reached over to the chair and grabbed my dressing gown with the red pepper humus stain down the front. I pulled it tight around me and as I opened the front door, I didn't even bother to hide the loud huff that left my lips.

There stood Angus. On my front doorstep. Outside my house. Angus.

I stared at him, then glanced past him over his shoulder and out to the road where his car was parked. "Angus? What? How did you…?" I was stunned to see this extraordinary man on my doorstep. It wasn't cold outside, yet my nipples were already standing to attention, such was the effect he had on me. I pulled my dressing gown tighter around me and folded my arms at my waist (remember, I had no bra on) as I had a strange sense of déjà vu.

"Louisa, I'm so sorry, I had to see you, I couldn't wait. I would never leave without seeing you but it's so difficult trying to get away, not seeing you is killing me. I think about you all the time, of the things we've done together, the moments we've shared. I've been sitting in my car for hours trying to pluck up the courage to knock on your door and speak to you."

I stepped to one side, speechless, and motioned for Angus to come in.

As he walked in, I noticed him noticing the debris of my crying session. I didn't apologise. I sat down on the sofa and Angus remained standing. We held each other's gaze for what seemed like minutes, but were only a few seconds, and then I broke the silence.

"Angus, please don't make this a 'goodbye'," I said, "I can't think that I may never see you again, let's just say it's 'so long for now, until we meet again'. This (and I pointed first to him and then to me) is torture. You got inside here (and I tapped the side of my head to demonstrate I meant my head) and you also got inside here (I thumped my chest, roughly where my broken heart lie bleeding). You are the only man to have affected me like this, leaving me so broken. I went through all our old messages, you promised me you'd always be here for me. You lied, Angus, because you're not going to be here for me, you're leaving me."

When I thought I had no more tears left, they came again. I was going to be so dehydrated in the morning!

He sat down next to me, enveloped me in a real Angus hug, and we cried together.

He kissed the top of my head, he kissed either side of my eyes, my lashes wet with tears, he kissed my cheeks and the tip of my snotty nose. I turned my face to his and kissed him gently on his lips. I leant into him, my limbs entwining his, my body melting into him so there was no space between us.

How bittersweet it was as we snuggled up on the sofa together. I closed my eyes and breathed in the familiar scent of this extraordinary man. I felt both euphoria and guilt, and they were sitting on each shoulder screaming in my ears – euphoria was telling me I was lucky to be in the arms of the man I loved, guilt was telling me that he wasn't mine to love. I pushed all thoughts of his wife waiting for him at home to the back of my mind. I didn't want to think about him kissing her the way he kisses me, or his fingers brushing her skin leaving an invisible trail in their wake the way he did with me.

I turned to Angus, kissed him full on the mouth and walked my fingers suggestively up his inner thigh.

As I stood up, I slipped my dressing gown down over my shoulder to reveal my fleecy pyjamas and with a cheeky grin said, "I'm just going upstairs to slip into something less comfortable!" He grinned at me and waggled his eyebrows as his phone bleeped the arrival of a text message.

Upstairs in the bedroom, I began to prepare myself for what I hoped would be a lust-filled evening. I pushed my guilty conscience to the back of my mind and focused on what I wanted. I could already feel the heat between my legs and I silently thanked the Gods of Wantonness that I had had the forethought to sort my lady garden! It was nicely trimmed with immaculate borders that tucked neatly away behind my knickers and as I'd bathed earlier and shaved my legs and armpits, I just needed a quick freshen up and I was all set to seduce him.

I stripped off, brushed my teeth and gargled some mouth wash to make sure my kisses were extra minty. Then I swept bronzing body shimmer across my décolletage and between my boobs and stepped into a pair of lacey knickers. Once I'd spritzed my perfume into the air and walked through the fragrant cloud a couple of times (I wanted to go with subtle and sensual, not overpowering and cloying), I was ready. I stood at the top of the stairs and could see Angus sitting on the sofa watching the TV. There was some home makeover programme on, and I could hear the presenter talking about swimming pools and the cost of cleaning them, so with a gentle tug on each nipple to get them erect and ready for action, I descended the stairs, boobs a-swinging!

I sashayed up behind Angus, thrust my ample bosoms forward and as I leant over him (remember, he's sitting down!), my boobs jiggled around and came to rest on his right shoulder, my nipples brushing his skin. It was at that moment that I saw he was on his phone.

On a Skype call.

To his mum!

I screamed, pulled away and jumped backwards, and at this point my boobs took on a life of their own. Each one moved independently and in the opposite direction to the other, and the most diabolical slapping sound emanated from my chest area. The momentum knocked me to the floor and as every inch of my skin burned with the heat of embarrassment, I could hear Angus's mum saying, "So that was the lovely Louisa, eh, Angus? I hadn't expected to see quite so much of her on our first introduction but hey-ho! Good to see you, Louisa."

I grabbed the throw from the back of the sofa and wrapped myself in it. It bought me no comfort as I sheepishly poked my head above the back of the sofa.

"Hello," I said, waving tentatively, "nice to, um… meet you."

Angus and his mum were by now laughing mercilessly at my misfortune. I, however, wanted the ground to open up and swallow me, shimmering breasts, lacy panties and all. My shame had reached new levels.

Once I had regained a little composure (a stiff drink helped) and Angus and his mum had stopped laughing, they promised to call each other again the next day. Angus's mum, whom by now I knew was called Cathy, said, "Before I go, Angus, could you put Louisa on for me please." Shit! She was going to call me a homewrecker, she was going to call me a…

130

"Louisa, I want to thank you," she said cutting into my anxious thoughts, "I know how much Angus loves you and I know how much of a comfort you have been to him. You've helped him through some truly dark and lonely times these last few months and it has been so important for me to know that you love and care for him so much. I know we haven't met in the, shall we say, most favourable of circumstances, but I sincerely hope that one day we will meet properly. I want you to make sure you get my contact details from Angus so we can keep in touch, I'm sure it would bring great comfort to him to know that you and I are in contact with each other. Especially as it's likely he won't be able to contact you himself, what with his controlling wife watching his every move!"

"I'd love to, thank you, Cathy," I said, still very aware of my near nakedness but instantly warming to this lovely lady who currently only exists to me through the jerky reality of Skype.

"See?" said Angus, as he disconnected the call after we bid his mum a fond farewell. There were lots of heartfelt 'love you lots', blowing kisses and waving to each other as the call ended. "I told you she likes you."

"Angus, that was so embarrassing, I'm so sorry," I responded, sitting down next to him. "I would never have come downstairs dressed like that if I'd known you were talking to your mum. I'm mortified, I don't think I'll ever be able to look her in the eye," I continued as I feel yet another flush of embarrassment creep up my face.

"Don't worry about it," he said grabbing my hand and laughing as he pulled me close, "she can look you in the nipples instead!"

"You shit bag!" I said, laughing along with him and slapping him playfully on the leg.

He put his hands either side of my face and looked intently into my eyes.

"I love you so much, Louisa Scott," he said as he leant in to kiss me.

"I love you too, Angus Pewk" I responded, and this time it didn't sound so funny saying his name.

As we kissed, I ran my hand up his inner thigh. The kissing became more forceful and passionate and as my hand reached his cock, I could feel it was already hard. I started gently rubbing it through his trousers and he spread his legs wider and groaned in pleasure.

I slowly undid the button on his trousers, then, as my hands moved to the zip and slid it down, he tilted his head back and gasped. I reached in and grabbed his cock and it willingly reacted to my touch.

We didn't speak as I took his hand and led him upstairs to my bedroom. This time, I was going to have this extraordinary man.

I pushed him down onto the bed and slipped his trousers and boxers off while he took off his shirt. Without waiting for any foreplay, I straddled him and slipped him into me.

This extraordinary man reached places no man has ever reached before. He literally filled me up! He put his hands on my hips and started to gently rotate me as I sat on him. I leant back slightly and shut my eyes and the pleasure intensified as he hit my sweet spot. Too quickly, I could feel my orgasm peaking, but it was unstoppable. I screamed as pleasure ripped through me, but he didn't let up with the hip swirling. I looked down at him and he had a ridiculous grin on his face.

"You liked that, huh?" he questioned.

"A little bit," I replied, and he playfully slapped my thigh. "Oh, so you want to play games do you, Angus? Well, I'm a very willing and able opponent!" and I leant forward, so my boobs fell tantalisingly close to his mouth.

"Jesus! Louisa! What are trying to do to me?" he groaned as he tried to catch a ripe nipple in his mouth.

I leant in closer and as I let his mouth envelop my nipple, I raised myself off him, almost slipping him out, then I pushed back down onto him, so his cock pushed back up inside me.

"FUUUUCK!" he yelled as I repeated the process.

"Yes, I think we are," I responded as he thrust his bum up off the bed and pushed harder and harder.

I could feel him touching the very top of me and it felt unbelievably good.

We both climaxed together and for good measure I squeezed him a little at the point of orgasm. I think it blew his mind!

As we lay together satiated on the bed, panting and laughing, cuddling and stroking, he traced his finger around my navel and up between by boobs, around my nipples and back down again. As he travelled further down to my naughty area, he slipped his fingers in and gently rubbed his thumb around my...

Oh. My. God!

We took a shower together afterwards and there was still lots of stroking and kissing as we took pleasure in each other's body. I had no hang-ups with Angus, no insecurities. This was me, and he appreciated every inch of me – several times!

When we were both dressed and back downstairs, he helped me make a pot of tea. I say 'helped' but what he actually did was stand behind me kissing and nuzzling my neck while I made the pot of tea. He would occasionally slide his hand into my dressing down and caress my boobs and my nipples would respond instantly to his touch, traitors that they were.

"Oh, Louisa, Louisa, Louisa," he sighed all melancholy as he rested his chin on my shoulder.

"Angus, don't," I responded as I turned to face him and put my finger to his lips.

"But I can't…" he said through the barricade.

"I know," I interrupted, "believe me, I know."

He hung his head.

This time it was my turn to take his face in my hands and kiss him.

"Remember," I said, "this is NOT goodbye."

"Louisa, I love you so much…" he said, before I interrupted.

"Angus I love you too. But you know that it will never work like this, I can't be just your 'bit on the side', it's not fair on either of us. You need to do what's best for you and your family, and yes, you're going to have to make some tough decisions, but you must do it. We all need to move on." I pulled my dressing gown around me; it didn't seem appropriate to be talking so frankly and still having the girls on show.

"As I see it, you have two choices," I continued as I picked up the mugs of tea, "one is to go back to Australia where both of you work on your marriage, sort out your problems, make a go of it and forget about us." I couldn't believe I was saying it and even he raised his eyebrows at my forcefulness.

"The other is to go back to Australia, you both admit that your marriage is over, and you start the separation process."

As I carried the tea into the front room, his phone rang.

I knew who it was, the same person it always was. I felt betrayed, as if he'd brought her into my house.

I left him in the kitchen talking to his wife. I had zero interest in what they were saying; I was tired of the whole situation. My fight was all gone. A minute later, Angus walked in and as I took a sip of tea, I looked up at him. He was crying.

"Louisa," he said as he started to sob, "It's done. The choice is made…"

The fate of Angus and Louisa now lies in your hands.

If Angus goes back to Australia to end his marriage, then turn the page to Chapter Twenty-Three.

If Angus goes back to Australia to work on fixing his marriage, then turn to Chapter Twenty-Eight page 161.

Angus returns to Australia to end his marriage...

Chapter Twenty-Three

I jumped to my feet.

"You what?" I questioned, startled and barely able to comprehend what he was saying.

"The decision has been made," he reiterated through his tears.

I stood up and started to pace around the small living room space. It was as much as I could do to not put my fingers in my ears and go 'la, la, la, la, la' to block out his words. I didn't want to hear his decision. Whatever it was, it wasn't going to end well for me. He was leaving for Australia very soon and he'd be out of sight and out of reach, but not out of mind. The time was fast approaching when all I'd have left of Angus was my memories. My body craved his touch so how was I going to cope with that loss.

"It really is over," he continued.

Oh my God, I was going to vomit. He was about to tell me he was going to stay with the evil bitch for the sake of the kids.

"I'm not going to stay with that evil bitch, not even for the sake of my kids."

See, I told you…

"Whaaaaaaat?" I screeched.

He took a step back. I must have sounded deranged.

"Louisa, I can't stay with her," he continued, "she has controlled every aspect of my life for the last twelve years, I can't do it anymore. It's destroying me."

"Angus, the kids. How are you going to…?"

"We are all going back to Australia, she's going to stay in the house and I'm going to find somewhere close by to rent and we will share custody of Charlotte and Ethan. I can't put them through this anymore, Louisa," he said as he sunk down onto the sofa.

"Our constant fighting is affecting them terribly. Charlotte is very clingy and tearful, and Ethan is developing anger issues at school. I feel like it's all my fault, I've treated Joanna like a princess for all these years and I've created a monster. My feeling is that the kids are better off in a single-parent household than a toxic household, and my marriage is truly toxic."

"Angus, my love," I soothed as I sat down next to him, "this is absolutely NOT your fault. She knows how to push your buttons and she's taking full advantage of you. But you need to be really sure that this is what you want. Your decision has massive consequences, are you ready for the fall out?" I asked, trying to be practical.

"Louisa, I have never had the courage to stand up to her. And I mean properly stand up to her. To question her morals and her judgements. But since I met you, I feel invincible. You've made me realise that this is not my lot and I don't have to take her shit anymore."

Oh dear, so this was all down to me then? I had an unsettling feeling working its way up from my toes, like icicles forming in my blood.

"Oh, um…" was all I could say.

"Do you know what her latest trick is?" he asked. It was a rhetorical question. "She promised them they could get a puppy when they returned to Australia as long as they told me they were homesick and wanted to leave England!"

My eyes widened in astonishment.

"But not only that," he continued, "we had an almighty row about her promising things to the kids and making life-changing decisions without discussing them with me first, and when I foolishly relented and agreed to a dog, she said 'of course, if Daddy really loved you, he'd let you have one each. But he doesn't, so you can't!' How could she use our children like pawns in her sick game, Louisa? What sort of mother does that?"

I had no possible explanation.

Chapter Twenty-Four
November 2016

The day Angus and I said goodbye was nothing short of heart-breaking. We talked a lot, we cried a huge amount and we hugged constantly. It hadn't really sunk in that Angus was going back to Australia until he looked at his watch and said, "I really need to go soon. Our flight is early tomorrow morning and Joanna's booked us a family room at the airport hotel. The kids are hyper and so excited about going home and I really should be there."

I could feel it in the pit of my stomach, intense sadness welling up and threatening to spill out unless I pushed it back down because if I let it all out, I was afraid I would never stop. The hardest thing, above all, was deciding that we wouldn't contact each other. It was for the best, we both knew that, but it didn't make it any easier to cope with. The time difference was about ten hours and my early morning was his early afternoon. Because Joanna monitors his phone/social media/emails, I had no way of contacting him and he certainly couldn't contact me. All communication would have to be through Cathy, his mum, and whilst I'd had many a conversation with her since 'nipple-gate' (as we affectionately called it) and we'd emailed each other every week, it still wouldn't be the same sending her messages to pass on to Angus. But still, it was better than nothing.

I had initially been angry with Angus for letting Joanna dictate to him. I shouted at him and said it was a breach of his privacy that she was allowed to get away with it and he should change his passwords. He pointed out that if he changed them then he looked guilty, as though he had something to hide, and it was better that she saw that he was not the philandering bastard she made him out to be. Whatever the reasons, cutting all contact was for the best and although I didn't like it, I would just have to suck it up.

I knew the weekends would be the hardest. When we worked together, I'd count the hours and minutes until I could be with him again. It's harder to keep busy at the weekends because I know he's there, with her. There's no love between them but at least she has him. I have to stop myself from thinking about what he's doing because I know that whatever it is, it will involve her. I torment myself with my thoughts, with the picture I have in my head of the two of them together.

"Angus, I can't say goodbye to you," I said as my tears start again, "I don't want you to leave me. I want to be selfish and keep you with me for ever," I choked out through my sobs.

"Louisa, when it's all over, I will come back for you. I promise," he said, tilting my head up and looking into my eyes. There was a fire dancing behind his eyes, a fire I had ignited. "Now, I need a cup of coffee and then I really am going to have to go. I love you," he finished as his kissed me softly on the lips. I didn't know it, but it was his goodbye kiss.

"I'll put the kettle on," I said, as I wiped the tears from my puffy, swollen eyes. I walked out into the kitchen and opened

141

the cupboard. "I have decaf or full caffeine. Which would you prefer?" I asked.

No response.

"Angus!" I called as I poked my head around the door. "I have decaf or…" I stopped short. I was just in time to see the front door close as this extraordinary man walked out of my life.

Chapter Twenty-Five

Thank goodness I had taken a few days' leave. The next morning, I was awake at 4am. so I got out of bed, made a coffee and sat with my knees pulled up under my chin whilst mind-numbing programmes played out on the TV. I wasn't taking any of it in, I was seeing it but not watching it. I was still smarting from Angus walking out on me; all I wanted was for him to put his arms around me and hug me. I wanted to feel safe again.

At 10:30 am, I had an overwhelming urge to drive to the airport and beg him not to go. To tell Joanna how selfish she is for having an extraordinary man and not appreciating him. To tell her to wake up and smell the Milo (an Aussie malt drink) and be thankful for her wonderful family. But I don't. I sit on the sofa, in a trance-like state, and think about how lost and lonely I feel.

Chapter Twenty-Six

As the hours turned into days and the days turned into weeks, the feeling of loss and anguish start to diminish a little. Life has to go on. I keep up to date with news from Australia as Cathy and I email or talk at least once a week and Angus keeps in touch with Joshua, one of our interns (and the only one Joanna will allow him to keep in his contacts as he isn't perceived as a 'threat'). They arrived safely in Australia and are doing well. Apparently, they are all very pleased to be back home and want to put the 'regret' of living in England behind them. That's what Joanna tells her family anyway, it's certainly not what Cathy tells me. They are looking forward to a family Christmas together. Angus has a contract position in an Aussie law firm and Joanna has a job stacking shelves in their local Woolworths (no pick and mix though!)

Oh, and they got two dogs.

I've been concentrating on getting my mind and body fit and healthy and have even enrolled on a Mindfulness course. It's really helping me to sort my head out and move forwards positively. I've taken up running and although it was a disaster at first, now I've got into the routine, I find it therapeutic. I like the sound of my feet pounding beneath me, it gives me a sense of pushing myself and I can't stop until I get home. If I do, I'm cheating. I push myself harder each time.

It's a wonder I didn't give up after the first session! I downloaded my 5K app onto my iPhone and as I activated Week 1, Day 1, I set off to the dulcet tones of a computerised American voice telling me to 'Keep going – you're doing great (haven't left the front door yet!) and 'Good jarb' (they mean 'job') and my favourite 'Now slow down and wok' (they mean walk, but again – digital American voice!). I slipped my phone into my sports bra and set off at a reasonable pace. I felt safe with it tucked away with the girls, they were keeping it secure and the app was amazing as it was counting the steps as I ran, I could hear them clicking up on the pedometer with each step. It was a great incentive and after 25 minutes of running and 'woking' just as computer-voice lady instructed, I got back to my front door red, sweaty and out of breath, and extracted my phone to see how many steps I'd done. Imagine my mortification when I discovered there was no pedometer counting my steps, the clicking noise was my camera. I had forgotten to lock my phone and had taken 736 pictures of my left breast!

I take the same route each time, it makes me feel safe. I see the same people out and about – the other runners, the teenagers on bikes and the two men who stand on the corner having a 'sneaky fag' (I wonder if anyone goes into a shop and asks for 'a packet of sneaky fags please!'?) I time myself at each point and push to get there quicker the next time.

Chapter Twenty-Seven
December 2016

I arrive home from work one Thursday after a particularly stressful day and after a quick swipe across my face with a make-up remover wipe, I pull on my tracksuit trousers and a baggy t-shirt (definitely not Lycra – Lycra on me not only highlights my 'problem areas' but also highlights the problem areas that have not yet become a problem!) and set off on my run. I was on Week 5, Day 5 and mere days away from being able to run a full 5K. Supposedly.

As I rounded the corner by the park bench, ready to take the path along by the river, the same route I always did, I glanced at my watch to see what time I had done it in. Fantastic! I had shaved ten seconds off my personal best and as I mentally patted myself on the back, my phone started to ring. I looked at the screen and was going to reject the call when I saw it was Cathy, Angus' mum. Shit! Why was she ringing me?

It was 4am in Australia.

I swiped to answer the phone and as I put it to my ear, my knees buckled and I fell to the floor. As my face struck the path, and a searing pain invaded my skull, everything went black...

Joanna's Story

I'm so sick of men thinking they are in control of me. They soon realise I'm so much stronger than them. Every man I've ever known has regretted the day he's tried to control me, from my ex-boyfriends to my father. My mother was weak and happy to be controlled by him; he expected her to cook, clean and keep house while he fucked other women and drank himself into an early grave. I will never be like my mother, weak and helpless, not able to speak out, being treated like shit. I am always in control. Always.

***

We got together in a nightclub in Caloundra. I was on a hen night and I saw him standing at the bar. Why do you think I'd suggested that the party goes onto a club? I knew the lads would end up there, it doesn't take much to persuade men to do what I want them to. The promise of a couple of beers was all I needed to get one of them to suggest the club, where I'd be waiting. I knew through a friend of a friend of a friend that he had had a couple of serious but disastrous relationships and was on the look-out for the mother of his children. He had money, an apartment in the city he'd bought cheaply, he was well educated and had a good job. I was sure I would be able to convince him to sell his bachelor pad and buy a family home, I'd give him children and in return my future would be secured. It was convenient for me. The only downside would be having to put up with the physical side of the relationship. I'm not keen on sex, it's so messy and I don't like intimacy, but to give him children it will be a means to an end.

147

I used to be married. Nobody in the group knows though; they assumed he was just a boyfriend if his name ever came up and I didn't correct them. He was a bastard. I got home from work one day and noticed that all his things were gone. He'd cleared out and moved in with another woman. It had been going on for 18 months I later found out, in fact ever since we got married. He worked for the Australian Army so being away from home wasn't unusual, I didn't know that he was lying about the number of leave days he had and was in fact spending most of them with her, not coming home to me. Within a couple of days, I received the divorce papers; he claimed I had a controlling behaviour and narcissistic tendencies – what a crock of shit! It wasn't my fault that I couldn't keep up with his desire for sex every night.

I just sidled up to Angus and told him I'd give him everything he needed. He's a man after all, weak and easily led, and the promise of providing him with everything he needed was the hook that enabled me to reel him in. It was that easy. I needed to get out of my current situation – I was living in a tiny apartment, behind on the rent, with a $15K credit card bill and a lazy bum of a boyfriend who was taking out cash advances on the card to fund his drug habit. He claimed I drove him to it as I was 'a cold-hearted and controlling bitch'. Whatever! I was working in a job I really hated, so hooking up with a man with money would mean I could give it up. The sooner I bagged me a rich man, the better. He'd have to bail me out first, I needed to clear my debts. If he sold his apartment, we could buy a nice family home in the suburbs and with the profit he made, he could clear my debts and have some spare. We'd get married quickly, they'll be lots of sex at first as I need to keep him satisfied and get pregnant, but then I'll cut right back on that shit. Once I'm pregnant, he'll be so overjoyed he'll do anything to keep me happy. I can't lose.

After about three months of us dating, I was bored with waiting, so I dropped loads of hints about getting married. I even had to pull the 'if you love me, you'd ask me to marry you' bullshit. It worked! I chose the ring and waited for the grand romantic gesture, the big lavish party with our friends who'd buy us great gifts. Angus, the idiot, had other ideas. Seriously, how could he possibly think that a walk up Sydney Harbour Bridge would be an acceptable place for a marriage proposal? There was nobody up there except us and the guides, nobody saw the 'big moment'. I was fuming and wholly disappointed. But I didn't let Angus see, I just accepted graciously and put out for him that night. I should've planned it myself and got what I really wanted.

I always knew he was a flirt but I can manipulate this to my advantage in any given situation. He likes to socialise, he's got lots of mates and we get lots of invites to parties, dinners and social occasions, but I don't get on with any of his bogan friends. Or their partners. The women all fawn over Angus, touching his arm, tucking stray bits of hair back, pushing their breasts together to give him an eyeful, all that kind of slutty stuff. I always cut short our nights out because Angus loves the flirting and returns it in spades, and I refuse to put up with that. The women don't talk to me very much, they're polite, but I know it's Angus they want to see. They make polite conversation but I shut them down; I'm only there to keep an eye on Angus and I don't need benign distractions and small talk. I have to keep my wits about me. I always note who leaves the room, how long they are gone for, who walks in with them, whether they look any different. Basically, I have to make sure that Angus is not meeting up with any of the women in the toilets and getting touchy-kissy with them. He needs controlling, it's the only way to keep him in check.

When I've had enough, I don't make a scene, I just get up and walk out and as Angus is my husband, I expect him to follow. He knows their flirting irritates me and yet he still encourages it, so it's up to me to put a stop to it. I always give him the choice – his friends or me – so obviously he chooses me and in turn he cuts contact with his friends. Or rather, they cut contact with him. It's an easy way to reduce the bad influences in his life. I'm the only one he needs, he will soon realise that, and if he doesn't? Well, I'll take everything he's got and leave him with nothing.

The only other influence I can't control is his mother, Cathy. It infuriates me that he constantly asks her for advice and reassurance, and I know they talk about me behind my back. She tried to come between me and Angus once; she was staying with us and instead of being grateful for my hospitality, she criticised me for wanting some time out when the kids were younger. She couldn't understand why I wanted a break and I tried to explain that I was with them all day and it was tiring. Angus always got a break; he went to work every day and didn't have to put up with the constant demands. When he got in from work, he'd want me to tell him in great detail what the kids had done that day, but I'd already lived through every second of it and didn't want to waste time recalling it so I used to take myself off to bed early in the hope of a decent sleep. It also meant I didn't have to put up with him pawing at me and trying to get me to have sex – I could pretend I was asleep when he came up to bed and honestly most of the time I was. It was handy that he was quite a light sleeper too; when the kids woke during the night, he'd be the first one up tending to their whimpers and sniffles so I could stay snuggled under the duvet feigning sleep. It was his responsibility, I had them all day so it was only fair he did the fatherly stuff during the night. Cathy didn't agree, but I soon put her straight. I don't take any shit from her and if she gets too involved in our lives, I just threaten that she won't see her grandchildren again. She soon backs off. She needs to know that I'm in control of our family, not her.

The perfect opportunity to remove every bad influence from his life, including his mother, came one day when he announced he'd been asked to take up a work placement in England. I was ecstatic, I've always wanted to live overseas and travelling around Europe had been a dream of mine. Plus, it meant that Cathy would be on the other side of the world and couldn't be that constant presence, poking around into every aspect of our lives and giving her opinion. We'd be leaving all his friends behind, and in turn the temptation of other women, and as we knew nobody in the UK, I could do and be whatever I wanted. He would have to rely on me 100%.

My friends were so jealous that I was moving to England. I posted countdowns to the big day on social media and regularly let them know what plans I was making. I told them we were going to live in London and posted pictures of the iconic London landmarks. I got so many comments and 'likes', I felt like a celebrity and decided not to let on that we were actually going to live in Kent. There was no harm in letting them believe that I was on the verge of a fantastic new start in an amazing city. I couldn't wait to get on that plane!

England was so fucking freezing! It was either cold and wet, or wet and windy. Where the fuck had the sun gone? Did it ever make it around to this godforsaken country?

Angus had a lot of sorting out to do when we arrived: he needed to finalise the new house (the other one fell through because apparently I didn't transfer the deposit in time but I know I told him to do it) and find the kids a school. I was happy to indulge my friends' desire for constant updates through social media and I'd spend many happy hours on the sofa posting pictures and 'checking in' while Angus sorted out the boring shit like work, cars and groceries. He spoke to his mother once a week on speakerphone at my insistence, that way I could monitor their conversation. I made sure she knew that we didn't need her. I was living my best life and each afternoon when I rang my mum in Australia, she'd congratulate me on my genius.

When Angus started at Williams & Bowman, I made sure I was ahead of the game. I knew who he worked with and what they looked like even before he did, that way I could determine whether they were a threat or not. There were a couple of women I knew I had to be wary of and if he started to talk about them at home, it was usually a sign that he was attracted to them and I'd have to investigate further. His wage was a lot less than his earnings in Australia and I had to bite the bullet and get a job to fund the holidays I wanted around Europe, but I had to suck it up. Again, it was a means to an end. I got a job as a picker/packer at a local supermarket and although it initially started off very mundane, it became so much more interesting when I noticed that some of Angus's work colleagues shopped there. I had almost full control of our life here and I now had a fantastic opportunity to be able to keep tabs on him whilst he was at work. I also knew that if I told his colleagues who I really was, they wouldn't be honest with me so I became a different person with a different name – pure brilliance on my part and they fell for it hook, line and sinker. It was so easy to bump into them while they were shopping and they thrived on gossip, so I got to know everything about everyone at the firm, including Angus.

As the stories from Williams & Bowman, recalled in great detail by Kelli and Louisa, got more and more juicy, I knew Angus was on the verge of an affair. For a while I'd been secretly monitoring his social media and emails but when he caught me looking one evening, it really kicked off. I knew then that he was fucking someone else (especially as he hadn't tried to get in my pants for a while) and whilst I struggled to control my anger at his betrayal, I knew I had to wait for solid evidence to gain proof of his infidelity. I could also use it as a bargaining chip when I decided that the time had come for us to move back to Australia.

Woe betide any little bitch that got Angus's cock twitching…

Present Day

What's going on? He's walked straight past me! I realise that with so many people around, he probably hasn't seen me, but I've been calling his name and he hasn't heard me. Then I see that Charlotte is sobbing as she grips the side of the trolley and Ethan is now in his arms and he's comforting him. Bless them, they're probably so tired. I can see he's struggling with all the bags, so I walk a little quicker hoping to catch up with him, although suddenly, there seems to be a lot more people around. As I try to dodge the wanderers and weavers, I am losing sight of him and these damn wedges were a great idea this morning but are now not conducive to a brisk walk through a busy airport. I can't let Angus out of my sight, he knew I'd meet him here and I don't understand why he's not waiting for me. I shout his name and he turns and looks back. Thank goodness! He's looking straight at me, so I wave and smile. He turns away and continues walking towards the exit. Tears spring from my eyes and I'm wiping them away, now not giving a shit about smudging my makeup, I just want to know why this man is leaving the airport without me. Confused and distraught, I finally get out of the terminal just in time to see him and his children getting into a waiting taxi. I stare in disbelief as my world collapses around me.

Thinking quickly (I don't know why I'd not done it before actually), I whip out my phone and call him. Damn! No service. In a fucking airport? Seriously? I notice that the taxi company collecting him is based in Maidstone and putting two and two together, I figure that this must be roughly where they are heading. But why? He knows I don't live anywhere near there. I run as fast as my wedges will carry me, pay for my parking, locate my car and exit the airport as fast as the speed limit will let me.

Luckily, the traffic is light and as I take a few deep breaths and calm down, I realise I can catch up with them. I hit redial on the Bluetooth in the car and curse as it goes to voicemail. I look skywards and roll my eyes. Someone up there doesn't like me! For the umpteenth time, I wondered why this day, which I had waited so long for, was going so catastrophically tits up.

As I weaved in and out of the traffic, I could see them just up ahead; Charlotte was looking out of the back window, her big brown eyes red with tears. What the hell was going on? These three people whom I love with all my heart had not only not waited for me as previously arranged (Angus had been very romantic and said he would meet me under the Burger King sign in arrivals!), but they had made no attempt to contact me. My head was spinning, and my imagination was going into overdrive as I hung back at a safe distance and waited to see where the taxi was taking them.

As we journey steadily along the M25, the traffic lessens once we get past the services and my heart leaps as I see Angus pick up his mobile, he must be calling me. I look at my dash display, waiting for the Bluetooth to kick in and announce his incoming call, but it doesn't happen. I overtake the van in front of me and move in behind a motorbike which is directly behind their taxi. For fuck's sake, I can see him talking on his phone. We haven't seen each other for eighteen months and I'm struggling to think who he'd need call before me, especially as we'd arranged a meeting place. Maybe he's calling his mum to let her know they've landed safely. Hold on a sec, how does he know I'm not still standing under the Burger King sign waiting for him…?

Shit! The motorbike has overtaken their taxi and I'm now directly behind them. Charlotte is looking straight at me so I grin and wave frantically, hoping that my enthusiastic actions will get her attention and she'll realise it's me and then she'll tell Angus that I'm behind them, and we'll pull over and all fall into each other's arms and there'll be happy tears and lots of 'I love you's' with lots and lots of Angus kisses. How I've missed his kisses. But she doesn't even recognise me and now I am seriously freaking out.

We come off the M20 and head towards Larkfield. What the hell is he doing? My irrationality properly kicks in and my mind goes into overdrive – he's got someone else and he's going to her before he comes to me. The shit bag, how dare he. He's probably going to get the taxi driver to wait while he sorts her out first, all the time his poor kids will be sitting waiting for him in the car while he gets his jollies, then he gets dropped off at mine. No fucking way, mister! How many women does he have on the go? The thought has never crossed my mind that there was anyone else, until now. His feelings always seem so utterly genuine and we've gone through so much to get to this point.

156

I'm jolted back to reality as I see the taxi pull up outside the florists in the High Street and Angus jump out and run inside. All my instincts tell me to follow him in, but I don't, I now want to see this through and find out exactly what this man is up to. I pull over a few car lengths behind the taxi and wait.

Less than two minutes later, Angus appears with a bunch of the most gorgeous flowers I have ever seen. The bouquet is eye-wateringly large and contains, amongst others, roses and gerberas – two of my favourite flowers. Oh God, no! How sick and twisted is it that he's giving another woman a bouquet containing MY favourite flowers? This is a whole new level of wrong. He jumps back into the waiting taxi and as it pulls out onto the main road, I move in behind it again. We drive up through the High Street and I'm crying so hard that I can barely see properly as I only just about register the taxi pulling off the road and coming to a halt in the churchyard. Oh, he's sneaky, there's a short cut to the estate through there, he's really trying to cover his tracks and throw me off the scent. But Angus, Charlotte and Ethan now get out of the taxi and start walking up the path through the churchyard.

I pull over and leave my car on the double yellow lines – I don't care now, I just want to know what the fuck is going on. I run around the corner and up the path into the churchyard where I practically bump into them just yards in front of me. You'd think that would make them notice me, but it still doesn't, it's as though I'm not even there. Anger and pain well up inside me and I open my mouth to shout out to them, but nothing comes out. I am quite literally speechless. I try again but there is no sound at all. Not even a rasp or a croak. I frantically try calling even loader, holding my throat in case that miraculously activates my voice box, but nothing. Not even a squeak.

Charlotte and Ethan are sobbing now, and Angus is wiping his eyes with the back of his hand. He passes them both a tissue and suddenly, the penny drops – they're not visiting another woman, they're visiting someone's grave. But he's never spoken about any family being buried here and as he leans down and places the bouquet in the vase in front of a newly-laid granite headstone, looking quite out of place amongst the old moss-covered stone ones and unkempt graves in the cemetery, he hugs his children tight and I get a feeling that I'm intruding on a very intimate and personal moment between the three of them. I hang back a few feet and hold my head in my hands, rubbing my face trying to stay composed, but the sight of this man and his children sobbing is heart-breaking. As they lean in to each other for comfort, I catch a glimpse of the name on the headstone.

With a smash to my chest, the air is ripped from my lungs and I can't breathe. I try to scream but no sound comes out. I can't form any rational thoughts; my mind goes completely blank. All I want is for Angus to slap me on the back one more time and call me 'mate'.

I am looking at my own grave.

****

I had imagined spending the rest of my life with Angus. He told me he would always love me even when his bones are in the ground. Turns out mine are there before his.

Love is just a word, until you give it meaning, and my life had meaning when Angus became a part of it.

He was my inspiration, he made me see what was holding me back, he helped me to fix me.

He will always be in my heart.

Our souls will always be connected.

When he suffers pain and loss, he will think of me and I will be there, watching over him.

Now I have to say goodbye to this extraordinary man.

The End

Angus returns to Australia to fix his marriage...

Chapter Twenty-Eight

I jumped to my feet.

"You what?" I questioned, startled and barely able to comprehend what he was saying.

"I've made my decision," he reiterated, through his tears.

I stood up and started to pace around the small living room space. It was as much as I could do to not put my fingers in my ears and go 'la, la, la, la, la' to block out his words. I didn't want to hear his decision. Whatever it was, it wasn't going to end well for me. He was leaving for Australia very soon and he'd be out of sight and out of reach, but not out of mind. The time was fast approaching when all I'd have left of Angus is my memories. My body craved his touch and I had no idea how I was going to cope with that loss.

"It really is over," he continued.

Oh my God, I was going to vomit. He was about to tell me he was going to stay with the evil bitch for the sake of the kids.

"I have to stay with her, for the sake of my kids, Louisa, I have to."

"Whaaaaaaat?" I screeched.

He took a step back. I must have sounded deranged.

"Louisa, I have to stay with her," he continued, "she will take the kids away from me if I leave her. They will go with her and live with her mum. I know that if that happens then Charlotte will be pregnant before she's 15 and Ethan will be on drugs by the time he's 10. It really is that simple. I must put my kids above everything else, and that means even my feelings for you. I am so sorry, Louisa. I can't put them through this anymore," he said as he sunk down onto the sofa.

"Our constant fighting is affecting them terribly. Charlotte is very clingy and tearful, and Ethan is developing anger issues at school. I feel like it's all my fault, I've treated Joanna like a princess for all these years and I've created a monster. Now I need to fix it.

"Do you know what her latest trick is?" he asked. It was a rhetorical question. "She promised them they could get a puppy when they returned to Australia as long as they told me they were homesick and wanted to leave England!"

My eyes widened in astonishment.

"But not only that," he continued, "we had an almighty row about her promising things to the kids and making life changing decisions without discussing them with me first, and when I foolishly relented and agreed to a dog, she said 'of course, if Daddy really loved you, he'd let you have one each. But he doesn't, so you can't!' How could she use our children like pawns in her sick game, Louisa? What sort of mother does that?"

I had no possible explanation.

It was goodbye, and it was heart-breaking. I could feel indescribable sadness welling up and threatening to spill out but if I let it, I was afraid I would never stop.

The hardest thing, above all, was deciding that we would never contact each other again. It was for the best, we both knew that, but it didn't make it any easier to cope with. We stood together, both on our phones blocking each other on Facebook and deleting each other as contacts. Neither of us spoke.

I was fuming with him for letting her dictate to him and for not standing up to her. What sort of example was he setting his children – that it's okay to treat someone like shit because the weaker person will always back down?

"Angus, I can't say goodbye to you," I say as my tears start again, "I don't want you to leave me. I want to be selfish and keep you with me for ever," I choke out through my sobs.

"Louisa, I can't," he said, tilting my head up and looking into my eyes. "If things had been different then…"

"Oh, no, you don't," I interrupted, "don't you dare do the 'if only' and 'if I could have my time over again' because it's all bollocks. You are responsible for your own destiny, Angus. You and only you can change it if you want to; using your situation with Joanna is just an excuse for not growing a set of bollocks and doing something about it. Your kids will not thank you for staying in a bad relationship for their sake. They will grow up and leave home and you and Joanna will be left with a hollow and loveless marriage, just muddling along. I can't believe that's what you want out of life, Angus. I've seen the flashes of lightning in your eyes, heard the thunder in your voice and you electrified me. Where has that man gone, that extraordinary man that literally knocked me off my feet? Where is he, Angus?" I was now shouting and shaking uncontrollably.

"Just know that I will always love you," he said.

And he turned and walked out of my life.
It was the end of the end.

Chapter Twenty-Nine
November 2016

Thank goodness I had taken a few days' leave. The next morning, I was awake at 4 am so I got out of bed, made a coffee and sat with my knees pulled up under my chin whilst mind-numbing daytime programmes played out on the TV. I wasn't taking any of it in; I was seeing it but not watching it. I was still smarting from Angus walking out on me, all I wanted was for him to put his arms around me and hug me. I wanted to feel safe again.

At 10:30 am, I had an overwhelming urge to drive to the airport and beg him not to go. To tell Joanna how selfish she is for having an extraordinary man and not appreciating him. To tell her to wake up and smell the Milo (an Aussie malt drink) and be thankful for her wonderful family. But I don't. As Angus leaves England for a life in Australia, I sit on the sofa in a trance-like state and think about how lost and lonely I feel.

Chapter Thirty

I knew the weekends would be the hardest. When Angus and I worked together, I'd count the hours and minutes until I could be with him again. It's harder to keep busy at the weekends because I know he's there, with her. There's no love between them but at least she has him. I have to stop myself from thinking about what he's doing because I know that whatever it is, it will involve her. I torment myself with my thoughts, so I try everything to erase the picture I have in my head of the two of them together.

****

As the hours turn into days and the days into weeks, the feeling of loss and anguish start to dissolve a little. Life has to go on. I keep up to date with news from Australia as Angus keeps in touch with Joshua, one of our interns (and the only one Joanna will allow him to keep in his contacts as he isn't perceived as a 'threat'). They arrived safely in Australia and are doing well. Apparently, they are all very pleased to be back home and want to put the 'regret' of living in England behind them. They are looking forward to a family Christmas together. Angus has a contract position in an Aussie law firm and Joanna has a job stacking shelves in their local Woolworths (no pick and mix though!).

Oh, and they got two dogs.

I've been concentrating on getting my mind and body fit and healthy and have even enrolled on a Mindfulness course. It's really helping me to sort my head out and move forwards positively. I've even taken up running and although it was a disaster at first, now I've got into the routine I find it therapeutic. I like the sound of my feet pounding beneath me, it gives me a sense of pushing myself and I can't stop until I get home. If I do, I'm cheating. I push myself harder each time.

It's a wonder I didn't give up after the first session! I downloaded my 5K app onto my iPhone and as I activated Week 1, Day 1, I set off to the dulcet tones of a computerised American voice telling me to 'Keep going – you're doing great' (haven't left the front door yet!) and 'Good jarb' (they mean 'job') and my favourite 'Now slow down and wok' (they mean walk, but again – digital American voice!). I slipped my phone into my sports bra and set off at a reasonable pace. I felt safe with it tucked away with the girls, they were keeping it safe and the app was amazing as it was counting the steps as I ran, I could hear them clicking up on the pedometer with each step. It was a great incentive and after 25 minutes of running and 'woking' just as computer-voice lady instructed, I got back to my front door red, sweaty and out of breath and extracted my phone to see how many steps I'd done. Imagine my mortification when I discovered there was no pedometer counting my steps, the clicking noise was my camera. I had

forgotten to lock my phone and had taken 736 pictures of my
left breast!

I take the same route each time, it makes me feel safe. I
see the same people out and about – the other runners, the
teenagers on bikes and the two men who stand on the corner
having a 'sneaky fag' (I wonder if anyone goes into a shop
and asks for 'a packet of sneaky fags please!'?) I time myself
at each point and push to get there quicker the next time.

Chapter Thirty-One
December 2016

I arrive home from work one Thursday after a particularly stressful day and after a quick swipe across my face with a make-up remover wipe, I pull on my tracksuit trousers and a baggy t-shirt (definitely not Lycra – Lycra on me not only highlights my 'problem areas' but also highlights the 'problem areas' that have not yet become a problem!) and set off on my run. I was on Week 5, Day 5 and mere days away from being able to run a full 5K. Supposedly.

As I rounded the corner by the park bench, ready to take the path along by the river, the same route I always did, I glanced at my watch to see what time I had done it in. Fantastic! I had shaved ten seconds off my personal best and as I mentally patted myself on the back, my phone started to ring. I looked at the screen and was going to reject the call when I saw it was Cathy, Angus's mum. Shit! Why was she ringing me? It was 4am in Australia. We only ever emailed so Angus didn't know we were in contact.

I swiped to answer the phone and as I put it to my ear, my knees buckled and I fell to the floor. As my face struck the path, and a searing pain invaded my skull, everything went black…

Joanna's Story

I'm so sick of men thinking they are in control of me, they soon realise I'm so much stronger than them. Every man I've ever known has regretted the day he's tried to control me, from my ex-boyfriends to my father. My mother was weak and happy to be controlled by him; he expected her to cook, clean and keep house while he fucked other women and drank himself into an early grave. I will never be like my mother, weak and helpless, not able to speak out, being treated like shit. I am always in control. Always.

***

We got together in a nightclub in Caloundra. I was on a hen night and I saw him standing at the bar. Why do you think I'd suggested that the party goes onto a club? I knew the lads would end up there, it doesn't take much to persuade men to do what I want them to. The promise of a couple of beers was all I needed to get one of them to suggest the club, where I'd be waiting. I knew through a friend of a friend of a friend that he had had a couple of serious but disastrous relationships and was on the look-out for the mother of his children. He had money, an apartment in the city he'd bought cheaply, he was well educated and had a good job. I was sure I would be able to convince him to sell his bachelor pad and buy a family home, I'd give him children and in return my future would be secured. It was convenient for me. The only downside would be having to put up with the physical side of the relationship. I'm not keen on sex, it's so messy and I don't like intimacy, but to give him children it will be a means to an end.

I used to be married. Nobody in the group knows though, they assumed he was just a boyfriend if his name ever came up and I didn't correct them. He was a bastard. I got home from work one day and noticed that all his things were gone. He'd cleared out and moved in with another woman. It had been going on for 18 months I later found out, in fact ever since we got married. He worked for the Australian Army so being away from home wasn't unusual, I didn't know that he was lying about the number of leave days he had and was in fact spending most of them with her, not coming home to me. Within a couple of days, I received the divorce papers; he claimed I had a controlling behaviour and narcissistic tendencies – what a crock of shit! It wasn't my fault that I couldn't keep up with his desire for sex every night.

I just sidled up to Angus and told him I'd give him everything he needed. He's a man after all, weak and easily led, and the promise of providing him with everything he needed was the hook that enabled me to reel him in. It was that easy. I needed to get out of my current situation – I was living in a tiny apartment, behind on the rent, with a $15K credit card bill and a lazy bum of a boyfriend who was taking out cash advances on the card to fund his drug habit. He claimed I drove him to it as I was 'a cold-hearted and controlling bitch'. Whatever! I was working in a job I really hated so hooking up with a man with money would mean I could give it up. The sooner I bagged me a rich man, the better. He'd have to bail me out first, I needed to clear my debts. If he sold his apartment, we could buy a nice family home in the suburbs and with the profit he made he could clear my debts and have some spare. We'd get married quickly,

171

they'll be lots of sex at first as I need to keep him satisfied and get pregnant but then I'll cut right back on that shit. Once I'm pregnant, he'll be so overjoyed he'll do anything to keep me happy. I can't lose.

After about three months of us dating, I was bored with waiting, so I dropped loads of hints about getting married. I even had to pull the 'if you love me, you'd ask me to marry you' bullshit. It worked! I chose the ring and waited for the grand romantic gesture, the big lavish party with our friends who'd buy us great gifts. Angus, the idiot, had other ideas. Seriously, how could he possibly think that a walk up Sydney Harbour Bridge would be an acceptable place for a marriage proposal? There was nobody up there except us and the guides; nobody saw the 'big moment' I was fuming and wholly disappointed. But I didn't let Angus see, I just accepted graciously and put out for him that night. I should've planned it myself and got what I really wanted.

I always knew he was a flirt but I can manipulate this to my advantage in any given situation. He likes to socialise, he's got lots of mates and we get lots of invites to parties, dinners and social occasions, but I don't get on with any of his bogan friends. Or their partners. The women all fawn over Angus, touching his arm, tucking stray bits of hair back, pushing their breasts together to give him an eyeful, all that kind of slutty stuff. I always cut short our nights out because Angus loves the flirting and returns it in spades, and I refuse to put up with that. The women don't talk to me very much, they're polite, but I know it's Angus they want to see. They make polite conversation but I shut them down; I'm only there to keep an eye on Angus and I don't need benign distractions and small talk. I have to keep my wits about me. I always note who leaves the room, how long they are gone for, who walks in with them, whether they look any different. Basically, I have to make sure that Angus is not meeting up with any of the women in the toilets and getting touchy-kissy with them. He needs controlling, it's the only way to keep him in check.

When I've had enough, I don't make a scene, I just get up and walk out and as Angus is my husband, I expect him to follow. He knows their flirting irritates me and yet he still encourages it, so it's up to me to put a stop to it. I always give him the choice – his friends or me – so obviously he chooses me and in turn he cuts contact with his friends. Or rather, they cut contact with him. It's an easy way to reduce the bad influences in his life. I'm the only one he needs, he will soon realise that, and if he doesn't? Well, I'll take everything he's got and leave him with nothing.

The only other influence I can't control is his mother, Cathy. It infuriates me that he constantly asks her for advice and reassurance, and I know they talk about me behind my back. She tried to come between me and Angus once; she was staying with us and instead of being grateful for my hospitality, she criticised me for wanting some time out when the kids were younger. She couldn't understand why I wanted a break and I tried to explain that I was with them all day and it was tiring. Angus always got a break; he went to work every day and didn't have to put up with the constant demands. When he got in from work, he'd want me to tell him in great detail what the kids had done that day, but I'd already lived through every second of it and didn't want to waste time recalling it so I used to take myself off to bed early in the hope of a decent sleep. It also meant I didn't have to put up with him pawing at me and trying to get me to have sex – I could pretend I was asleep when he came up to bed and honestly most of the time I was. It was handy that he was quite a light sleeper too; when the kids woke during the night, he'd be the first one up tending to their whimpers and sniffles so I could stay snuggled under the duvet feigning sleep. It was his responsibility, I had them all day so it was only fair he did the fatherly stuff during the night. Cathy didn't agree, but I soon put her straight. I don't take any shit from her and if she gets too involved in our lives, I just threaten that she won't see her grandchildren again. She soon backs off. She needs to know that I'm in control of our family, not her.

The perfect opportunity to remove every bad influence from his life, including his mother, came one day when he announced he'd been asked to take up a work placement in England. I was ecstatic, I've always wanted to live overseas and travelling around Europe had been a dream of mine. Plus, it meant that Cathy would be on the other side of the world and couldn't be that constant presence, poking around into every aspect of our lives and giving her opinion. We'd be leaving all his friends behind, and in turn the temptation of other women, and as we knew nobody in the UK, I could do and be whatever I wanted. He would have to rely on me 100%.

My friends were so jealous that I was moving to England, I posted countdowns to the big day on social media and regularly let them know what plans I was making. I told them we were going to live in London and posted pictures of the iconic London landmarks. I got so many comments and 'likes', I felt like a celebrity and decided not to let on that we were actually going to live in Kent. There was no harm in letting them believe that I was on the verge of a fantastic new start in an amazing city. I couldn't wait to get on that plane!

England was so fucking freezing! It was either cold and wet, or wet and windy. Where the fuck had the sun gone? Did it ever make it around to this godforsaken country?

Angus had a lot of sorting out to do when we arrived: he needed to finalise the new house (the other one fell through because apparently I didn't transfer the deposit in time but I know I told him to do it) and find the kids a school. I was happy to indulge my friends' desire for constant updates through social media and I'd spend many happy hours on the sofa posting pictures and 'checking in' while Angus sorted out the boring shit like work, cars and groceries. He spoke to his mother once a week on speakerphone at my insistence, that way I could monitor their conversation. I made sure she knew that we didn't need her. I was living my best life and each afternoon when I rang my mum in Australia, she'd congratulate me on my genius.

When Angus started at Williams & Bowman, I made sure I was ahead of the game. I knew who he worked with and what they looked like even before he did, that way I could determine whether they were a threat or not. There were a couple of women I knew I had to be wary of and if he started to talk about them at home, it was usually a sign that he was attracted to them and I'd have to investigate further. His wage was a lot less than his earnings in Australia and I had to bite the bullet and get a job to fund the holidays I wanted around Europe, but I had to suck it up. Again, it was a means to an end. I got a job as a picker/packer at a local supermarket and although it initially started off very mundane, it became so much more interesting when I noticed that some of Angus's work colleagues shopped there. I had almost full control of our life here and I now had a fantastic opportunity to be able to keep tabs on him whilst he was at work. I also knew that if I told his colleagues who I really was, they wouldn't be honest with me so I became a different person with a different name – pure brilliance on my part and they fell for it hook, line and sinker. It was so easy to bump into them while they were shopping and they thrived on gossip, so I got to know everything about everyone at the firm, including Angus.

As the stories from Williams & Bowman, recalled in great detail by Kelli and Louisa, got more and more juicy, I knew Angus was on the verge of an affair. For a while I'd been secretly monitoring his social media and emails but when he caught me looking one evening, it really kicked off. I knew then that he was fucking someone else (especially as he hadn't tried to get in my pants for a while) and whilst I struggled to control my anger at his betrayal, I knew I had to wait for solid evidence to gain proof of his infidelity. I could also use it as a bargaining chip when I decided that the time had come for us to move back to Australia.

Woe betide any little bitch that got Angus's cock twitching…

Present Day

Heathrow Airport, Terminal 2 Arrivals

What's going on? He's walked straight past me! I realise that with so many people around, he probably hasn't seen me, but I've been calling his name and he hasn't heard me. Then I see that Charlotte is sobbing as she grips the side of the trolley and Ethan is now in his arms and he's comforting him. Bless them, they're probably so tired. I can see he's struggling with all the bags, so I walk a little quicker hoping to catch up with him, although suddenly there seems to be a lot more people around. As I try to dodge the wanderers and weavers, I am losing sight of him and these damn wedges were a great idea this morning but are now not conducive to a brisk walk through a busy airport. I can't let Angus out of my sight, he knew I'd meet him here and I don't understand why he's not waiting for me. I shout his name and he turns and looks back. Thank goodness! He's looking straight at me, so I wave and smile. He turns away and continues walking towards the exit. Tears spring from my eyes and I'm wiping them away, now not giving a shit about smudging my makeup, just want to know why this man is leaving the airport without me. Confused and distraught, I finally get out of the terminal just in time to see him and his children getting into a waiting taxi. I stare in disbelief as my world collapses around me.

Thinking quickly (I don't know why I'd not done it before actually), I whip out my phone and call him. Damn! No service. In a fucking airport? Seriously? I notice that the taxi company collecting him is based in Maidstone and putting two and two together, I figure that this must be roughly where they are heading. But why? He knows I don't live anywhere near there. I run as fast as my wedges will carry me, pay for my parking, locate my car and exit the airport as fast as the speed limit will let me.

Luckily, the traffic is light and as I take a few deep breaths and calm down, I realise I can catch up with them. I hit redial on the Bluetooth in the car and curse as it goes to voicemail. I look skywards and roll my eyes. Someone up there doesn't like me! For the umpteenth time, I wondered why this day, which I had waited so long for, was going so catastrophically tits up.

Chapter Thirty-Two

As I weaved in and out of the traffic, I could see them just up ahead; Charlotte was looking out of the back window, her big brown eyes red with tears. What the hell was going on? These three people whom I love with all my heart had not only not waited for me as previously arranged (Angus had been very romantic and said he would meet me under the Burger King sign in arrivals!) but they had made no attempt to contact me. My head was spinning, and my imagination was going into overdrive as I hung back at a safe distance and waited to see where the taxi was taking them.

As we journey steadily along the M25, the traffic lessens once we get past the services and my heart leaps as I see Angus pick up his mobile, he must be calling me. I look at my dash display, waiting for the Bluetooth to kick in and announce his incoming call, but it doesn't happen. I overtake the van in front of me and move in behind a motorbike which is directly behind their taxi. For fuck's sake, I can see him talking on his phone. We haven't seen each other for eighteen months and I'm struggling to think who he'd need call before me, especially as we'd arranged a meeting place. Maybe he's calling his mum to let her know they've landed safely. Hold on a sec, how does he know I'm not still standing under the Burger King sign waiting for him…

Shit! The motorbike has overtaken their taxi and I'm now directly behind them. Charlotte is looking straight at me so I grin and wave frantically, hoping I'll get her attention and she'll realise it's me and then she'll tell Angus that I'm behind them, and we'll pull over and all fall into each other's arms and there'll be happy tears and lots of 'I love you's' with lots and lots of Angus kisses. How I've missed his kisses. But she doesn't even recognise me and now I am seriously freaking out.

We come off the M20 and head towards Larkfield. What the hell is he doing? Suddenly my irrationality kicks in and my mind goes into overdrive – he's got someone else and he's going to her before he comes to me. The fucking shit bag, how dare he. He's probably going to get the taxi driver to wait while he sorts her out first, all the time his poor kids will be sitting waiting for him in the car while he gets his jollies, then he gets dropped off at mine. No fucking way, mister! How many women does he have on the go? The thought has never crossed my mind that there could be anyone else, until now. His feelings always seem so utterly genuine and we've gone through so much to get to this point.

I'm jolted back to reality as I see the taxi pull up outside the florists in the High Street and Angus jump out and run inside. All my instincts tell me to follow him in, but I don't, I now want to see this through and find out exactly what this man is up to. I pull over a few car lengths behind the taxi and wait.

Less than two minutes later, Angus appears with a bunch of the most gorgeous flowers I have ever seen. The bouquet is eye-wateringly large and contains, amongst others, roses and gerberas – two of my favourite flowers. Oh God, no! How sick and twisted is it that he's giving another woman a bouquet containing MY favourite flowers? This is a whole new level of wrong. He jumps back into the waiting taxi and as it pulls out onto the main road, I move in behind it again. We drive up through the High Street and I'm crying so hard that I can barely see properly and I only just about register the taxi pulling off the road and coming to a halt in the churchyard. Oh, he's sneaky, there's a short cut to the estate through there, he's really trying to cover his tracks and throw me off the scent. But Angus, Charlotte and Ethan now get out of the taxi and start walking up the path through the churchyard.

I pull over and leave my car on the double yellow lines – I don't care now, I just want to know what the fuck is going on. I run around the corner and up the path into the churchyard where I practically bump into them just yards in front of me. You'd think that would make them notice me, but it still doesn't, it's as though I'm not even there. Anger and pain well up inside me and I open my mouth to shout out to them, but nothing comes out. I am quite literally speechless. I try again but there is no sound at all. Not even a rasp or a croak. I frantically try calling even louder, holding my throat in case that miraculously activates my voice box, but nothing. Not even a squeak.

Charlotte and Ethan are sobbing now, and Angus is wiping his eyes with the back of his hand. He passes them both a tissue and suddenly, the penny drops – they're not visiting another woman, they're visiting someone's grave. But he's never spoken about any family being buried here and as he leans down and places the bouquet in the vase in front of a newly-laid granite headstone, looking quite out of place amongst the old moss-covered stone ones and unkempt graves in the cemetery, he hugs his children tight and I get a feeling that I'm intruding on a very intimate and personal moment between the three of them. I hang back a few feet and hold my head in my hands, rubbing my face trying to stay composed, but the sight of this man and his children sobbing is heart-breaking. As they lean into each other for comfort, I catch a glimpse of the name on the headstone.

With a smash to my chest, the air is ripped from my lungs and I can't breathe. I try to scream but no sound comes out. I can't form any rational thoughts; my mind goes completely blank. All I want is for Angus to slap me on the back one more time and call me 'mate'.

I am looking at my own grave.

Chapter Thirty-Three

With a gasp, I am awake. I can hear bleeping and pinging noises close to my head as my eyes try to focus and I can just make out the image of someone moving around nearby, the smell of disinfectant assaulting my nostrils. I have excruciating pain in my head and as I feel something being pulled out of my throat, my gag reflex kicks in, bile rises and threatens to spew out. A choking sensation makes my fingers curl and grip in panic and I gasp for breath. It feels like someone is holding my hand, but I can't be sure.

As I cough and gag, I hear a voice I don't recognise.

"Take it easy, hun," says the soft, female voice, "I'm just removing this tube and then we can see how you're doing."

I panic and try to sit up, but it feels like a wrecking ball is swinging against the inside of my skull. A groan escapes my lips.

As my vision improves, I see I am in a hospital room. A nurse stands over me with a tube in her hand; I think she's just pulled it out of my throat.

"Welcome back, Louisa, you've had quite a time of it," the nurse says. I see her name badge; she's called 'Jas'.

"What happened?" I croak. My mouth feels so dry, my lips are swollen and sore and are stuck to my teeth, and my voice is barely a whisper.

"All in good time, sweetie, I'll get the doctor to explain everything to you," says Jas kindly. "But right now, you need rest. I'll get you some ice and we can melt a little on your lips and your tongue. Then you can progress to sips."

Progress to sips? What the fuck happened?

Someone comes into my room, but they are obscured by Jas. I see them sit in the chair next to me and as Jas moves to the end of my bed to write in my notes, I see the owner of the familiar voice. It's Angus' mum. What the hell is she doing here?

"Hello, my lovely," she says as she leans over and kisses my forehead. "We've been so worried about you. How are you feeling?"

"Hit…. by…. train!" I rasp.

She smiles at me, but I can see pain in her eyes.

"Cathy?" I say, as little tears hug the rim of my eyes. This is the first time I've met her in person and in my dreams it was under far nicer circumstances than this.

"What happened? Please, tell me," I ask, feeling a little panicked.

"Let's let the doctor check you over first, and then I'll fill you in," she replied softly, standing up. "I'm going to make a couple of phone calls, then I'll be back." She stood up, kissed my forehead again, smiled and said, "Welcome back," and walked quietly out of my room.

"You've been through quite an ordeal, young lady," said the doctor, getting straight to the point.

184

"I'm Doctor Cooper and I've been looking after you for the last six weeks."

WHAAAAAT???????

Six weeks? Six frigging weeks? He's lying. That means I've missed Christmas. How can I have missed Christmas? And New Year. Oh God, what's happening?

I try to sit up but the pain in my head keeps me firmly on the pillow.

"How much do you remember, Louisa, about your accident? What's the last thing you remember?"

I can't think. I'm panicking. How have I been here six weeks? My brain must be playing tricks on me.

"I remember going out for a run, along the river. I remember rounding the corner and checking my timings. Then my phone rang. Now I'm here." I stare at him wide-eyed like a frightened rabbit.

"That's good that you remember," said Dr Cooper. "Now, you'll need to talk to the police. They've got some questions for you about the minutes leading up to the phone call. Something might jog your memory. Would you like Cathy to sit with you when they speak to you?"

"The police?" I questioned. "Why do I need to speak to the police?"

Dr Cooper didn't get to answer as a female police officer entered the room with Cathy.

"Hello, Louisa," said the police officer, "I'm DI Jemma Conglarves. I'm so glad you're back with us and I'm sorry to do this but I've got some questions for you. Cathy wants to sit in on the interview, if that's OK with you?"

"Interview? What's all this about?" I croak.

DI Conglarves and Cathy glance at each other. This isn't going to be good. Cathy sits on the chair beside my bed and holds my hand; DI Conglarves remains standing.

"Louisa, can you explain to me what happened on the afternoon of Thursday 8th December?" she asks.

"Like I told Dr Cooper," I respond, "I remember going out for a run. I rounded the corner to jog along the river as usual and my phone rang. I remember seeing it was Cathy, but I don't remember anything after that."

"Do you remember anything about the conversation with Cathy?" DI Conglarves continues, "Anything at all?"

"No, I don't," I reply. "I don't recall having a conversation. Look, can you please tell me what this is all about and how I ended up here?" I was getting frustrated and really anxious because nobody was telling me anything useful, like how I came to be in hospital with these injuries.

"It seems that you suffered some sort of a blow to your head in the moments just before or just after you answered the phone," DI Conglarves stated. "Fortunately, Cathy heard everything but she couldn't see what was going on so she called the police and an ambulance. Thanks to her quick thinking, she probably saved your life."

Shocked and lost for words, I looked at Cathy for some answers.

"I heard it all," Cathy confirmed, stroking my hand, "the sickening thud as you fell, your phone clattering to the floor. Thank God the line was still open and the emergency services could trace your location. And also…"

"What?" I interrupted, "also what, Cathy?"

"Now, now, we can't be sure of this" cut in DI Conglarves as she looked over at Cathy and held out her hands in a sort of 'calm down, hold back' gesture. "We are still looking at the CCTV footage from the river and the two men are part of the ongoing investigation."

"Ongoing investigation?" I rasp, "Can someone please tell me what exactly has happened?"

"Look" says DI Conglarves as she rubs her forehead with her fingertips and closes her eyes. "There were two men down by the river when you went running and it seems that they may have approached you as your phone rang and, according to Cathy, they may have informed you that they had something for you. Some sort of a message maybe?" DI Conglarves looks at me as though she's waiting for me to fill in the blanks. I am still none the wiser.

"I know what I heard" says Cathy, chipping in, "but it all happened as you answered the phone and as you fell" she says, turning to me and squeezing my hand.

I was so confused and my thoughts weren't forming rationally.

"As I said" DI Conglarves says rather forcefully, interrupting my thought process, "we don't have any evidence of an altercation or assault. CCTV footage from the river is very grainy but we can see both men approach you and we can see you falling. There doesn't appear to have been a blow struck by either men, they don't appear to have any kind of weapon to strike you with but they were very careful to block the camera view. All we know is that you suffered a head injury following this encounter and the specific cause of your injury is unknown. You could've struck your head as you fell, possibly you tripped as you answered your phone. Lack of concentration perhaps. Until we find these two men and they can answer our questions, we have nothing else to go on, there were no witnesses. Louisa" she continues, in a softer tone, "if there is anything, anything, you remember please do be sure to get in touch with me" and she handed me a business card with her contact details on. With a nod of her head to Cathy, she walked out, leaving me in complete disbelief and utterly dumbstruck.

"Oh Louisa, I'm…"

"Cathy, what did they say? You said you heard them. What did they say?" I interrupted.

"Don't you worry about it my love" replied Cathy, "It all happened so quickly I was probably mistaken and…"

"WHAT. DID. THEY. SAY?" I demanded.

Cathy signed heavily and her shoulders dropped.

"They said 'This is from Joanna'" she replied.

Chapter Thirty-Four
February 2017

A week later, I am well enough to leave hospital. Cathy is amazing and is staying on to help me recover. We are going to have a belated Christmas together and as you can imagine, I had a lot of questions about the incident. DI Conglarves came to see me with some interesting news. It turns out that Joanna paid someone her family knows to 'rough me up' a little and warn me to stay away from Angus. The two men I used to see having a 'sneaky fag' every time I went running were paid to have a quiet word with me, to let me know that if I had any contact with Angus they would up the ante, but all they got to say was 'this is from Joanna' before I apparently tripped over my own feet as I answered my phone, hitting my head on the concrete plinth the bench was secured to as I fell. They fled the scene before the rest of Joanna's message could be conveyed. Apparently, they spent a week or so following me and learning when and where I went jogging. And there was me thinking that sticking to the same predictable route was safe! Thankfully the two wannabe hitmen had an attack of conscience and voluntarily turned themselves in at the nearest Police station. They both confessed to having been hired to carry out the attack but said they didn't physically assault me. CCTV footage corroborates their story. As they didn't actually commit the intended crime but still fled the scene of an incident, they were given a suspended sentence in exchange for the names and addresses of the ones who had hired them, dropping Joanna's family right in the shit!

Cathy and I spend many an evening reflecting on recent events. I feel so comfortable in her company and we even talk about Angus and his marriage. It's cathartic for both of us and when I told her how much I loved Angus, we both cried. I miss him so much. She said she knew he loved me because she could see it in his eyes. Apparently, they twinkled whenever he talked about me. Obviously not when Joanna is within earshot!

Cathy told me all about Angus and how he'd agreed to work on his relationship with Joanna, but that she had to try too. She'd insisted that it was all down to him and that he treated her unfairly and didn't look after her. She's invited a succession of relatives to stay at their house and they sit of an evening drinking wine and slating Angus and telling Joanna how she's better off without him and she should leave him and take his children away. They are very happy to accept his hospitality though. I sense Cathy's rage, she said she is so sickened by Joanna's behaviour, she has told her that she wants nothing more to do with her. She sees Charlotte and Ethan when Joanna allows Angus to visit her.

I asked her if Angus was going to stay with Joanna and she replied, "It's not Joanna he wants, Louisa, he's got a plan but there's hurdles he needs to get over first. Let's just take it one day at a time and if it's meant to be, it will happen!"

The dream I regularly had while I was in hospital, I think was down to the medication I was on, but at the time it felt so real. I was following Angus out of the airport and he couldn't see me. I couldn't get hold of him on the phone, it was almost as if my fingers couldn't dial the numbers, and I could see a gravestone with my name on it. It freaked the shit out of me initially, it was so vivid and for a while I worried every night about going to sleep as I would invariably wake up sobbing my heart out and soaked in sweat. But as each day passed and I got stronger, the dream become fuzzier until I could barely remember it at all.

Epilogue

Cathy finally flew back to Australia last week and we had a very emotional goodbye at Heathrow. She phoned me the day after she landed and said that Angus had visited her and wanted to know all about me and how I was doing. She said the wheels were in motion and that I'd find out soon enough. It was all very cloak and dagger.

The Police couldn't prosecute Joanna, she was so far down the chain it would've been very difficult to bring charges against her, especially as she was in Australia, but she will have to live with her guilt, knowing her behaviour had nearly ended a life, and for me that was punishment enough.

***

I went back to work two months after leaving hospital and was greeted by the familiar faces of my work colleagues. It was so good to see everyone again and to get back into a routine. Kelli and I had a good talk; there were lots of tears and she was racked with guilt and remorse. I forgave her.

Angus' office remains dark and empty, and I'm okay with it. I miss him like crazy but my regular contact with his wonderful mum keeps me sane and I welcome her updates. The kids are doing really well at school and Angus has finally secured a partnership in an Australian law firm, so it's all good.

I hope one day that I will see him again, or that he'll unblock my number from his phone/Facebook/all social media and I'll be able to talk to him, but I'm not holding my breath.

The exciting news here is that one of the senior partners is retiring and we have some 'fresh blood' joining the company. She is called Kimberley and is a talented conveyancing lawyer. I'm going to be her PA and the job comes with a hefty pay rise. Result!

I leave home extra early on Monday, Kimberley's first day, so I can get into work and set up ready for her arrival. Unfortunately, the A2 has other ideas and a 45-minute journey takes me nearly two hours. I pull into the carpark and everyone else is already in. I can see a swanky new Audi in the partners' space and am mortified to realise that Kimberley is in before me. How unprofessional do I look now?

I rush from my car into the office and am greeted by Kay and Vickie on the front desk.

"Oh, so nice of you to join us!" they chorus. I smile, flip them the birdie and mouth 'FUCK YOU' as I walk past their office, just as he walks out of their office.

He is not a stunning man. No chiselled jaw sporting designer stubble, or perfectly coiffed just-the-right-length hair. He isn't wearing a designer suit with handmade Italian brogues and he definitely doesn't smell of sandalwood and citrus. He smells of Right Guard, sweat and sheer hard work.

I stare in disbelief.

"There's that look again, Vickie," says Kay with a huge grin on her face. "Priceless! Looks like Louisa has just met 'Kimberley', our new partner!"

This extraordinary man then gets down on one knee, holds my hand in his, looks into my eyes and says, "Louisa, mate! Would you do me the honour of…?"

I gasp.

"Blowing my mind – again…?"

The End

Help and support

- women can call The Freephone National Domestic Abuse Helpline, run by Refuge on 0808 2000 247 for free at any time, day or night. The staff will offer confidential, non-judgemental information and support
- talk to a doctor, health visitor or midwife
- men can call Men's Advice Line on 0808 8010 327 (Monday and Wednesday, 9am to 8pm, and Tuesday, Thursday and Friday, 9am to 5pm) for non-judgemental information and support
- men can also call ManKind on 0182 3334 244 (Monday to Friday, 10am to 4pm)
- If you identify as LGBT+ you can call Galop on 0800 999 5428 for emotional and practical support
- anyone can call Karma Nirvana on 0800 5999 247 (Monday to Friday 9am to 5pm) for forced marriage and honour crimes. You can also call 020 7008 0151 to speak to the GOV.UK Forced Marriage Unit
- in an emergency, call 999

You can also email for support. It is important that you specify when and if it is safe to respond and to which email address:

- women can email helpline@womensaid.org.uk. Staff will respond to your email within 5 working days
- men can email info@mensadviceline.org.uk
- LGBT+ people can email help@galop.org.uk

If you are worried that you are abusive, you can contact the free Respect helpline on 0808 802 4040.

There are many organisations who provide support for you if you self-harm and the NHS can point you in the right direction
https://www.nhs.uk/mental-health/feelings-symptoms-behaviours/behaviours/self-harm/getting-help/
There are many organisations who provide support for you if you have an eating disorder and the NHS can point you in the right direction
https://www.nhs.uk/mental-health/advice-for-life-situations-and-events/how-to-help-someone-with-eating-disorder/